Library of
Davidson College

THE ENGLISH TRAVELLER IN AMERICA
1785—1835

THE ENGLISH TRAVELLER IN AMERICA

1785—1835

BY
JANE LOUISE MESICK, Ph.D.

GREENWOOD PRESS, PUBLISHERS
WESTPORT, CONNECTICUT

917.3
M578e

Originally published in 1922
by Columbia University Press, New York

First Greenwood Reprinting 1970

Library of Congress Catalogue Card Number 74-109790

SBN 8371-4280-6   72-1389

Printed in the United States of America

TO THE MEMORY
OF MY FATHER
AND MY MOTHER

PREFACE

IN undertaking this study of conditions in the United States in the fifty-year period after the Revolution, as seen through the eyes of English travellers, the author has attempted to produce a book which will be useful and interesting alike to the student of history and of literature. The English attitude toward America has been variously and frequently determined; such widely different works, for instance, as Henry T. Tuckerman's "America and Her Commentators" (1864) and John Graham Brooks' "As Others See Us" (1908) are well-known examples of this type of interpretative literature. But books of this kind, while affording much bibliographical material, usually attempt to cover the whole field of foreign criticism of America and are necessarily superficial in their discussion of the various phases of American life. It is this difficulty that the present work attempts to obviate by the limitation of its subject.

The bibliography of English travel in America, appended to this book, includes the works which were drawn upon by the authors. The original spelling, punctuation, and capitalization of the books of travel have been preserved in the titles and in the quotations throughout the book. While the titles were secured from many fruitful sources, the most useful work in this connection was the bibliography of Professor Lane Cooper's chapter "Travellers and Observers" in the Cambridge History of American Literature.

Grateful thanks are due to Dr. Carl Van Doren, Literary

Editor of *The Nation* and Associate in English at Columbia University, who suggested this study and who read both the manuscript and the proof; to Professor William P. Trent of Columbia University, who read the proof; also to Professor Dixon Ryan Fox, Assistant Professor of History, Columbia University, whose careful criticism has been of great assistance. Acknowledgement must be made of the help given by the New York State Library at Albany, which generously lent its large collection of travel literature. The author is indebted, too, to her sisters, Maude M. Benson and Katharine M. Bennett, and to her friends, Mary Loomis Cook and Dr. Ruth Lansing, for practical aid in the inevitable drudgery which a book of this kind involves.

CONTENTS

CHAPTER I
MOTIVES AND GEOGRAPHY 1

CHAPTER II
THE EMIGRANT AND THE TRAVELLER 26

CHAPTER III
MANNERS AND CUSTOMS 64

CHAPTER IV
THE CARE OF THE UNFORTUNATE 108

CHAPTER V
SLAVERY 122

CHAPTER VI
AGRICULTURE, MANUFACTURE, AND INDUSTRY 149

CHAPTER VII
TRADE AND FINANCE 181

CHAPTER VIII
EDUCATION AND LITERATURE 203

CHAPTER IX
RELIGION 246

CHAPTER X
FAMOUS CONTROVERSIES 270

CHAPTER XI
CHARACTER 299

CHAPTER XII
THE FUTURE OF THE UNION 321

CHAPTER XIII
CONCLUSION 336
BIBLIOGRAPHY 347
INDEX 353

THE ENGLISH TRAVELLER IN AMERICA

1785—1835

CHAPTER I

MOTIVES AND GEOGRAPHY

WE of the twentieth century shall perhaps experience no modern equivalent of the attitude which prompted the European interest in America in the early days of the Republic. If we could, we should find the outlook extremely interesting. Seldom shall we witness such a fascinating experiment in government in these sophisticated days when the world impresses us as having been conquered and re-conquered many times. Here was a startling venture in statecraft. The new nation was made up of a heterogeneous collection of more or less truculent colonies, each of which had already manifested a tendency to develop according to its own geographic and economic needs. The unassimilated confederation was staggering under an enormous public debt, with no prospects of immediate resources. When we add to these difficulties the great extent of territory, the disparity in race and language of the people, the lack of sympathetic religious and political relations, and the local jealousies, and survey the accumulated burden, we do not wonder that the question foremost in the mind of the American as well as of the European was,—what is to be the result of all this? or, how long will this union last? Some of the most interesting chapters of travel literature at the time deal with this question of the future of the United States. Many optimistic European visitors saw in the young nation the nucleus of a future world power—a power which was destined to engage in a death grapple with England for the supremacy of the seas; others, judging by what they actually saw, foretold a speedy shipwreck on the rock of the slavery question, or of equal suffrage, or of the inability to populate such a vast tract of land. It was inevitable that, owing to the practical difficulties which prevented an easy communication between Europe and America, ignorance of the real state of affairs should prevail, and that preconceived ideas should govern the attitude of many a professedly truthful traveller. When we remember that even within the memory of our own generation the European mind has pictured the Indian stalking in blanket and war-paint through the streets of our large cities, we are likely to look with tolerant eye on the overdrawn and often prejudiced accounts of American life of more than a century ago. Significant, perhaps, of the knowledge of America which prevailed in England immediately after the Revolution is a statement in the preface of a curious little book published in 1789—"Historical Review of North America—by a gentleman immediately returned from a tour of that continent" (W. Matthews). "It is a country hitherto little known. The perfidious French while they retained any power in North America, took every method to keep the English in ignorance, even by publishing false maps with false names and false accounts annexed to them; probably (says Carver) the greatest part is entirely unexplored."[1]

[1] Matthews, W., Preface, p. xiv.

At any rate, with whatever eyes the European tourists surveyed America, survey it they did, and the bibliography of travel literature reveals an ever-increasing list of visitors to these shores, beginning directly after the Revolution, decreasing perceptibly during the war of 1812, and receiving a new stimulation after the independence of America was fully established by the peace of 1814. As it became more and more evident that the United States was becoming a power with which to reckon, European eyes were turned westward more curiously than ever. Correspondingly, books of travel multiplied and the list of works for the facilitation or the discouragement of emigration grew apace. Guide books for the new land were a natural consequence. Travellers vitally interested in some particular form of occupation,—agriculture, trade, etc., could not resist the temptation to tell of the new and promising field for such ventures.

The most obvious motive which led the British to seek America was relief from the state of affairs in Europe and especially in their own land. This cause operated less immediately after the Revolution than after the second war with Great Britain. In 1798, however, we find Isaac Weld writing in the preface to "Travels through the States of North America and the Provinces of Upper and Lower Canada": "At a period when war was spreading desolation over the fairest parts of Europe, when anarchy seemed to be extending its frightful progress from nation to nation, and when the storms that were gathering over his native country in particular rendered it impossible to say how soon any one of its inhabitants might be forced to seek for refuge in a foreign land, the Author of the following pages was induced to cross the Atlantic, for the purpose of examining with his own eyes into the truth of the various accounts which had been given of the flourishing and happy condition of the United States of America, and of ascertaining whether in case of further emergency, any part of those territories might be looked forward to as an eligible and agreeable place of abode."[2]

The wars which were "spreading desolation over the fairest parts of Europe" had after-effects which the British Empire was to feel more deeply than it did the conflict itself. Not only was England left with a war debt of over eight hundred and thirty million pounds, but she was forced to face and to solve many domestic problems which had been held in abeyance during the Napoleonic struggles. Her ministry was inharmonious and weak; her export trade was at a low ebb. The introduction of machinery and the establishment of the factory system were throwing thousands out of employment. The Corn Law of 1815 was a rankling grievance; the poor took to rioting and rickburning, and although sporadic attempts at rebellion were checked, discontent was general. This condition of affairs accounts for the vast number of British emigrants who yearly sought American shores. In 1817, Henry Bradshaw Fearon was deputed by thirty-nine English families to go to America "to ascertain whether any, and what part of the United States would be suitable for their residence." In the "Introductory Remarks" to his "Sketches of America" he makes a significant statement in regard to the condition of affairs in England. "Emigration had at the time of my appointment assumed a totally new character: it was no longer merely the poor, the idle, the profligate, or the wildly speculative who were proposing to quit their native country, but men of sober habits and regular pursuits; men of reflection who apprehended approaching evils; men of upright and conscientious minds to whose happiness civil and religious liberty were essential; and

[2] Weld, Isaac I., Preface, pp. iii-iv.

men of domestic feelings who wished to provide for the future and prosperity of their offspring."[3]

In 1830, Joseph Pickering published a book called "Inquiries of an Emigrant, being a narrative of an English farmer from the year 1824-30," in which he devotes his introduction to the discussion of the causes of emigration. "The first and by far the most prominent one," he says, "is privation and its consequent distress. The next, perhaps, is dissatisfaction under real or fancied political grievances; some few emigrate for a warmer, drier or healthier climate and others for no reason but a love of change."

The best known examples of those who sought a new home for themselves, and who encouraged imitation of their own example were Morris Birkbeck and George Flower. Birkbeck was a Quaker farmer who decided on account of troubles in England to emigrate to America. He inspired with enthusiasm his friend George Flower, who went before Birkbeck to investigate conditions. Birkbeck met Flower in 1817 in Virginia and together they made their way to the Ohio, and thence to the region of the Illinois. Here they assumed responsibility for a huge tract of land, 16,000 acres stretching northward from the Ohio. Farms were laid out, cabins built, and emigration encouraged to a district which, by its proximity to the Mississippi River, offered infinite possibilities for the transportation of produce to the markets of the world. Two optimistic books issued by Birkbeck in 1817 and 1818, "Notes on a Journey in America from the Coast of Virginia to the Territory of the Illinois" and "Letters from Illinois" stimulated great enthusiasm among the discontented in England, and the "English Prairie," as it was called, was the scene of active colonization. It was also

[3] Fearon, Introductory Remarks, pp. xi-xii.

destined to become later the point of dispute in a literary war. It is quite natural that many of Birkbeck's emigrants should have been disappointed in their expectations, and equally natural that they should in that case have tried to prevent other people from following their unfortunate example; on the other hand many considered the venture a successful experiment and were loud in their praises of it. William Blane, after travelling through Birkbeck's settlement in 1822, says, "While in Albion I read all the books and reviews that had been written both for and against this settlement. One traveller described it as an earthly paradise, another as a miserable, unhealthy swamp; the truth is midway between these extremes."[4]

Many travellers whose interest was not primarily philanthropic and who cared nothing for the cause of emigration in the abstract, nevertheless looked upon it in the light of their personal needs. Such a one was Thomas Cooper who, as early as 1794, came "to determine whether America and what part of it was eligible for a person like myself with a small fortune and a large family to settle in—and having completely satisfied my own mind upon the subject, I left part of my family there and have returned (probably for the last time) to fetch away the rest."[5]

One of the most amusing accounts of those who sought a personal refuge from England's evils is that of the Rev. Isaac Fidler who, dissatisfied with ecclesiastical conditions at home, crossed the ocean confidently expecting to find an Episcopal benefice waiting for him on this side. He found not only that two years' residence was required for an alien to hold such a benefice, but that his secondary

[4] Blane, William, "An Excursion Through the United States and Canada During the Years 1822-1823," p. 157.

[5] "Some Information Respecting America, Collected by Thomas Cooper, Late of Manchester," Preface, p. iii.

scheme of disseminating knowledge of Sanscrit and other ancient tongues was not more practicable. His disgust knew no bounds, and the resulting diatribe against American stupidity constitutes an interesting though unreliable source of information concerning the condition of religious affairs in America.[6]

A limited number of travellers came to investigate certain specialized fields of activity such as trade or commerce or manufacture. One of the most important and authoritative of these visitors was John Melish, who in 1806 tried to open a line of cotton trade with Savannah, Georgia. At the accession of Charles James Fox as the head of the ministry in 1805, Melish deemed the time ripe for friendly commercial relations between England and America, and embarked on his new enterprise. Later, in 1812, he writes, "Having occasion to travel extensively through the interior of Georgia, I extended my remarks, and found an opinion forced upon me, that should the restrictions of commerce be of long duration, America would become a manufacturing country and consequently would be in a great measure independent of Europe. That opinion received strength and confirmation during a residence in New York in 1810, when I was fruitlessly employed in looking for mercantile employment."[7]

With the knowledge gained in a month's leave of absence from his ship in Halifax, Lieutenant the Honorable F. Fitzgerald de Roos of the Royal Navy ventured to publish in 1827 a "Personal Narrative of Travels in the United States and Canada." His purpose was to inspect the

[6] "Observations on Professions, Literature, Manners, and Emigration in the United States and Canada." By the Rev. Isaac Fidler (1833).

[7] "Travels in the United States of America in the Years 1806 and 1807, and 1809, 1810 and 1811." By John Melish, I, Preface, p. viii.

dockyards with a view to establishing certain facts in regard to the American navy, facts which he makes clear—namely, that the reports of the naval powers of the United States have been greatly exaggerated, that the new country will never "cope with Great Britain in maritime warfare—far less dispute with her the Dominion of the Seas."[8]

A much more charming personality, a man blessed with a singular openness of mind, was John Bernard, a popular English comedian who became one of the first American stage managers. Driven from England in 1797 "by the failure of two or three managerial speculations and the patronage of an extensive circle of fashionable acquaintances," he sought a new field for the propagation of his beloved art. "On reaching Boston," he says, "I met many London acquaintances at the theatre there who varied in the reception they gave me. One said I had come too late by five years; another that I was a great fool to come at all; a third, that as I looked a florid habit, there was every chance of my being packed in a black box before the spring. The better tempered cheered me in the way an army agent does a cadet in war time. 'The yellow fever,' said they, 'thins the Green Room of at least twenty every summer, so that in a short time the field will be your own.' "[9]

Although it is true, as we have seen, that many of America's visitors came to her with a definite purpose in mind, by far the largest class was made up of those who were actuated by the same motives that impel many of us today to visit foreign countries—they sought pleasure and

[8] See De Roos, pp. 218-219; Boardman (Preface, p. v) also came for commercial reasons.
[9] "Retrospections of America, 1797-1811." By John Bernard (edition of 1887), p. 23, also pp. 25-26.

the gratification of their curiosity. How great that curiosity was is difficult to comprehend. Aside from the interesting political experiment that America represented, there was also the novelty of strange manners and customs, the mystery of the fast dying-out race of Indians, the lure of unexplored depths of forest and prairie. Curiosity drew to America some of the most interesting of her commentators and some of the most bigoted of her detractors. Actuated, at least in the case of many, by no serious purpose, they let their imaginations run riot, and the result was often a tale worthy of the Arabian Nights.

One of the most delightful embodiments of the spirit of adventure came to America in 1798 in the person of John Davis. Professedly literary in his inclinations, he wandered from New York to South Carolina, acting as tutor to earn his living. In his pedestrian travels he covered fifteen states, jotting down in his journal interesting though sometimes unreliable information about the people with whom he was associated, and particularly, many facts concerning the literary conditions of the time. The vivacity of his descriptions, the spirit of the writer, and his racy mixture of fact and fiction make the book a landmark on the oftentimes monotonous road of travel literature.[10]

In 1856, there appeared the posthumous journal of Francis Baily, at one time president of the Royal Astronomical Society. Baily had as a young man of twenty-two undertaken a tour of two years' duration (1796-7) through the unsettled parts of North America. Impelled by the spirit of adventure, he intended to make this journey serve as an apprenticeship to later travels, preferably in Africa, in the exploration of which he hoped to equal Mungo Park.

[10] "Travels of Four Years and a Half in the United States of America, During 1798, 1799, 1800, 1801, and 1802." By John Davis.

Taking time to satisfy his curiosity, he drifted leisurely through most of the explored regions of the Middle West and through vast tracts of virgin forests as well. His experiences are always interesting, some of them intensely so, as for instance, when he passed from Pittsburg to New Orleans in an open boat occupying in transit about fifty days and nights "not reckoning landings."[11]

There are, in the history of travel in America, three or four especially notorious names—notorious in the sense that they represent authors whose accounts of American life were either so scathing as to provoke indignation and frequent reprisals on the part of the natives, or so imaginative that no value could be attached to some of their statements. In this latter class is the name of Thomas Ashe who, driven by curiosity which took the form of an interest in archæology, made a journey in 1806 in the region of the rivers Allegheny, Monongahela, Ohio, and Mississippi. As we thrill with anticipation while he is uncovering an Indian mound, or while we take with him the chute of the falls of the Ohio, we forget that he was everywhere advertised as an impostor, and that such marvellous descriptions, as that of the falls of the Ohio in a thunder storm, had little, if any, foundation of fact.[12]

If we consult a table of dates of travel in this country, we find, as has been said before, that there is a decided gap in the records of the years during which occurred the second war with Great Britain. As relations with the latter country became strained, travel decreased; especially is this true of the type now under discussion, that is, that undertaken from motives of curiosity. In the six years

[11] See Baily, Francis, Preface, p. viii.
[12] See, for instance, Ashe, Thomas, "Travels in America Performed in 1806, . . ." pp. 238-239.

from 1810-1816, there were few Englishmen who evinced enough temerity to travel in the United States for pleasure. About 1816 or 1817, we see the beginning of the great western movement which was destined to receive its first real check in the circumstances of the World War. The impetus was manifold; the removal of the embargo of 1807, the growing appreciation of the possibilities of the New West, and the increased facilities in the shape of canals and highways, led Europeans to turn to America, and drove forth the settlers already there to seek fresh fields along the Ohio and in the Mississippi valley.

The uncertainty in the minds of Europeans concerning the real state of affairs in the United States called forth such works as Bristed's "Resources of America" (1818). In it, the author discusses the various opinions of travellers of all nations, their conflicting accounts, and the true state of affairs in various lines of activity, such as commerce, manufacture, government, literature, etc. Again and again were lovers of America forced to refute in print what was published in London and Edinburgh, and if it was true, as even Captain Basil Hall admitted, that the Americans were uniformly forbearing in their attitude toward the discontented and fault-finding wayfarer, their patience often came to a sudden end when they were able to set down their grievances on paper.

Lieutenant Francis Hall's book of travels in 1816 is one of the first signs of re-awakened interest in American affairs. After an extended tour through Canada, he entered the United States on the Niagara frontier, from which he penetrated through New York and Pennsylvania down as far as Charleston. His work is distinctive because of its organization. It is no hastily scrawled journal, as are so many of the accounts, but adds to the separate chapters for the different localities appendixes in which such subjects as slavery and traits of American character are discussed fully and dispassionately.[13]

The next writer of any note, who enjoys too the added distinction of being the first Englishwoman who wrote down her impressions of America, was Madame Frances Wright D'Arusmont, or Fanny Wright, as she was more familiarly known. She visited America in 1818 and again five years later, when she became interested in the slavery question and founded a colony of free negroes near Memphis. Her book, "Views of Society and Manners in America," a highly laudatory account of travels through the East and South, appeared in London in 1821.

It was in the second and third decades of the century that pleasure-seekers began to visit America in noticeably large numbers, and at that time too, began in earnest the literary war between those who wrote scoffingly of America and those who defended her. William Blane, who wrote a sympathetic account, came in 1822. Isaac Candler in 1824 published a "Summary View of America" in which he set forth concisely and clearly his observations during a trip through the New England, Middle Atlantic, and Southern states. His book met with praise from both English and American reviewers. Captain Basil Hall, a visitor in 1827-8, was the arch-traitor to American hospitality in the opinion of those who had tried to endure his fault-finding during his leisurely journey with his family over most of the known territory of the United States. Around his book, "Travels in North America in the years 1827 and 1828," there sprang up a young growth of literature that repeated or attacked his views.

After 1830, the travel literature increased as rapidly as did the number of the curious. This is the decade of Mrs.

[13] "Travels in Canada and the United States in 1816 and 1817." By Lieut. Francis Hall.

Trollope, who journeyed to the banks of the Illinois ostensibly from motives of the ordinary sight-seer, in reality for the benefit of a private business venture. Her book "Domestic Manners of the Americans" was estimated by her son Anthony Trollope to be "the first of a series of books of travel of which it was probably the best and certainly the best known."[14] In this period too, belongs Henry Tudor, an English barrister, who came to see the only quarter of the globe he had never visited and especially to behold "the magnificent cataract of Niagara."[15] Appreciative accounts of American life were written by Tyrone Power the actor[16] (1836), and by Harriet Martineau, the latter of whom was welcomed everywhere as a celebrity.[17] Godfrey Vigne, an English barrister, in 1832 came "alone, unbewifed and unbevehicled, as a man ought to travel, and with the determination of being, as far as an Englishman can be, unprejudiced." His intention was to see all he could of the United States in the space of about six months, and after reading his succinct, straightforward, almost curt account, one does not wonder that he covered as much ground as he did in the comparatively short space of time.[18]

It is impossible to individualize all the books of this class, especially those that were written in the twenties and thirties. Yet one hesitates to omit at least a bare mention of the books by such men as Charles Augustus

[14] See Trollope, Anthony, "Autobiography," Chap. II, for discussion of her work.
[15] Tudor, Henry, "Narration of a Tour in North America, in a Series of Letters Written in the Years 1831-2." (1834.)
[16] Power, Tyrone, "Impressions of America During the Years 1833, 1834, and 1835." (1836.)
[17] Martineau, Harriet, "Society in America." (1837.)
[18] Vigne, Godfrey, "Six Months in America." (1832.)

Murray, S. A. Ferrall, and Thomas Hamilton. Murray's interest led him to spend a summer with the Pawnee Indians in the remote Missouri Territory;[19] Ferrall's long "ramble" of 6,000 miles was undertaken through the sheer love of novelty,[20] while Hamilton as an "independent observer" seems to have found in American institutions and experience only a dangerous precedent for possible imitation by England.[21]

When we turn to the consideration of the motives which prompted these travellers to put down on paper what they saw and how it impressed them, we find that few were thinking of the writing of the book as a literary exercise. Many of them were careful to disclaim any pretense to literary ability, and there are indeed, very few whose excellence of style is so marked that it distracts our attention from the facts and the writer's point of view. It is amusing to see how many of the authors have "yielded to the solicitations of friends," having kept their journal of travels with no thought of publishing it. So numerous are these modest writers that one is in a humor to appreciate a statement like the following with which Charles Augustus Murray prefaced his book: "It is very seldom that the journal of a traveller appears before the public unaccompanied by a prefatory declaration that it was not his original intention to publish, and that he had been reluctantly induced by the importunities of his friends to inform the world of the extent and particulars of his travel. A statement of this kind meets with as much credit as the laboured impromptu of a wit: or the professions of dif-

[19] Murray, The Hon. Charles Augustus, "Travels in North America During the Years 1834, 1835, and 1836." (1839.)
[20] Ferrall, S. A., "A Ramble of 6,000 Miles through the United States of America." (1832.)
[21] Hamilton, Thomas, "Men and Manners in America." (1834.)

fidence made by a practised speaker: as it is a matter in which the public are so little interested, I am surprised that authors should take so much pains in attempting to explain it. Most travellers keep a record of the scenes through which they pass without having at the time definite intentions as to publication, leaving their after-decisions to be determined by circumstances; this is generally the case with persons who travel without any scientific object and is probably applicable to the following narrative."[22]

Many Englishmen, having travelled more or less extensively with professedly unbiased judgment, felt that it was their duty to enlighten their fellow countrymen on the subject of the evils of emigration. An enthusiastic detractor of this type was Thomas Brothers, who signed himself a resident in the United States for fifteen years and who gave his book the beguiling title of "The United States as They Are, not as They Are Generally Described: Being a Cure for Radicalism." The American system of government was his point of attack. Others exposed the faults of American society and domestic manners, as Mrs. Trollope and William Faux,[23] the latter of whom was designated by *Blackwood's* reviewer as "a simpleton of the first water,....a capital specimen of a village John Bull, for the first time roaming far away from his native valley —staring at everything and grumbling at most."[24]

The influence of these men was offset by that of a group of writers who looked at the United States through rosy spectacles and who encouraged emigration thither. Many

[22] Murray, C. A., Preface, p. v.
[23] Faux, William, "Memorable Days in America." (Thwaites, XI, XII.)
[24] See *Blackwood's Magazine*, XIV, 562, 565. (November, 1823.)

of these had a favorite place of residence, the superior advantages of which they enthusiastically set forth.

Many writers had no other aim than to produce an account of the unusual things that they had witnessed. Inveterate observers and travellers like Isaac Candler or Francis Baily took notes on "those things which attracted attention either by their novelty or importance," notes which were published later for their intrinsic value. Some made a special appeal to young people, with the hope of administering the wholesome pill of useful information disguised by the jelly of amusing or exciting adventures.[25] To many of the English travellers, publication was evidently a safety valve, the result of a natural desire to narrate their personal adventures or to publish their diaries or part of their correspondence. Especially is this true in the case of many of the women writers on America, Fanny Wright, Frances Kemble, and Harriet Martineau; it is also true of two of the most famous actors who visited America, John Bernard and Tyrone Power.

By far the greatest number of travellers wrote to answer questions or to set forth the real state of affairs in America. Their name is legion; each purports to be telling the absolute truth about what he has seen and heard, to be swayed by no prejudices, and to be desirous only of improving upon the accounts that have antedated his work. Some are favorable to America, some quite otherwise; in some cases the expressed determination to tell the truth has a grim and sinister ring; in others, the account is prefaced by a relation of the shocking impositions regarding America already practised on unsuspecting Englishmen.

[25] See Wakefield, Priscilla, "Excursions in North America. Described in Letters from a Gentleman and His Young Companion, to Their Friends in England." (1806.) Also, a compilation by William Bingley, "Travels in North America." (1821.)

That the majority of these writers were sincere, one cannot doubt after reading their books, but the natural disposition of the traveller often played an all too important part in determining his attitude. Though the length of the sojourn in America might vary from one month to four or five years, not even the most casual observer doubted his ability to pass judgment on what he had seen.

The difficulty of dealing with this class of material is that it is almost impossible to reconcile the different views, to lend credence to a Blane and to a Fearon at the same time, for instance, when each insists that he is telling the truth. When we turn to native books on the same subject, in an endeavor to justify some of these statements, we are still at a loss because of the prejudiced views of the sensitive American authors of the time. We hesitate to judge by instances of agreement of opinion on individual subjects discussed by several authors, but we are often obliged to take refuge in this unsatisfactory method of solving the problem.

Let us suppose that our traveller has braved the dangers of a sea voyage of several weeks' duration, and has arrived in America with rather well-defined ideas as to what parts of this land he is to visit. He has, of course, taken this voyage in a sailing vessel and has to a great extent provided for himself en route, carrying with him enough "necessities" to dismay the soul of the modern traveller. He may have in mind as an objective a limited area of land where he hopes to find a home, or he may contemplate a journey over tracts of thousands of miles, so great is the variation in the extent of land covered by different travellers.

Usually the stranger landed in New York or at Boston, after passing the Newfoundland banks. A few had their first sight of the new world from the harbor of Savannah, of Newport News, or of New Orleans, but nearly all chose the more conventional route, unless influenced by some consideration of trade or convenience. From New York or Boston, the main-travelled roads led of course westward and southward. The traveller by water resorted to the sloop or steamboat; the journey by land was perforce accomplished by stages or carriages or on horseback, as before 1830, when the South Carolina railway was built to be run by locomotive, there were only spasmodic attempts at railroads equipped with wooden rails and operated by horses.

When the Englishman landed in New York, he had the choice of two alternatives: he might go up the Hudson by sloop or by stage coach, or he could take a boat to New Brunswick en route to Philadelphia on his way to the south and west. If he went north he usually followed a beaten track, first to Albany, then across the state to Buffalo by stage or by canal boat. At the close of the Revolution, the western interior of New York State was practically a wilderness. While there was water communication between Lake Ontario and the Hudson by means of the Mohawk River, the only road in the state leading westward was the one which had been made by the Indians—the so-called Iroquois Trail. The famous Genesee Road which still survives in the Genesee Street of several cities in the central part of the state, was built westward from Fort Schuyler, or Utica, in 1794 and was extended to Buffalo in 1798. The usefulness of this road, which at its best was very poor, was much diminished by the building of the Erie Canal, begun in 1816 under the direction of DeWitt Clinton. On October 26, 1825, the first boat, "The Senecan Chief," passed from Buffalo to New York by water. So cheaply was freight carried, and so popular was canal travel that by 1836, the waterway had turned into the state treasury more than its cost. Its contribution to the prosperity of New York cannot be estimated.[26] It was inevitably destined later to be superseded by the railroad, but during the period under discussion, the canal and the Genesee Road were the two beaten paths to western New York.

A visit was, of course, always made to Niagara Falls. This most popular landmark in American scenery impressed the English traveller of the early nineteenth century much as it impresses us today. Some reacted to the sight positively and enthusiastically, often prolonging their stay to view the cataract under varying conditions, others were manifestly disappointed and did not pause to look the second time.[27]

If the traveller wished to turn back at this point, he could proceed eastward along the southern shore of Lake Ontario and thus to the waterways of central New York; if, on the other hand, a visit to Canada were contemplated he now crossed the border near Niagara. Approximately one-half of the English travellers included Canada in their itinerary. Some of these had a desire to visit the comparatively new and flourishing colonies; others seriously weighed the relative advantages of these provinces and the States, as a place of abode. The visit completed, our Englishman usually proceeded down the St. Lawrence, over land to Lake Champlain, then to Lake George, and thence back to the Hudson, sometimes stopping at Saratoga Springs, which was for many years the fashionable sum-

[26] See Shirreff, "A Tour Through North America" (p. 307), for a good account of the Erie Canal.

[27] For some descriptions of Niagara Falls, see the following: Harris, p. 165; Fowler, p. 138 ff.; Mrs. Trollope, II, 257-260; Power I, 391 ff.; Hall, F., pp. 141-147; D'Arusmont, pp. 173-180; Boardman, p. 136 ff.; Hall, B., I, 177-213; Coke, II, 28-35; Hodgson, I, 342-346; Alexander, II, 143-146; Blane, pp. 396-406; Weston, pp. 259-260.

mer place for the wealthy, not only in its vicinity but in the South as well. The Southern planter is often reported to have lived with strict frugality during the winter months, that his family might make the greater impression during their summer stay at Saratoga or Ballston Spa.[28]

From Saratoga or from Albany the wayfarer, if he were so inclined, could visit Boston, travelling by stage or by privately hired carriage. Sometimes he took short side trips into the White Mountains.[29] His route from Boston usually took him south through Providence, New London, and New Haven, finally bringing him back to New York.

Only those who were limited in time or who perhaps intended to spend some time in Canada, contented themselves with this short journey. If curiosity did not carry one as far as the Mississippi, at least it often took one to Philadelphia, and especially to Washington. To visit these cities, one usually embarked at New York on the Philadelphia boat which descended the bay, turning westward into the strait that separates Staten Island and New Jersey, then into the Raritan River, and so to New Brunswick, where stages were taken to Philadelphia via Trenton.[30] Failing this, one might take the boat from New York to Perth Amboy on the Jersey coast, from which there was a stage line running to Philadelphia. Baltimore was reached by what Melish in 1812 called "land and water stages."[31] Later it was possible to go entirely by water. Thirty-eight miles from Baltimore lay Washington, the focus of several coach lines. No sight-seeing tour was complete without a visit to Washington's tomb, in which the

[28] For Saratoga, see Hall, B., II, 24-25; Power, I, 422-424; Tudor, I, 188-194; Murray, I, 62; Shirreff, pp. 57-58.
[29] See, for instance, Tudor, I, 412 ff.; Coke, II, 145-153.
[30] Blane, p. 14.
[31] Melish, I, 177.

stranger, by the way, was invariably disappointed.[32] From Washington, the beaten track led south, through Richmond to Charleston. Often the traveller turned aside to visit the Natural Bridge. In a few instances, as in the case of Lambert in 1806, the journey was made by water from New York to Charleston, but the favorite route was overland by stage. Apparently he who penetrated as far south as Charleston more often than not projected a journey across Georgia toward the Mississippi. In that case, he went to Savannah, usually by boat. We are given an account of such a voyage by James Stuart in 1833. "The voyage to Savannah may be said to be entirely inland, the course for a considerable space passing through no less than sixteen rivers, some of them not much wider than the boat itself . . . and in other places being at sea behind no less than thirteen islands. Several of the cuts from river to river were made by the British during the Revolutionary War in order to facilitate the conveyance of military stores."[33]

From Savannah, a stage and horseback route led across a comparatively unsettled country of swamps and pine forests to New Orleans. The last stage of this journey could be accomplished by boat from Montgomery, Alabama. Safely arrived at New Orleans, the wanderer entered upon an easier route to follow. The Mississippi opened to him areas of thousands of miles; he might ascend as far as the mouth of the Ohio, or he might, like Miss Martineau, enter the mouth of the Cumberland River and explore the Tennessee and Kentucky region. Very few English travellers

---

[32] For remarks on Washington's tomb, see the following: Finch, p. 218; Tudor, I, 68; Hodgson, I, 14; Hall, F., p. 203; Murray, I, 106; Coke, I, 100. See also *North American Review*, XIX, 120, for defence of the tomb.

[33] Stuart, II, 79.

went beyond the western banks of the Mississippi. In 1809-11, John Bradbury, in search of natural history specimens, followed the course of the Missouri for some distance and returned to St. Louis after a not very successful expedition. Blane and Latrobe visited the prairies around St. Louis, but did not go far from the river. Generally exploration, as far as the English were concerned at least, confined itself to the east bank of the river.

We have the record of only one English traveller who ventured to penetrate into the forest wilderness north and northeast from New Orleans. The scientist, Francis Baily (1796-7), having descended the Mississippi, intended to return by the same means, but as there was no boat for some time, he became impatient and set out on horseback through the wilderness. After great difficulty and many exciting experiences, he reached Knoxville and from there took his way over the Cumberland Mountains.

From the mouth of the Ohio, the way stretched eastward to Pittsburg and the road across the Alleghanies. This was the route usually taken, though a few travellers went either by a more southern route from the Ohio to Virginia, or north to Lake Erie, and then to New York State. A stage ran from Sandusky on Lake Erie to Cincinnati, a distance of about 200 miles. The use of the Great Lakes belongs to a later time when steam navigation was more nearly perfected, though Harriet Martineau took the trip from Buffalo in 1837. Patrick Shirreff, in 1835, used the lakes to cross from Canada directly to Detroit on his way to Chicago which, though at that time it was a hamlet of only 150 wooden houses, was already the subject of brilliant prophecies for the future.[34]

A choice of several routes was offered to the traveller who wished to go west from Pennsylvania, Maryland, or

[34] Shirreff, p. 226.

Virginia. He could go through New York State to Buffalo, then by steamboat on Lake Erie to Sandusky, and from there cut across by stage to the Ohio River. One of the favorite projects of this period was the building of a canal between Lake Erie and the Ohio; the realization of this dream, which later materialized, opened a complete watercourse between New York and New Orleans. The Ohio River was obviously the most important factor in travel routes to the west. All roads led to "la belle rivière," as the early French settlers called it. A. B. Hulbert in "Historic Highways" emphasizes the fact that the western movement was by river valleys; through the most important of these, the Ohio, there passed for half a century a great stream of travel that changed materially the future history of the country.

Reaching to the Ohio from the east was an ever-increasing number of roads. Three or four represent the favorite routes and were most often taken by the traveller or emigrant to the West. All of them were originally Indian trails which had been widened by the passing of pack trains. The oldest of the thoroughfares was a trail called Braddock's Road. This was first opened by the Ohio Land Company and was utilized by Washington in 1755 on his way from the upper Potomac to Fort Duquesne, at the behest of Gov. Dinwiddie. This route was widened by the unfortunate Gen. Braddock, who marched over it to defeat.

A more direct route, however, and one at the present time taken by the Pennsylvania Railroad, was the turnpike called "Forbes' Road," built in 1758 under the direction of General Forbes, whose experiences are worthy of being incorporated in a romance. This road became the great military highway to the West during the Revolution. Afterward, it was improved and for thirty years was the main thoroughfare across the mountains. Most of the travellers whose views we are to discuss took this road if they visited the West.

This whole matter of western emigration was an especially fertile field for the display of state jealousy in the early days of the republic. We have seen that Virginia and Pennsylvania both had, at the close of the Revolution, a well-defined road to the Ohio. Not to be outdone by them, Maryland in 1806-18 secured the building of a national thoroughfare from Cumberland to Wheeling, West Virginia, on the Ohio. This was known as the Cumberland Road and was supposed to be very fine. Many of the better known English travellers like Mrs. Trollope, Fearon, and Blane took this route.[35] These three roads, with the addition of the old "Boone's Trail," which after 1769 marked a rather indistinct course from North Carolina to Kentucky, constituted the chief means of access to the West in the early days of emigration. As we approach the end of this period, we find that it is characterized by several new ventures in road-building as well as by an increased interest in artificial waterways, which, supplanting in many cases the older land-trail, were in turn superseded by the railroads. One of the most important of these waterways was the Chesapeake and Ohio Canal which was to be built between Washington and Cumberland. From its inception it had a formidable rival in the Baltimore and Ohio Railroad, which ran from Baltimore to Cumberland and on to the Ohio. On the same day, July 4, 1828, ground was broken for each in Washington and in Baltimore respectively. The subsequent history of these two travel routes is one of failure for the canal, which could not compete with the more rapid railroad.

It is quite probable that the completion of the Erie Canal and the prosperity which it brought to the New

[35] See Blane, p. 86; Fearon, p. 186; Mrs. Trollope, I, 271.

York region influenced the public-spirited of other states. At any rate, there was begun in 1826 the Pennsylvania Canal, which was to cross the state from Philadelphia to the Allegheny River at a point a short distance above Pittsburg. Advantage was taken of the Susquehanna and Juniata Rivers, and for the use of locks there was substituted an ingenious scheme in the shape of Alleghany Portage Railways on which boats were elevated or lowered by means of inclined planes.[36] Tunnels were bored beneath the peaks of the Alleghanies. This whole was completed by 1835 and was in use, with modifications, until the completion of the Pennsylvania Railroad in 1854.

These were some of the attempts to penetrate beyond the Alleghany ridge, which as James Hall said, "presented a formidable barrier, and those who crossed it found themselves in a new world where they must defend themselves or perish. It was the Rubicon of the adventurous pioneer."

[36] Murray, I, 135; Power, I, 291.

CHAPTER II

THE EMIGRANT AND THE TRAVELLER

THE emigrant and the traveller in America encountered of course much the same conditions and the same difficulties, but their individual experiences, owing to the difference in their aim, were likely to be very dissimilar. Thus they lend themselves to a certain amount of separate treatment, though a great deal that is said of the emigrant applies equally well to the traveller, and vice versa.

Let us imagine ourselves in the position of the middle-class Englishman who, dissatisfied with conditions at home, casts expectant eyes toward this El Dorado of which he has heard so much. He wishes to know the truth about America, and if he is a thoughtful man, he weighs the evidence set forth in the travel literature and the numerous books of advice to the prospective settler.

Besides the generally unfavorable condition of affairs in Europe, there were several good substantial considerations that induced Englishmen to emigrate to the United States. The most obvious was perhaps the fact of the uncongested breadth of the land—a land that was practically unlimited in extent. It was seldom that anyone held such a view as did Ashe that "from the vast extent of America, the industry of man cannot for centuries effect a visible change in the general and primitive face that it bears."[1] The lack of population usually acted as an encouragement to emigration rather than as a deterrent. Here the man of small means might procure by easy payments to the gov-

[1] Ashe, p. 33.

ernment sufficient acreage for himself and his descendants for the moderate price of two dollars per acre. If he found himself surrounded by undesirable neighbors, he had the opportunity to sell out and secure another tract in a more favorable, and perhaps a more remote district. The mere extent of land free from overlordship or supervision of any kind was a strong factor in determining emigration.

Freedom from taxes and tithes was, as has been said, another strong inducement.[2] The rapid reduction of the national debt after the establishment of the new republic, the constantly increasing self-sufficiency of the United States in regard to her imports, the unrestricted internal trade, the lack of a state church—all of these considerations helped to reduce the taxes to a minimum amount. This sum was chiefly applied to the repair of existing roads and the construction of new ones. Certain luxuries, as gold watches, for instance, beyond the reach of the average person of the time, were subject to a tax. Immigrants paid no import duty on their clothes, books, household furniture, and tools or implements of their trade. "Thus," says Thomas Cooper, in 1794, "they may begin their commerce, manufacture, trades or agriculture on the day of their arrival upon the same footing as a native citizen."[3] It is very evident that the lack of the customary English church tithes was an attraction. A late traveller comments on the generous salary ($700) which the Independent Church at Hartford, Conn., offered its minister, and adds, "The Americans are said to have no religion because the state is not its nursing father; perhaps they pay so much for religion because they want it, while others want it be-

[2] See, on this point, Welby, p. 297; Harris, p. 77; Cooper, pp. 52-53; also, pp. 209-210; Kendall, I, 135; Flint, p. 174; D'Arusmont, p. 136.
[3] Cooper, p. 218.

cause they pay so much for it."[4] This exemption from tithes was the direct result of the perfect freedom in the whole matter of religion. This seems to have been always a source of astonishment to the visiting European, who never fails to mention the fact. Practically all comment on it, some seeing in it the secret of much that was good in American life; others deploring it as indicative of instability and consequent failure in the new experiment.

The lack of actual poverty, in fact, equality in every form, whether in wealth, social position, or political rights, is much emphasized. Many observers comment on the astonishingly small number of beggars met with on their travels.[5] The number never exceeded three or four, and more usually there was a single specimen the sight of whom emphasized to the visitor the fact that he was the sole exception to the general rule. Equality in political rights was rather well understood from the very nature of the republican government, but the uniformity of the social life was often a source of astonishment and sometimes of chagrin. English people travelling with servants found themselves helpless in preventing the rapid absorption of republican principles on the part of maids and valets.[6] It was rather embarrassing to both master and servant to find that they were placed side by side at an inn table and that they were generally regarded as equals. To the discontented lower-class Englishman at home, however, who read of this fact, it was indicative of a condition that was very alluring.

James Stuart, after his visit to Mr. Flower's settlement in Ohio in 1830, put the freedom from anxiety in regard to

[4] Abdy, I, 248-249.

[5] For some mention of lack of beggars, see Boardman, p. 12; Tudor, II, 412; Fowler, p. 218; Alexander, II, 126-127; Rich, p. 87; Fearon, p. 6.

[6] See, for instance, Fidler, p. 82.

the future at the head of all the assets of emigration.[7] The fact that the English farmer or mechanic could bring his family to a place where possible resources seemed unbounded, and where every man of industry might earn a competence to distribute among his children, made the outlook very bright to those who were accustomed to look forward with dread to the future.

All of these considerations, combined with the attraction of the natural resources of the land and the fertility of the soil, helped to turn westward an ever-swelling tide of hopeful souls.

The factors which operated against emigration were just as numerous, but perhaps not so effectual. A very obvious and practical deterrent, especially in the early days of the period, was fear of the Indian tribes, who made emigration seem a dangerous venture to many. The most was made of this terror by unsympathetic writers who, it is probable, actually prevented a certain amount of emigration.[8]

Much more effectual arguments were those that had to do with the conditions confronting the mechanic and the farmer.[9] In the East in the latter part of this period, there was constant complaint of lack of employment among mechanics. Immediately after the Revolution, while there was not much opening for certain kinds of manufacture, such as woolen, linen, etc., the Americans showing a predilection for articles of British manufacture, there was a great demand for workers in the production of such com-

[7] Stuart, II, 241; see also Cooper, pp. 52-53.

[8] Parkinson, p. 160; also the refutation by James Hall, "Letters from the West," p. 350.

[9] For facilities for employment see the following: Duncan, I, 338; Holmes, pp. 127-128; Hodgson, II, 101; Faux, p. 80; Cooper, pp. 59-60; Kingdom, p. 3, also p. 7; Fearon, p. 25, also pp. 224-226; Bradbury, p. 323.

modities as glass, gunpowder, and paper. Cooper in 1794 mentioned the fact that there were 400 silversmiths in Pennsylvania alone. We judge from later accounts that this state of affairs did not continue. Faux tells in 1827 that in Philadelphia there were more laborers than could be paid. Eleven thousand men were in a state of unemployed pauperism, while in one prison there were 600 thieves and incendiaries. Fearon in 1817 says that in Cincinnati there was great stagnation of business owing to the surplus of shopkeepers, and that in New York, when he visited that city, he found a great lack of business among cabinet makers, timber merchants, and builders, owing to competition. The same state of affairs was noticed around Boston where no one was advised to come who could not bring from five hundred to a thousand pounds, as many were unemployed and nobody was satisfied.[10]

If the emigrant were a farmer, he had very serious problems to solve. Land was cheap, and the unwary newcomer, with an eye to its future value, often indulged in vast tracts. Then he found that superfluous acres were worse than useless [11] because if he employed help sufficient to cultivate such an extent of land, there were no profits left for himself at the end of the year; besides, there was often no market for the produce that remained after supplying the needs of his family. When access to markets was easy, these markets were flooded. With no better fate did the ordinary farm laborer meet. There is evidence that in the Atlantic States at least, the market of farm labor was overstocked. Adam Hodgson (1819-21) says that laborers should not come to America no matter how uncomfortable

[10] Faux, p. 55.
[11] Dalton, pp. 221-222; Parkinson, II, 26-27; Duhring, p. 173. Darby ("Emigrants' Guide," pp. 297-298) issues a warning against this.

their condition might be; "five out of ten may wander about for weeks or months in the agricultural districts of Pennsylvania without finding regular employment or the means of supporting themselves by their labor."[12]

Granted that the material conditions were favorable, there were still unsurmountable difficulties in the way of enjoyment of the new life. These were sometimes concerned with climate, the extremes and sudden changes of which the Englishman was ill-prepared to endure.[13] The frequent lack of even decent accommodations, of English comforts and pleasures, was not to be ignored. The difference in manners, the daily annoyances to which he was subjected, irritated the Englishman beyond measure. These last considerations often gave pause to the most enthusiastic of lovers of America and produced very often the cautious statement that if a man were at all comfortable and happy in England, he was not encouraged by the writer to leave that country.

Granting, however, that emigration could not be checked, few of those who wrote could abstain from advice to the Englishman who was seeking a new home in America. Some of these advisers, for the most part self-constituted, wrote primarily, some only incidentally, for the emigrant. In the former class were many Americans who tried to direct into the right channel the activities of the newcomers. Men like Benjamin Franklin, for instance, realized the importance of the movement and foresaw its bearing on the future of the United States. Franklin's "Information to Those Who Would Remove to America" was referred to constantly by both Americans and Englishmen, and was considered extremely practical in its

[12] Hodgson, II, 101.
[13] For extremes of climate, see Holmes, p. 124; Candler, p. 494 ff.; Davis, Stephen, p. 29.

advice. A much read and very useful book of this type was William Darby's "Emigrant's Guide" (1818) written for those who sought a home in the western and southwestern states and territories. It comprised all the information one might need, in "one portable and cheap volume."[14] Not only was it literally a guide book as to roads, etc., but it made a point of explaining a subject little understood by the average emigrant—land-tenure in the newly settled regions. Comprehensive, practical, and unbiased, this book is a fine example of its kind of literature. Most of the American books are of local interest only, and set forth the condition of affairs in only a limited section. This is true of Drake's "Account of Cincinnati," of Stoddard's, of Brackenridge's, and of Darby's "Louisiana." It was not until a later date that more comprehensive works appeared.

Another individualized type of guide was that drawn up by such groups of people as the Shamrock Society of New York to encourage emigration. In 1817, this organization published "Hints to Emigrants from Europe who intend to make a permanent residence in the United States, on subjects economical and political." This tract offers much useful advice to the emigrant, under three heads: "First, what relates to his personal safety in a new climate; secondly, his interests as a probationary resident; and thirdly, his future rights and duties as a member of a free state."[15]

Many of the English books written for the emigrant's direction divided the honors between the United States and Canada; several of them, in fact, urged the superior advantages of the British province.

One of the earliest of books written especially for the

[14] Darby, "Emigrants' Guide," Preface, p. 1.
[15] See "Hints to Emigrants," p. 7.

emigrant was Thomas Cooper's "Some Information Respecting America" (1794). While the author confined his travels to the East, he set forth fairly the relative advantages of each part of the country; for further aid to his readers, he quoted Franklin's tract, "Information to Those Who Would Remove to America." Pickering's "Inquiries of an Emigrant," though dealing with Canada primarily, had much that was useful to all emigrants. John Palmer (1818) affixed to his journal of travels in the United States and Canada a great amount of information relative to all the chief cities in America, together with a variety of other useful information. He declares his aim to have been information to emigrants. The books, however, both American and English, which were written primarily to disseminate information, are in the minority. With most writers, the advice was incidental and found a place in scattered passages or in an appendix. These admonitions make sometimes very amusing reading, and are never the least interesting part of the author's reaction to the new country. They range from the discussion of the dangers of drinking too much cold water to information in regard to the best part of the country for settlement.

Of course, one of the first decisions which the emigrant had to make concerned the time of year when he should travel. Generally, he was advised to make his journey in the early spring to avoid the extreme heat of the American summer. In that case, he might land at New York; if he started later, he was advised to land as far north as possible, namely, at Boston. The choice of a port depended too on whether the emigrant was going west after his arrival. If his destination was Ohio or any other point in that region, he was advised to land at Philadelphia or Baltimore as being more on the direct route westward.[16]

[16] Cooper, p. 80.

John Bradbury in 1818 took a journey to the western country in search of data on American natural history. On his return to England, he felt impelled to help obviate the distress he had witnessed on his travels,—distress due to the ignorance of the emigrant. He says that the first step necessary to the prospective settler is to "provide himself with a proper certificate setting forth his trade or profession, and testifying that he has never been employed in manufactures, or machine making, or in works of brass, iron, or steel pertaining to manufacture." This certificate was to be signed by the minister and church wardens of his parish and was intended to satisfy the English law prohibiting the emigration of manufacturers and machinists to the United States.[17]

In 1798, cabin passengers were obliged to pay from twenty-five guineas to thirty pounds, for which they were "found" in everything except bedding and linen; steerage passengers escaped with a payment of eight to ten pounds, children at half price.[18] There were other advantages in travelling steerage; the emigrant's baggage escaped the custom house officers, as his goods were entered by the captain of the ship on which he crossed. Later, the steerage passenger found his own provisions.[19] He was admonished to remember, in making out his list, that he and his family would probably be seasick and unable to cook, therefore enough cold food for the voyage must be provided. Tea, coffee, sugar, biscuits, butter, cheese, hams, salt, soap, and candles were part of the essentials, with some oatmeal and molasses if there were small children—of all these things there must be enough to last eight weeks at least. Bottles of vinegar for disinfection of ship's quarters were

[17] Bradbury, pp. 318-320.
[18] Cooper, p. 80.
[19] Flint, p. 115.

included; to that same end, a red-hot piece of iron dipped into a kettle of pitch was often employed when practicable.[20] Cooper advised the traveller to take plenty of lemons and apples or other fruit that would keep, as they were invaluable in cases of seasickness. Of the latter he says, "This complaint is not dangerous, and is better submitted to than prevented. It goes off earlier by exercise upon deck in the open air than by staying below in the cabin; and it is better cured by gentle dilution than by loading your stomach with food or by any preventive or curative medicines. On landing, your health will be better for having been sick at sea. This is at least as true with respect to females as the male sex." [21]

Little furniture was carried by the newcomer as it was for the most part cheaper in the United States than in Great Britain.[22] Bedding was taken of course, as it had to be provided for the voyage. Small articles like glasses and crockery were to be packed in large boxes or trunks, preferably the latter, as they were the easier to handle. Clothes enough for a year's wear were recommended. If a man intended to farm in America, he often took seed wheat or hay seed with him for convenience. His farming implements were all made in America.[23]

Arrived at an American port, the emigrant presented his letters of introduction, if he possessed them, and prepared to find a place in which to settle.[24] Whether he was a farmer or a mechanic he was advised to go westward. In 1812 the expense of travelling by stage from Philadelphia to Pittsburg was $20, and 12½ cents for every

[20] Bradbury, Appendix, pp. 321-322.
[21] Cooper, p. 82.
[22] Bradbury, Appendix, p. 320.
[23] Cooper, pp. 83-84.
[24] Bradbury, Appendix, p. 322.

pound of luggage beyond fourteen. "The charges by the way," says Melish, "are about $7. The whole distance is 297 miles and the stage travels it in six days. The expense of travelling by waggon is 5 dollars per cwt. for both persons and property; and the charges by the way are about 12 dollars. A waggon performs the journey in about twenty days."[25] If the man of the party chose to walk over the mountains, the family went much more cheaply. Provisions were cooked in a camp kitchen set up by the roadside, and a comfortable bed was available in the wagon.[26] These vehicles had "a canvass cover stretched over hoops that pass from one side to the other, in the form of an arch. The front is left open to give the passengers within the vehicle the benefit of a free circulation of cool air."[27] If the newcomer went as far as the Ohio and wished to descend the river, he was advised to buy an ark for the purpose, in partnership with three or four other families. These arks were flat-bottomed and square at the ends, and were all made with the same dimensions; fifty feet in length and fourteen feet in breadth. They were covered, and were managed by a steering oar. The usual price was seventy-five dollars and they were often sold at the end of the journey for nearly what they cost.[28]

That the unsuspecting emigrant again and again fell into the hands of rascally speculators, of whom the western country particularly was full, is very evident from the repetition of admonitions to look well to one's purse, and to invest carefully. The man who came into the new country with even a little money must use caution to conceal the

[25] Melish, II, 52; Holmes, p. 141.
[26] Bradbury, p. 324; Harris, p. 123; Kingdom, p. 2.
[27] Flint, p. 65.
[28] For the Ohio River ark, see Bradbury, pp. 324-325; Flint, pp. 96-97; Baily, pp. 152-153.

existence of it or he would prove a victim to the importunities of landsharks of all nationalities.[29] Money was provided in gold and silver rather than in notes, especially in those of distant states.

A besetting sin to which the emigrant often yielded, and against which he was warned, was intemperance. Much is said of the cheapness of spirits and the facility of obtaining them. There was a theory in Europe that the intense heat of the American summer forbade the use of cold water and that the natives took to strong drink instead. This theory is the basis of much that is said about the intemperance of the Americans, as we shall see later.

By such intimate and detailed information did those who were interested in emigration, whether native Americans or travelled Englishmen, try to guide the thousands of weary but eager feet that sought Utopia. Courage was needed for the enterprise, and a sense of humor, and adaptation to circumstances. All of these were enjoined on the traveller and emigrant. He was warned that he would meet with many hardships to which he was unaccustomed, and that nothing could be gained in America without labor, and plenty of it.

What classes of men, then, were to surmount these difficulties and eventually to become prosperous and desirable citizens of the republic? For what types of people was such a change beneficial?[30] The extreme poor, of whatever trade or occupation, were always bettered by emigration to America if they were industrious and willing to work. Except in the eastern congested districts, it was al-

[29] Bradbury, p. 329.
[30] For a discussion of the classes of people who should, or should not emigrate, see Fearon, pp. 437-442; Davis, Stephen, pp. 146-147; Duhring, pp. 171 and 175; Cooper, pp. 58-59, 62-64; Candler, pp. 494-495; Wilson, C. H., Appendix, p. 1078; Weston, pp. 168-169.

ways possible to find employment with a tradesman as an apprentice, or with farmers who had more land than they could manage to cultivate. In a year a man was generally proficient in his new trade. Manufactures of other than useful articles found slight foothold in America in the earlier part of the period under discussion. Luxuries had little place in American life, and the production of them was relegated to countries with wealth to buy them and leisure to enjoy them. Merchants, tradesmen, and shopkeepers, unless they had previously formed connections, found it hard to establish a patronage until they had served a sort of local apprenticeship. Once established, they usually succeeded, though shopkeeping became, as we have seen, an occupation very much overdone. Most professional men were in the early days decidedly out of their element, unless an exception is made in the case of lawyers, who seem to have been always extremely busy with the vast amount of litigation over land titles, etc. Divines apparently succeeded as schoolmasters rather than in their original capacity. The student of the fine arts and the literary man as such seem to have had small reason for coming to this country.

The introduction of English servants was not generally encouraged. They seem to have been too sophisticated to be a success in the employ of the average American; indeed, most foreign servants, not understanding conditions, seem to have been generally at a loss and unsatisfactory.[31] The most useful class were the German and Swiss peasants, many of whom came to Pennsylvania, and beginning as assistants to farmers and country gentlemen, soon earned enough to buy a home and thus to become landed proprietors. Bradbury says that the reason for the greater success of the German, Dutch, and Swiss was not their greater

[31] D'Arusmont, p. 338.

industry or economy but their more judicious mode of settling. They were more likely to plan ahead and usually engaged an agent. When arrangements were made, they moved over in a body.[32]

In the selection of the region to which they were to emigrate, newcomers had a wide field for choice. This selection was governed by several important considerations. For instance, we find very few new settlers emigrating to the Southern states. Though curiosity often led travellers thither, almost none sought a new home there. One great drawback was the enervating climate, another greater one was the presence of slavery with all its accompanying evils as the European saw them.[33]

In the more thickly populated states on the seaboard, land became so dear as to be beyond the means of the majority, and early reached its maximum value as an investment. Those who felt that they could afford to settle here were again limited by their aversion to the cold climate of Maine and the mosquitoes and agues of New Jersey. Western Pennsylvania was an extremely attractive location, as it possessed "a healthy climate, a good soil, abundance of coal, iron-ore, limestone, sandstone, and salt springs," but he who settled there had no market facilities for disposing of his produce. The same was true of western New York until after the Erie Canal was completed in 1825.[34] Besides, the winters of New York were more severe than those of Pennsylvania. In the seventeen nineties, an English colony was proposed in Pennsylvania on the Loyalsock Creek, about 170 miles west of Phila-

[32] D'Arusmont, p. 342; Sutcliffe, p. 34; Bradbury, p. 338.
[33] Holmes, p. 142; Cooper, p. 7.
[34] Flint, pp. 181-183; Cooper, p. 16. "New York State laws do not permit aliens to purchase, transmit or convey landed property," see also on this, Holmes, p. 142.

delphia. This site was supposed to represent the most favorable situation in the whole state, in climate, in height above sea level, and in fertility of the soil.[35]

The great crowds that pressed westward over the Alleghanies were significant of a condition which was made more manifest by the fact that so many thousands of inhabitants of the Eastern states joined the throngs of new arrivals. John Palmer in 1818 remarked on the fact that Vermont and New Hampshire were but slowly increasing in population, for so many people emigrated to the new states. Some towns had lost as many as forty families in a year. "In several instances," he says, "I have seen elderly people about to quit good farms on which they were getting a living, to go and form new connections in the west. This is carrying the thing to excess, but Americans on any part of the continent are at home; and it certainly is better for their children, as in the west there is a milder climate and plenty of room for centuries to come." [36]

The country north of the Ohio was very fertile and attracted great numbers of people. Blowe says it was settled not with regard to health but for gain.[37] Mechanics and farmers were very much in demand here, but the wise settler chose a site at some distance from the river, as the tendency of the Ohio to overflow its banks caused fever and ague, which rendered the victim practically incapable of employment. All settlements along the Western rivers were unhealthful; all swampy places were to be shunned by the prudent settler.

Proximity to the Ohio offered, however, a very practical

---

[35] Cooper, pp. 73-74.

[36] Palmer, p. 202; also see, on emigration from New England, Bradbury, pp. 309-310, 318; Blowe, p. 163; Cooper, p. 79.

[37] Blowe, p. 163.

advantage; it provided a free water route to New Orleans, a city which was expected to rival and indeed to surpass New York in commercial activity. Many curious facts are revealed by travel literature in regard to the prevailing attitude toward New Orleans. Unhealthful to an extreme, a veritable pest hole of yellow fever, this city was called "the wet grave," as it was built so near the level of the water that graves dug for the reception of the dead were filled with water before the coffin could be lowered.[38] Yet there seems to have been something extremely fascinating to the stranger in the gay life, the mixed population, the atmosphere of romance that shed a glamor over the vice and dissipation, and above all, in the practical commercial possibilities of the city.

The land south of the Ohio presented a marked contrast to the northern tract. True, it too was extremely fertile, and therefore offered great advantages, but these were offset by local drawbacks. A very serious one to the farmer, especially, was the prevalent insecurity of land titles. The Kentucky region was surveyed very early and very poorly, and mistakes were constantly being made in regard to the possession of the land. Therefore, the region was the scene of endless and complicated litigation, which fact kept it in bad repute.[39] In the second place, the wildness of the country, its isolation in spite of the fact that one of the roads to the West passed through it, gave a peculiarly uncivilized character to the inhabitants, and many were the wild tales narrated of the gouging and gander-pulling, drinking and gambling of these people to whom the travellers, albeit reluctantly, had to concede the virtues of generosity, hospitality, and warmth of character.[40] Fevers of all sorts

[38] Alexander, II, 30.
[39] Winterbotham, p. 315; Flint, p. 184, also note; Ouseley, p. 138.
[40] Melish, II, 94; Fearon, p. 243.

were prevalent here. Fearon says that about every twelfth house in Louisville in 1818 was a doctor's.[41] Slavery, too, proved a drawback to settlement in this region.

Though little was known in the period under consideration of the region along the Missouri, it was supposed to be rich in coal, silver, lead, and other minerals, and was credited with great advantages in soil and climate.[42] Flint says that the difficulty of navigating the river deterred many.[43] Most of the people along both banks of the Mississippi were "squatters"; many of them maintained a precarious ague-stricken existence by supplying wood to the Mississippi steamboats. They were credited by people who passed on the river with being outcasts, criminals, and "men of broken characters, hopes and fortunes who fly not from justice, but contempt."[44]

The section which seems to have represented a combination of the good features of other places, with few of the drawbacks, was the territory of the Illinois. One authority says: "There is perhaps no country in the world where a farmer can commence operations with so small an outlay of money and so soon obtain a return, as in Illinois."[45] The land was cheap and of great fertility. In 1830, there were only 150,000 people occupying a tract of land greater than England. It united the advantages of rich soil, a ready market for produce, good climate, no slavery, and a proportionally great number of schools and churches. James Stuart advised all who wished to settle in that region to take certain precautions: "What I would recommend to the stranger emigrating to this country would be that he

[41] Fearon, p. 243.
[42] Bradbury, p. 250 ff.
[43] Flint, p. 191.
[44] Hamilton, II, 187.
[45] Shirreff, p. 446.

should apply at the land offices at Springfield or at Vandalia, or at any other of the land offices, and get the surveyors to show him those situations which they look on as most desirable; *first*, in point of health; *secondly*, in point of soil; *thirdly*, in being provided with good water and a sufficient quantity of wood, which is not always the case in the prairie land, and ought most especially to be attended to, strong wooden fences being indispensable; and *fourthly*, in point of convenience of situation, including the neighborhood to a town, schools and churches and the means of communication by roads and rivers."[46]

Evidently, therefore, the region west of Pittsburg and the Alleghanies offered more advantages to the emigrant than did the more densely populated east. To the farmer the superiority of this section was obvious; to the man in trade, the profits in business were greater and the expense of living much less; to the European generally, the climate, lacking the extremes of heat and cold of the Atlantic States, was much more suited to his constitution. The benefits accruing to the man who had the courage to make the journey with his family seem in most cases to have more than repaid him for the toil and hardship undergone.

The settler's first care after acquiring his new land was to cut down trees for his log house, which was often finished in a few days and at a moderate cost for labor, if he could secure labor at all. The next task was to clear the land, to root out underbrush and small trees, which were burnt upon the land. Next came the felling of trees immediately around his house, both for the sake of living conditions and for the necessary supply of fence rails. The land was then lightly ploughed or scratched with a harrow, the grain was sown, and the new life begun. Later a frame building replaced the log hut, more and more land was cultivated as

[46] Stuart, II, 223.

resources increased, communities were formed, churches and schools built, and the locality took on a definite character, largely determined by the nature of the previous life of the settler and the part of the world from which he had emigrated.

Before bringing to an end this discussion of the emigrant, we must notice one particular type of settler who is mentioned frequently in travel literature. This is the "redemptioner," a foreigner who could not afford to pay his passage to America and who, as a result, became "bound out" for a certain number of years to the captain of the vessel on which he sailed.[47] This master, in turn, sold the services of these unfortunates to settlers who needed them. A great deal is said of this practice, and the cruelty of captains to their victims was made a subject of reproach to Americans. Parkinson even went so far as to say that the men who published the favorable accounts of the United States were hired by Americans to contract with captains of ships to bring over such as were unable to pay their passage that they might buy them when they arrived in America.

These redemptioners were supposedly governed by very severe laws formed for English convicts before the Revolution. Irish and German societies tried to mitigate the cruelty of them, and did a great deal toward alleviating the distress of their countrymen. The Irish especially came over in great numbers. Priest mentions that he saw at Baltimore in 1802 a large vessel from Ireland, that he found three at Newcastle and one in Philadelphia. Each vessel probably held about 250 passengers. He tells a harrowing tale of cruelty that was perpetrated on a ship loaded

[47] For "redemptioners," see Janson, pp. 461-462; Parkinson, I, Introd. p. 20; Priest, p. 142 ff.; Fearon, pp. 148-151; Palmer, pp. 164-170; Weld, I, 120-122; Sutcliffe, pp. 32-34.

with Irish redemptioners. Owing to the small provision of food and water doled out by the captain, a contagious disorder broke out on board, which carried off great numbers. Priest saw and talked with one of the survivors, who confirmed all that he had heard.

Fearon's disgust with this practice was extreme, and was expressed with his usual emphasis. While at Philadelphia, he visited a vessel of this type. "As we ascended the side of this bulk a most revolting scene of want and misery presented itself. The eye involuntarily turned for some relief from the horrible picture of human suffering which this living sepulchre afforded. Mr. —— enquired if there were any shoemakers on board. The captain advanced; his appearance bespoke his office; he is an American, tall, determined, and with an eye that flashes with Algerine cruelty. He called in the Dutch language for shoemakers, and never can I forget the scene which followed. The poor fellows came running up with unspeakable delight, no doubt anticipating a relief from their loathsome dungeon. Their clothes, if rags deserve that denomination, actually perfumed the air. Some were without shirts, others had this article of dress but of a quality as coarse as the worst packing cloth. . . . Such is the mercenary barbarity of the Americans who are engaged in this trade that they crammed into one of those vessels 500 passengers, 80 of whom died on the voyage. The price for women is about 70 dollars, men 80 dollars, and boys 60 dollars. When they saw at our departure that we had not purchased, their countenances fell to that standard of stupid gloom which seemed to place them a link below rational beings." Even after a century, it is pleasant to know that Robert Walsh took up this statement of Fearon's in "An Appeal from the Judgments of Great Britain" (1819), and showed that not only were the ship and the captain English, but that of the vessels that entered the port of Philadelphia in the years 1816 and 1817, laden with redemptioners, the greater number were foreign, of which half were British.

Other Englishmen, while deploring this custom, gave a less prejudiced view of it. R. Sutcliffe, a Quaker who visited America in 1804, 1805, and 1806, was a guest in a family who employed two servants of this class. He says that though the situation of these redemptioners naturally aroused a feeling of compassion, they generally enjoyed kindly treatment. John Palmer, in 1818, saw great numbers of redemptioners in the streets of Philadelphia. He says that captains sometimes treated them with great cruelty, but that this barbarity was an incidental circumstance and that laws were already being framed to protect this unfortunate class of people. Nine-tenths of them were bought out by their own countrymen and treated with kindness during the period of their servitude, which was usually three years.

It remains to discuss in more detail the conditions of travel that presented themselves to both the emigrant and the stranger whose stay in America was limited in length. We must therefore enter into a discussion of the means of transportation from place to place, the houses of entertainment, and the reception accorded the stranger by the native American.

In this period, one had small choice in the means one was to take to cover distance. The two conveyances most often used in travel were the stage coach by land, and, after Fulton's invention, the steamboat by water. It is true that one might enjoy a pedestrian journey, as did John Davis or Isaac Candler, but most travellers found this too slow and too arduous. One travelled sometimes on horseback and sometimes in one's private hired carriage, but the majority of people who came to see the new country were obliged to mingle with their fellow travellers in the enforced intimacy of the stage coach. Of this useful vehicle in its palmy days we have many descriptions.[48] Most of us probably are familiar with pictures of it standing before an inn door, as it was usually represented, while the driver, in a hat which was a cross between a western sombrero and the old fashioned "beaver," obligingly cracked his long whip over the backs of the four stationary horses. Though the Englishman was acquainted with his native stage coach, he was continually surprised at the changes which the Americans had made in evolving their type. The latter was a ponderous sort of vehicle; the body was swung on great leather straps which served as springs. The top was rounded, therefore no baggage was carried except at the back, where the impedimenta rested on broad leather thongs. The American coach that was typical throughout most of this period carried nine people inside, and one on the low seat beside the driver in front. No one rode outside, perhaps because it was considered dangerous on account of the roughness of the roads. The nine inside passengers sat in three seats, facing the front of the coach. The three people who occupied the middle seat used for a back a broad leather strap which passed across the coach. Vigne says that this occasionally became unhooked as the vehicle passed over a forest road, and that the heads of the passengers on the middle seat were instantly thrown in contact with the stomachs of those who were behind them. Side panels of either leather or oilskin were let down in wet weather, but seem to have been generally unsuccessful in preventing discomfort. The choice seat for the traveller

[48] For a few of the descriptions of the American stage coach, see the following: Palmer, p. 11; Fidler, p. 119; Vigne, I, 60-61; Duncan, II, 6 ff., also 316; Hamilton, I, 146-148; Mrs. Trollope, I, 270; Candler, p. 40; Boardman, p. 121; Twining, T., p. 59.

was the one beside the driver; not only could one elicit useful information from the latter, who was often an interesting character, but he could foresee all the bad places in the road and fortify himself against much of the jolting and other discomfort.[49]

In 1794, Wansey, in going from Boston to New York by stage, paid four pence a mile and was allowed fourteen pounds of baggage.[50] Thomas Cooper, at about the same time, estimates that the expense of travel between Philadelphia and New York, both as to carriage and living by the way, was about one-third cheaper than between the metropolis and any of the great towns of England.[51] The fares were collected piecemeal because of the frequent changes from one vehicle to another, of which travellers often complained.

Where stage lines were not available, the traveller himself had to assume the responsibility for his transportation. Candler says (1824): "In the newly settled parts, and in the bye-roads of the older, the traveller must content himself as well as he can in a light tilted wagon, in which, if the road be rough, he will experience a jolting painful to flesh and bones. Great command of temper is necessary for one who . . . is for the first time seated in one of these wagons when travelling on what is technically called a gridiron road, that is, a road formed . . . of trunks of trees placed across from side to side, covered with a layer of soil. On such a road, I have found the jolting so great as to knock my head violently against the sides and top of the vehicle, besides its making my hip bones quite sore."[52] This type of wagon was sometimes called the "coachee"—we have one detailed description of it. "The body of the coachee is rather longer than that of the coach; the front of it is

[49] Abdy, II, 294.
[50] Wansey, p. 31.
[51] Cooper, p. 140.
[52] Candler, pp. 40-41.

quite open, down to the bottom; and the driver sits on a bench under the roof of the carriage: within are two seats for the passengers, who are placed with their faces toward the horses: the roof is supported by props; it is likewise open above the pannels on each side of the doors, and as a defence against bad weather, it is furnished with a leather curtain which encloses the open part."[53]

The horses which drew the stage were many times the subject of admiring comment. Much was said of their remarkable qualities,—their endurance and sagacity, and of the perfect understanding which seems to have existed between themselves and their drivers. Seldom did a traveller see a blind, spavined, or lame stage horse.[54] The driver, too, was the recipient of universal if sometimes reluctant admiration. He could be trusted in all sorts of difficulties by the way; nothing disturbed his equanimity or his good nature, though his vehicle broke down repeatedly in the course of one day's journey, and the time-honored robbing of the snake fences for rails with which to extricate the party from a bad mud hole, had to be perpetrated ad infinitum. He was often poorly dressed and wore no indication of his profession; "a man in rusty black, with the appearance of a retired grave-digger"—thus Thomas Hamilton describes the driver of his coach. He might be almost anybody—a district judge, a farmer, or a captain in the army, and many a traveller discovered incidentally that he was being driven to his destination by one of the most influential citizens of the community.[55]

[53] Wakefield, p. 11.
[54] On stage horses, see Palmer, p. 42; Wansey, p. 36; Hamilton, I, 147.
[55] For interesting descriptions of the stage driver, see De Roos, pp. 98-99; Twining, p. 64; Weld, I, 38; Hamilton, I, 148; Shirreff, p. 49; Holmes, pp. 357-360.

The stages were necessarily built heavy and very strong to resist the effects of travel over the notoriously bad roads. Everywhere, one meets with mention of this condition of the thoroughfares, and each traveller, as he goes through the country, believes that he has discovered the worst road in America—until he has occasion to take the stage again in another locality. Weld said, just after the Revolution, that the worst roads in the United States were undoubtedly in Maryland.[56] Here the stage passengers were obliged to shift from side to side constantly, on signal from the driver, to prevent the coach from overturning in the ruts. Later Francis Hall claimed the same distinction for Virginia, with its stiff clay soil through which the traveller floundered helplessly.[57] Harriet Martineau could conceive of nothing worse than the roads of Georgia, unless it were those of the Michigan woods.[58] New Jersey, western Pennsylvania, and even Massachusetts, received their share of condemnation; indeed there is very little favorable mention of any of the American roads unless it were those of central New York, which met with occasional praise.[59] James Stuart expressed astonishment that the thoroughfares were as good as he found them, considering the method of building them. They were usually made and kept in repair by the inhabitants themselves. Small stones were not used, as in the present method, but holes were filled with clay, and brush and saplings were pressed into service in muddy spots. When possible, the way led over a ridge as being more likely to remain dry here than on low land.[60]

[56] Weld, I, 37; see also Palmer, p. 41.
[57] Hall, F., p. 208.
[58] Martineau, I, 215.
[59] Hamilton, I, 148, also II, 308-309; Melish, II, 355.
[60] Stuart, I, 180; Holmes, pp. 320-321; Duncan, II, 8; Weld, I, 37.

Mention has already been made of the gridiron or corduroy roads. These connected isolated communities or led from them into the more settled parts. Despite the harm which they did to both the body and the disposition of the unfortunate wayfarer, they seem to have been looked upon for many years as the only expedient. Tudor says of them (1831): "They are formed of many miles in succession of the stems of trees placed together transversely, and afford to a person troubled with indigestion an excellent opportunity for the due secretion of the gastric juice, though like all other remedies of a medicinal nature, accompanied by somewhat of inconvenience; for the unceasing jolts occasioned by passing over them threatened not infrequently to counter-balance this advantage by a rather uncomfortable dislocation. These anti-bilious communications . . . are designated corduroy roads, and I think the unhappy wight who has once travelled over them would never be inclined to wear a garment made of the stuff whence the name is borrowed, however fashionable it might become, from the ungrateful association that would always be connected with it; as a sympathetic ache of the bones would naturally accompany the direction of the eye when regarding its mimic ridges."[61] There was a story current that a Scotchman, packing his baggage for a stage ride, unwisely left some silver dollars in his clothes. When he arrived at his destination, he found that the coins, from the continual jolting, had escaped from their confinement and had literally cut his clothes to pieces.[62]

Lambert attributes the excellence of the central New York roads to the existence of turnpikes. These came to be very much in evidence in the Northern and Middle States. They were roads made in the more settled districts by stock companies; "the expenses are defrayed," Lambert says,

[61] Tudor, II, 434.   [62] Palmer, p. 45.

"by shares subscribed by a certain number of persons who form themselves in a company under an act of the legislature. It is a speculation that few have failed in, for the traffic on the road soon increases the value of the capital."[63] These roads were of course supported by tolls. "Turn pike tolls were not payable by persons going to and from public worship, funeral, grist-mill or blacksmith's shop—for physician or midwife, or passing on public business as jurors, electors or militiamen. There is an exemption for those who reside within a mile of the gate, except carriers, etc."[64]

When interest in the new railroad system was at its height, we find that many hitherto popular roads became neglected and almost impassable, because so great were the hopes entertained of the new venture that it was not considered necessary to repair and keep in order the old highway. This seems to have been especially true of the roads in Pennsylvania and New Jersey.

The difficulties of travel were increased in the isolated parts by the lack of bridges, or their poor quality where they existed.[65] Usually a stream had to be forded; if a bridge had been made, it was of slippery logs, so poorly put together that the unwary passenger often found himself thrown from his vehicle into the stream or driving through water which came up to the seats of the wagon. Basil Hall had the latter experience when he tried to cross the Yam Grandy River in Georgia. He and his party had to maintain a footing on a bridge that consisted for part

[63] Lambert, II, 33; Hamilton, II, 308; Maude, p. 33; Twining, pp. 62-63; Palmer, p. 178; Melish, I, 125.
[64] Abdy, I, 327 (note).
[65] For difficulties with bridges, see Martineau, I, 217-218; Flint, p. 131; Melish, I, 257-258; Hall, B., III, 265 ff.; Duncan, II, 9; Twining, pp. 60-61.

of the way of one log, while his driver took his chances with the carriage fording the stream.

Less difficulty confronted the traveller who journeyed by boat on the water courses of the United States. Before the days of the steamboat, the sloop was, in the East, much in evidence. This was a safe but slow means of transportation. Its place was taken on the Western waters by the keel boat, or the flat boat, of which some mention has already been made. After 1810, the Americans could offer to the travelling European a means of locomotion of which they themselves were extremely proud, and which met with universal admiration from the travelling public.[66] The steamboats that navigated the Hudson were especially commended. The "Chancellor Livingston," Fearon says, (1818) "was equalled by none in the world." It was a "floating palace," with an eighty-horse-power engine. Much wonder was expressed at the speed of these boats ("five miles an hour against wind and tide"), the luxurious furnishings, the general air of elegance, the good food, and the cheapness of it all. Palmer travelled on the "Chancellor Livingston," and paid a fare of seven dollars from Albany to New York, plus a state tax of one dollar toward the expense of building the Erie Canal. Though he grumbled slightly at this extra charge, he considered that the fare was extremely reasonable. After 1810, no visitor to America who had not travelled on one of these boats between Albany and New York deemed his trip complete. The only complaint seems to have been that no separation was made on these boats between the genteel and the less polished people.[67] Rules for behavior, however, were many and

[66] For praise of the American steamboat, see Lambert, II, 37; Daviss, p. 78; Fowler, pp. 38, 168; Stuart, I, 40-42; Duncan, II, 314; Martineau, II, 21; Fearon, p. 75; Flint, p. 46; Neilson, p. 44; Duncan, I, 306-307; Palmer, pp. 247-248.   [67] Candler, p. 39.

strict, playing cards and smoking in the cabin were forbidden, and the only dissipation seems to have been heated political controversy, which no man could have checked by any rules, even if he had wished to do so.[68]

It was estimated that in the period from 1811 to 1831, there were over 300 steamboats built to navigate the great Western rivers.[69] The awkward and dangerous keel boat was quickly supplanted by this new mode of locomotion, which shortened the voyage from Louisville to New Orleans and back from six or seven months to a little over three weeks.[70] The Western boats were comfortable, but were generally conceded to be less luxurious than those on the Eastern rivers. They burned wood exclusively, usually a cord an hour, at a cost of about three dollars a cord. The "Constitution" on which James Stuart travelled in 1830, burned twenty-six cords a day. The trip from St. Louis to Louisville took a little over eleven days and the fare was thirty dollars.[71] In 1830, Ferrall paid twenty-five dollars to go from Louisville to New Orleans in a very comfortable boat, and was "found in everything except liquors."[72] Much has been written about the dangers of navigating the Mississippi, and the pilot of the steam vessel found that increased speed of travel did not meet with a corresponding accession of safety in navigating. The treacherous "sawyers" and "planters" of the Mississippi lay in wait for the steamboat as well as for the slower flat-boat, and the shifting sediment on the banks often brought her to grief. To these dangers was added that of falling

[68] Lambert, II, 43; also Hamilton, I, 131 ff.
[69] Martineau, II, 21.
[70] Tudor, II, 36.
[71] Stuart, II, 154; Alexander, II, 51; Hall, B., III, Chap. XV (entire).
[72] Ferrall, p. 179.

sparks from her smoke-stacks; the history of early inland navigation is full of instances of the burning of steamers, especially on the Western rivers.[73] Nevertheless, the early form of steamboat played a great part in opening up the New West to the pioneer of the first part of the nineteenth century.

Much more typical of the new country than the means of transportation were the places of entertainment by the way. Though improvements were constantly being made in conditions throughout this period, the housing and feeding of the stranger was always accompanied by compromise and often much inconvenience on the part of both host and guest. The average English gentleman could not appreciate the advantages of the public parlor, where he was greeted with frank curiosity and with clouds of tobacco smoke, any more than he could reconcile himself to the frequent necessity of sleeping between sheets that a problematical number of people had used before him or of sharing his room or even his bed with a stranger, or strangers. Even if he good-naturedly tolerated any of these conditions, he did not like them, and he usually said as much.[74] If he stopped at an inn, he was more than likely to be expected to sleep in a room with several other people; he was fortunate if he could get a bed to himself. In times of great congestion, as for instance when land sales were going on in the neighborhood, or when the stream of western pioneers was especially great, he was often glad to accept a bed made up on the barroom floor, or some other uncomfortable makeshift.[75] Lambert says, in 1816, that the practice of putting two or three in a bed was largely discontinued, except in

---

[73] Alexander, II, 72; Stuart, II, 16 ff.
[74] Flint, p. 73; Blane, pp. 154-155; Hamilton, II, 175; Ferrall, p. 117.
[75] Martineau, I, 259.

the more isolated regions. The prevailing custom was to offer the hospitality of a large room with several single beds.[76]

Even with conditions at their best, the Englishman suffered greatly from petty annoyances, ranging from the prevalence of vermin down to the lack of curtains to his bed. Many were the anathemas hurled at the public wash basin, usually kept under the inn pump in the yard as being a central location, at the miserable little rags of towels, the narrow bed clothes, the flabby pillows, and the feather beds, to the last of which the Englishman could not become reconciled.[77] Harriet Martineau's progress through the new country seems to have been marked by a continual struggle for clean sheets and fresh water in her bedroom. There were no bells in an American inn, and a corresponding dearth of attendance existed.[78] Thomas Hamilton tells of his bedtime experience in a tavern in Worcester, Massachusetts, in the early thirties: ". . . in America there are no bells, and no chambermaids. You therefore walk to the bar and solicit the favor of being supplied with a candle, a request that is ultimately, though by no means immediately, complied with. You then explore the way to your apartment unassisted. . . . Your number is 63, but in what part of the mansion that number is to be found you are of course without the means of probable conjecture. Let it be supposed, however, that you . . . at length discover the object of your search. If you are an Englishman, and too young to have roughed it under Wellington, you are probably what is called in this country 'almighty particular,' and rejoice in a couple of comfortable pillows to

[76] Lambert, II, 29.
[77] For general conditions, see De Roos, pp. 5-6; Stuart, I, 88; Hall, B., III, 271; Martineau, I, 215, 219, 255; Weld, I, 114.
[78] Holmes, p. 342; Stuart, I, 88; Martineau, I, 219.

say nothing of a lurking prejudice in favor of multiplicity of blankets, especially with the thermometer some fifty degrees below the freezing point. Such luxuries, however, it is ten to one you will not find in the uncurtained crib in which you are destined to pass the night. Your first impulse is to walk downstairs and make known your wants to the landlord. This is a mistake. Have nothing to say to him. You may rely on it, he is too busy to have any time to throw away in humoring the whimsies of a foreigner; and should it happen, as it does sometimes, in the New England States, that the establishment is composed of natives, your chance of a comfortable sleep for the night is about as great as that of your gaining the Thirty Thousand pound prize in the lottery." [79]

This indifference of servants and of innkeepers puzzled more than one newcomer. In the former class there were very few native Americans, as none but the most indifferent characters remained in house service, which they considered degraded and suitable only for negroes. European emigrants of that class quickly imbibed the current ideas regarding independence and equality and persisted in the occupation only until they had earned a competence for some sort of business of their own. These facts explain to a great extent the attitude of the American servant class.[80] When the stranger, however, learned to *ask* for what he wanted rather than to order it, he found that his request was complied with, with a reasonable amount of good grace. Then, too, the lack of the "tipping" system helped to propitiate the impatient stranger.[81]

There was just as little privacy to be gained at meals as at any other time. Seldom indeed was a meal served in

[79] Hamilton, I, 249-250.
[80] Weld, I, 29; Boardman, p. 35.
[81] Holmes, p. 355; Dalton, pp. 242-243; Palmer, p. 150.

the private room of the guest at an American tavern. Every one ate in one large room, and at the same time, and it behooved the hungry man who did not wish to wait twenty-four hours for his dinner to be on time. A delay of even ten minutes was likely to prove fatal. The guests congregated before the bar or in the public parlor to await the ringing of the bell which signified that the dining room doors were about to be opened. Here is an account of the typical meals at a Southern inn in 1819:

"Usually about half past eight o'clock the bell rings for breakfast, and you sit down with 60 or 80 persons to tea and coffee, and every variety of flesh, fowl and fish, wheat bread, Indian-corn bread, buckwheat cakes, etc. Every one rises as soon as he has finished his meal and the busy scene is usually over in ten minutes. At two or three o'clock the bell rings, and the door unlocks for dinner. The stream *rushes* in and *dribbles* out as at breakfast and the room is clear in less than a quarter of an hour. . . . The waiters, who are numerous, civil and attentive, carve, few people appearing to have leisure to assist their neighbors. There are decanters of brandy in a row down the table, which appeared to me to be used with great moderation and for which no extra charge is made. Tea is a repetition of breakfast, with the omission of beefsteaks, but in other respects with almost an equal profusion of meat, fowls, turkey-legs, etc. . . . The picture which I have given you of the meals at taverns is not an inviting one: they more resemble a school boy's scramble than a social repast."[82]

The landlord's family made part of the company at the table, the wife or daughter presiding at the teapot and the

---

[82] For interesting accounts of meals, see Hodgson, I, 30-32 (quotation); Palmer, pp. 150-151; Duncan, II, 319; Janson, p. 80; Tudor, I, 37; Harris, p. 66; Fearon, pp. 247-248; Fowler, pp. 120-121; Shirreff, p. 34; Alexander, II, 101-102; Boardman, p. 25.

landlord attending to the introduction of strangers, especially if a distinguished person were present.[83] The American host was often a prosperous farmer as well as an innkeeper, and he was quite likely to be a field officer of the militia and altogether a most influential citizen.[84] The daughters,—indeed all the women of the family,—won almost universal commendation from strangers for their dignity and reserve.[85]

It has already been indicated that the food was plentiful in quantity.[86] Seldom is there a hint of insufficient provision in an American inn. Substantial items, such as veal cutlets, beefsteaks, chickens, ham, eggs, and cheese, and a variety of sweetmeats figured on the table at all of the daily meals. In the more unsettled regions a profusion of game and fish was added to the menu. The dishes were not always cooked and served to the Englishman's liking,— especially did he detest the American fondness for greasy food. The heavy diet and the use of animal food at every meal was looked upon by the English as the cause of many American diseases.[87] Every house of entertainment had a bar. Basil Hall says that there were usually two on every steamboat; that even the museum at Albany had one, and at the Cauterskill Falls there was one on either side of the cataract![88]

[83] Candler, p. 45; Dalton, p. 131.
[84] For the American landlord, see Holmes, p. 139; Janson, p. 442; Hall, F., p. 38; Duncan, II, 320; Weld, I, 114; Neilson, p. 232; Alexander, II, 127.
[85] Hall, F., p. 38; Hall, B., I, 121.
[86] For accounts of plentiful food, see Stuart, I, 53-54; Hamilton, I, 248; Duncan, II, 318-319; Hall, F., p. 38; Finch, p. 13; Weld, I, 41-42; Ashe, p. 193; Howison, p. 299.
[87] Shirreff, p. 269; Lambert, II, 40; Holmes, pp. 356-357; Priest, p. 33.
[88] Hall, B., I, 125-126; Coke, I, 213.

James Flint's "Letters from America" (1818-20) give a good description of a typical backwoods tavern. "A small degree of aversion to frivolous detail does not prevent me from describing a backwoods tavern. Like its owner, it commonly makes a conspicuous figure in its neighborhood. It is a log, a frame, or a brick house, frequently with a wooden piazza in front. From the top of a tall post, the signboard is suspended. On it a Washington, a Montgomery, a Wayne, a Pike, or a Jackson is usually portrayed, in a style that might not be easily deciphered except for the name attached. On the top of the house is a small bell, which is twice rung before meals." [89]

If shelter in a tavern were not available, the traveller could always find a household that would take him in for the night. Accommodations were usually worse here than at an inn; he was generally obliged to sleep either in a room occupied by members of the family or on the dirt floor, and he had to content himself with whatever food happened to be available. Never was he turned away, though the consent to stay was sometimes given grudgingly. He must be prepared too to care for his own horse, for which sometimes very scanty provision was made.[90]

In the unsettled regions, board was very cheap—in the first decade of the century one might live on two dollars a week and for fifty to one hundred dollars a year.[91] The best inns charged fifty cents a day for lodging with three meals. The American quarter of a dollar was much in demand and constituted a convenient price for the average single meal by the way. Many times the charge was less. Lambert in 1809 paid the large sum of a dollar and a half to two dollars a day in Albany at Gregory's Tavern, a

[89] Flint, p. 161.
[90] Weld, I, 114; Palmer, p. 150; Janson, p. 80.
[91] Ashe, p. 193.

hostelry which Lambert says was "equal to many London hotels." [92] Ten years later, Fearon paid as much as two dollars a day or eighteen dollars a week, exclusive of wine, in a New York boarding house.[93] A private fire in one's room in the later days was a luxury, as Fidler discovered in 1833 when he was charged four dollars weekly for fire and candles in a New York house. As he was then paying twenty-one dollars a week for two poorly furnished rooms, three meals a day, and water to drink, for himself, his wife, two children, and a servant, he thought himself very much abused.[94]

The reception given the English traveller differed greatly, according to circumstances, though it was usually admitted that courtesy on the part of the stranger met with a corresponding willingness to be obliging on the part of the native Americans. Even Basil Hall speaks repeatedly of the kindness shown his family during their long tour. The welcome was always especially cordial if the stranger carried letters of introduction to an American family; all houses in the vicinity were open to him and he was treated as a friend of the family. Bradbury says that he travelled nearly 10,000 miles in the United States and never received the least incivility or affront. "Let no one here," he says, "indulge himself abusing the waiter or hostler at an inn: that waiter or hostler is probably a citizen and does not, nor can he, conceive that a situation in which he discharges a duty to society, not in itself dishonorable, should subject him to insult; but this feeling, so far as I have experienced it, is entirely defensive." [95] "From my first landing

[92] Lambert, II, 39.
[93] Fearon, p. 7.
[94] Fidler, p. 16. For prices of board, see also Duncan, II, 242-243; Abdy, I, 249; Finch, p. 13; Neilson, pp. 16-17.
[95] Bradbury, pp. 312-313.

in the country till the present," says James Flint, "I have enjoyed intercourse with people of eminence in society and have uniformly met with the most polite reception, and on many occasions, with such marks of kindness that I can never have sufficient opportunities to requite."[96]

There were many complaints of the prevailing reserve or "cold civility," especially in the lower classes. This, however, did not interfere with the satisfying of the traveller's need. Many strangers propitiated the Americans by tactfully keeping to the native customs as much as possible, and by asking no special favors. Tudor tells of his amusing struggle with an American landlord on the subject of washing in his room, a struggle in which the Englishman yielded rather than to go unwashed indefinitely.[97] Candler advised his fellow countrymen to make themselves familiar with the people of the house where they were stopping; he himself, he said, had been much more so than he would have thought of being in England with the family of an innkeeper.[98] Undue familiarity and condescension, however, never met with success; the Americans were generally conceded to be excellent judges of manners, no matter what their own defects in that respect were. They could detect audacity and condescension very quickly, but if the stranger successfully passed their examination and scrutiny, nothing in the way of hospitality was too good for him.

If for no other reason than sheer weight of opinion, we must believe that the prevailing policy among the English was "live and let live." Most of them were broadminded enough to take things philosophically as they found them; sometimes because of frank interest in the unusual mode of living which they witnessed, more often, perhaps, because such a line of action was the better policy and gained them

[96] Flint, pp. 291-292. [97] Tudor, I, 466-467. [98] Candler, pp. 53-54.

more in the end. At any rate, the prevailing opinion seems to have been that if the Americans were treated well, they, in turn, would give the English as little to complain of as possible.[99]

[99] Hamilton, I, 122-123; Dalton, p. 113; Duncan, II, 320; Holmes, p. 139.

CHAPTER III

MANNERS AND CUSTOMS

THE American mode of life and the traits of American behavior were interesting subjects for speculation on the part of the European visitor. In the first place, these were different from anything of the sort that the traveller had before experienced; then they offered a fascinating problem in causes, a problem which the visitor invariably tried to solve. The fact that the latter stayed usually at an inn or boarding house had both its advantages and its drawbacks; such an arrangement favored observation, at the same time limiting the range of the observer. Many accounts of American life were drawn exclusively from that form of it seen in public houses.

The stranger, on his arrival in America, was inevitably impressed by two or three salient characteristics of the new society. The first in importance and obviousness was the spirit of equality which has previously been referred to. He could not enter a house of entertainment or a stage coach without feeling it and seeing evidence of it. It was forced upon him at the public dining table as well as in whatever private social life he enjoyed, and in all his intercourse with those whom he would naturally have considered his inferiors. This spirit could be traced to many sources; the most evident one, as it seemed to the traveller, was the republican nature of American institutions and government.[1] This was not an unmixed blessing to the English

[1] Tudor, II, 395; Abdy, I, 70.

gentleman; his sufferings at the hands of some one from whom he had attempted to exact a menial service left sometimes more of an impression than did the contemplation of the delights of liberty. As he went from place to place, he saw other evidences of the existence of this spirit. One was the lack of great wealth in the hands of any one man or company of men. There were few very rich men and correspondingly few beggars. Often this fact in turn provoked inquiry, and the primary cause was proved, to the traveller's satisfaction at least, to be the absence of the law of primogeniture.[2] By the constant division of property among the members of the usually large families, the wealth of each was kept moderate and thus equality was assured.

Another general trait that was very noticeable was the reserve with which the native American treated strangers. Very few of the latter, like Fearon, took this so seriously that they allowed it "to freeze the blood and disgust the judgment,"[3] but many agreed with Captain Thomas Hamilton when he said, "It seemed as if each individual were impressed with the conviction that the whole dignity of his country were concentrated in his person."[4] This reserve may have had its source in the more or less unsettled condition of international affairs until after the effects of the War of 1812 had worn off; it was probably stimulated by the injustice which the Americans were undoubtedly suffering at the hands of Englishmen in books and periodicals. It melted away rapidly, however, when the stranger entered the private house; here he perceived not only an almost invariable kindliness and consideration among the members of the family, but felt it extended to him as well. The general affability which prevailed among native Americans was sometimes ascribed to the fact of universal suf-

[2] Hamilton, I, 102.   [3] Fearon, p. 11.   [4] Hamilton, I, 26-27.

frage and frequent elections. An American never knew when he might wish the political support of his neighbors; therefore it behooved him to be agreeable.[5]

This reserve was closely connected in the traveller's mind with another trait, a certain stiffness in social forms, an awkwardness and lack of ease which the European felt at once in American society.[6] This was far removed from vulgarity, and revealed itself especially when the Americans chose to assume a formality to which they were unaccustomed. It was rather to be expected in a new republic, where an established code of social law was yet in the making, but its cause might lie in many different considerations. One of these was the lack of a court to standardize and unify social observance; another was the general absorption in business on the part of the young men of the nation, and the consequent lack of the social graces. This intense interest in business and in politics was much criticized, and many gratuitous warnings were thrown out to this nation of workers who did not know how to play, or, at least, how to play gracefully. Lack of interest in music and the fine arts, or of the facilities for cultivating such an interest, the absence of a travelled class of people and of those who had held intercourse generally with the more civilized nations of the globe—these were looked upon as reasons for the peculiar state of American manners. Young men were urged to seek experiences in lands other than their own America; women were exhorted, too, to raise the standards of society by educating themselves. "It certainly is not to be wished," says one writer, speaking of the education of women, "that mathematics or

[5] Flint, p. 292.
[6] Hamilton, I, 270-271; Power, T., I, 241 and II, 346; Birkbeck, M., "Notes on a Journey," p. 107; Vigne, I, 131; Hall, pp. 176-179; Murray, II, 212.

metaphysics should be discussed in their company; but polite literature in its various departments may be introduced with great propriety.'' [7]

These were some of the general and more frequently noticed traits of American life. It remains to discuss the details of this new state of society as the Englishman saw them.

As the stranger went from place to place, he noted great local differences in the tone of society and manners. Peculiarities of custom and of character were still at this period rather well-defined, and the distinctions were very marked to the eye of the foreigner. The most obvious fact in regard to the attitude of the traveller toward these differences in manners is the preference of most strangers for the South. It has already been noted that that part of the country received almost no consideration from the home-seeking emigrant. Perhaps the very limitations that kept it in bad repute as a permanent abiding place for the settler, made it the more delightful to the temporary visitor. Slavery, the great drawback of the South to the mind of the emigrant, helped to produce a class of people with leisure to attend to the more graceful and less strenuous things of life, and to offer unlimited and unsurpassed hospitality.[8] The manners of the Southerners were considered decidedly superior to those of any other people in the United States. Perhaps, as one author suggests, this was because they were more dependent on social intercourse and were thus at greater pains to render it agreeable.[9] They showed less caution than did the other Americans in admitting the stranger to their firesides; had more wit and vivacity, and by education and tradition were more like the

[7] Candler, p. 60.
[8] Martineau, I, 201; Davis, J., p. 97.
[9] Hamilton, II, 283.

English themselves. Many of them, especially those of the older stock, were products of English universities and had travelled extensively. Englishmen were impressed too, by the fact that Southerners took the intelligence of the traveller for granted, to a gratifying degree. Captain Hall said that in Baltimore it was a comfort to learn how little was urged upon him in the way of "sights."[10] It is not to be wondered at, that after a visit to bustling New England, the stranger was sometimes satiated "with institutions, jails, schools and hospitals" for which, it is feared, his attention and his admiration were exacted to a burdensome degree.

Charleston seems to have been the most agreeable and the most admired of the Southern towns.[11] It was declared to be the only place in the Southern states which realized the English idea of a city. C. A. Murray says that in 1835 it was nearly as well known to the civilized world as Bristol or Liverpool. The best society there was considered much superior to anything else of the kind found in America, and was much like that of England in its Episcopal religion, its people of English birth, and its regard for established institutions. Richmond and Baltimore, too, had their share as centres of a refined social life, while Washington appeared to the best advantage in the winter; in summer it was practically deserted.[12] New Orleans was looked upon as a gay place where gambling halls and drinking places abounded. There was much wealth and a great deal of social life of a certain kind among the extremely cosmopolitan population. The "Western Gazetteer" said that the universe was to be seen in miniature on the levee fronting New Orleans, and that the city's docks were

[10] Hall, B., II, 392-393.
[11] Hamilton, II, 278; Murray, II, 186; Hodgson, I, 48-49.
[12] Hall, B., II, 2; Power, T., I, 240.

crowded with vessels from every part of the world. The mixture of classes, the unhealthy climate, the prevalence of vice and lawlessness possessed an unwholesome fascination for the stranger. Harriet Martineau estimates that in New Orleans in 1834, "there were more duels than there were days in the year—fifteen on one Sunday morning; in 1835 there were 102 duels fought between January 1 and the end of April, . . . all but one of the 102 were for frivolous causes." [13]

Georgia and Alabama did not meet with the same approval as their neighbors, the Carolinas. The people were more impoverished, more rude in their manners, and more given to horse-jockeying and to fighting.[14] The same was true to an even greater degree in some parts of Virginia and in Kentucky, and, as a matter of fact, in all the Western country except that part which had been brought under advanced cultivation.[15] William Wirt in "The Old Bachelor" says that no people were more grossly misrepresented by foreigners than were the Virginians.[16] They and their Western neighbors, the Kentuckians, were looked upon by the English as types parallel to the wildest kind of Irishmen, and it is interesting to see how often the similarity in open heartedness, rude hospitality, generosity, wit, and love of lawless behavior, is emphasized. In the Kentucky region, the shops were reported to be filled with dirks. "Fights," says James Flint (1818), "are characterized by the most savage ferocity. Gouging or putting out the antagonist's eyes by thrusting the thumbs into the

[13] Martineau, H., II, 189.
[14] Hodgson, I, 153; Martineau, I, 221-222; Lambert, II, 260.
[15] Melish, II, 182, 205-206; Wilson, C. H., Appendix, p. 110; Twining, pp. 89-90; Faux, p. 117; Janson, p. 300; Hamilton, II, 175-176; Birkbeck, "Notes on a Journey," pp. 89, 115; Alexander, II, 33.
[16] Wirt, W., "The Old Bachelor," p. 171.

70   THE ENGLISH TRAVELLER IN AMERICA

sockets, is a part of the *modus operandi* . . . kicking and biting are also means used in combat; I have seen several fingers that have been deformed, also several noses and ears which have been mutilated by this canine mode of fighting."[17] Timothy Flint accounted for the great amount of duelling that went on in the West by the statement that it was the fiery, ambitious characters that emigrated to those parts. A chaos of political elements, too, thrown together with no immediate prospects of assimilation, offered unlimited chances for fistic argument. This lack of assimilation should have prevented some of the generalizing statements concerning the manners of the people west of the Alleghanies. The region was populated by representatives of a great number of foreign nations, together with emigrants from every state in the Union. Each group carried with it the customs, traditions, and ideals of its old life; a great many of these persisted in the new environment, as in the case of the habits of the New Englander, which were very marked in the West. Emigrants from New England carried with them always the interest in the church and the school, as well as thrift and commercial ability. Shirreff tells of seeking shelter in Illinois with a family that had originally come from New England. "Everything in the house," he says, "was particularly clean and neat. The manners of the inmates were calm and dignified, a smile never playing on their countenances, or an emphatic sound proceeding from their lips."[18]

The isolation of the Western settlements did a great deal to effect the demoralization of American manners in that part of the country. This is partly accounted for by the fact that the average Western emigrant was adventurous

[17] Flint, J., p. 138.
[18] Abdy, I, 281; Shirreff, p. 235; Winterbotham, p. 63; Bristed, p. 427; Bernard, p. 180.

by nature and was not dependent on the refinements of life for his happiness. In the West, he had very little incentive except his own self-respect to keep him from falling into a semi-barbarous state. To the lack of restraint of a polite society and even of law add his hand-to-mouth existence; it is no wonder that his personal pride forsook him after a very short time and that he went unwashed and unshaven, living with his family in the midst of dirt and squalor, doing only what was necessary to get daily bread.[19]

In the large cities of the East, the state of society was much the same as in the large towns of Great Britain.[20] Thomas Cooper said as early as 1798 that New York was a perfect counterpart of Liverpool. Society there was much more tinged with European manners than that of any other American city, though European luxuries and conveniences abounded in all parts of the East. Boston, too, early in this period had already achieved an atmosphere characteristic enough to cause comment.[21] The same was true of Philadelphia, which was a very distinctive town. Much was said of the neatness of the prim rows on rows of brick houses with spotless marble thresholds and steps, of the gravity, even sadness, of the demeanor of the inhabitants, and the reserve of society manners, which most visitors mistook for coldness.[22]

The rural classes of the North and East were usually characterized by gravity and reserve, but there was no hint of the simple rusticity that the European was accustomed to see in the peasant class of his own country.[23] Inter-

[19] Faux, pp. 198, 230, 291.
[20] Cooper, T., pp. 48-49; Tudor, II, 400-401; Vigne, II, 244.
[21] Hodgson, II, 146-147; Hamilton, I, 233.
[22] Hamilton, I, 379-380; Weld, I, 20-21; Hodgson, II, 20; Harris, W. T., p. 36; D'Arusmont, p. 35.   [23] Lambert, II, 500.

course with thrifty neighbors preserved the Eastern farmer's pride in the neatness of his property and of his personal appearance. The laboring classes were generally admitted to be "civil and respectful, though not crouching." [24] Harriet Martineau maintained that village manners in New England were some of the best and sweetest in America, and that the only evidences of vulgarity that she saw on her travels were displayed by a few of the wealthier class.[25] Adaptation had done its work in the East, and had already given a distinct character to the people of that part of the country.

It is unfortunate that human beings are so constituted that a comparatively insignificant objectionable personal trait will influence the relations of one person with another, assuming an importance which makes it overshadow all other considerations. Many of the smaller details of American social life and manners acted as dust in the eyes of travellers, blinding them to the greater issues. The constant use of tobacco was, to the Englishman, undoubtedly the most objectionable of all the American idiosyncrasies. Certainly more is said about it, and the attendant spitting, than about any other habit, and many writers agreed that it was what detracted most from the refinement of American manners.[26] There was a theory among strangers that Americans had taken to incessant smoking to ward off yellow fever. It was also said to be due to the nervous strain, the daily wear and tear of American life. Candler said that the idea of the soothing tendency and consequent

[24] Candler, p. 61.
[25] Martineau, II, 215-216.
[26] For this habit, see Fowler, p. 217; Lambert, II, 82; Candler, p. 57; Martineau, II, 265; Tudor, II, 421; Coke, I, 154; Moore, Thomas, "Epistle to Thomas Hume, Esq."; Kendall, I, 317; Sutcliffe, p. 88.

utility of smoking in concentrating thought, was urged in its favor, but he goes on to say, "The most active minds need not its assistance. Bonaparte never smoked." Robert Sutcliffe, a visiting Quaker, was horrified to see even children of five and six going about smoking "segars," though it must be admitted that he is almost the only traveller who notes the corruption prevailing at such an early age. There were plenty of observers, however, to comment on the fact that young men went about from morning till night with cigars in their mouths "when in the house, and not infrequently when walking the street. A box full is constantly carried in the coat pocket and handed occasionally to a friend, as familiarly as our dashing youths take out their *gold box* and offer a pinch of snuff."[27] Writers who refuted Mrs. Trollope's most sweeping denunciations of American life and exposed her charges as ridiculous, still admitted that this great fault in American manners was too noticeable to be ignored. Miss Martineau despaired of convincing her hosts of the seriousness of the situation. "Of the tobacco and its consequences," she says, "I will say nothing but that the practice is at too bad a pass to leave hope that anything that could be said in books would work a cure. If the floors of boarding houses, and the decks of steamboats and the carpets of the Capitol do not sicken the Americans into a reform; if the warnings of physicians are of no avail, what remains to be said?"[28] It was indeed only too well known that the floor of the Senate Chamber in Washington was not exempt, nor the pews in any of the churches, though we find some Americans refusing to admit that this disgusting habit prevailed, and professing to be very much surprised when their attention was called to it. Some writers attempted to justify it by pointing out that the habit existed in other lands as well.

[27] Lambert, II, 100.   [28] Martineau, II, 200.

74 THE ENGLISH TRAVELLER IN AMERICA

Boardman and Fowler noted that it did not extend to the better class of educated people, but they are the only travellers who at all qualify their condemnation.[29]

In conjunction with this criticism of the use of tobacco, we almost always find a denunciation of the habit of constant drinking. It was a source of wonder to the stranger that in spite of the dram-drinking that went on at all times and in all places, there was almost no sign of real drunkenness.[30] In the few cases that were observed, the culprit was quite likely to be a foreigner, or sometimes a degenerate Indian. James Stuart testified that in three years he did not see a dozen intoxicated men in America.[31] Hodgson did not see six, and was therefore inclined to believe that the sin of intoxication prevailed less extensively in America than in England.[32] The habit of constant "tippling" extended to children, if we are to believe William Cobbett, who says that even little boys at and under twelve years of age went into stores constantly and "tipped off their drams."[33] Janson, too, very often saw "wealthy boys intoxicated, shouting and swearing in the public streets."[34]

The habit of constant "tippling" was ascribed to the effects of the extreme heat, which forbade the use of ice water without the addition of spirituous liquors. Faux tells in his "Journal" of some Englishmen who fell dead at the city fountains in Washington in consequence of

[29] Hodgson, II, 36-37 (note); Tudor, II, 422; Candler, pp. 58-59; Boardman, p. 177; Fowler, p. 217; Shirreff, pp. 275-276; Mrs. Trollope, I, 19-20.
[30] Finch, J., p. 13; Fearon, p. 29; Flint, J., p. 60; Neilson, p. 67; Melish, II, 51; Winterbotham, p. 71.
[31] Stuart, II, 311.
[32] Hodgson, II, 249-250.
[33] Cobbett, p. 212.
[34] Janson, pp. 297-299.

drinking too much cold water. "To avoid this danger," he advises, "it is only necessary to drink a wine glass half full of brandy first and a pint of water immediately after. Thirst is thus safely quenched with much less water than would be necessary without the spirits."[35] The extreme heat was by no means the only inducement to much drinking; another consideration which constantly tempted the American was the ease with which liquor was obtained, and its great cheapness. The habit was accounted for also by tracing it back to a very practical and indisputable source, the great amount of salt food that the native American consumed.

We have mentioned the ease with which liquor was obtained. The average American, however, was not convivial in his habits, and was much absorbed in business; he did not linger, therefore, over his glass at the table, though brandy bottles figured largely at public and private meals, and guests helped themselves as they wished.[36] Outside the larger towns, the common beverage was spirits and water, taken without sugar, or "cyder" which was always available in the more settled regions where apple-trees had a chance to grow. Large quantities of molasses imported to New England in trade with the West Indies furnished plenty of rum. In parts of the country where the chief agricultural product was grain, the spirit used was distilled from it, usually from rye. In the South, peach and apple brandy, made usually at the private still of the plantation owner, warmed the heart of the traveller. Much was said about the amount of conviviality in the South

[35] Faux, pp. 129-130. See, also, Melish, II, 51; Duncan, II, 322-323; Neilson, p. 67; Winterbotham, p. 71; Fearon, p. 29; Stuart, II, 311.

[36] Hamilton, I, 42-43; Candler, p. 80; Neilson, p. 69; Melish, II, 51; Abdy, II, 242; Fearon, p. 28.

and the fondness of the Southern gentlemen for liquor. Basil Hall says that in Virginia, during a journey of seventeen hours, the stage stopped at ten different houses, and at each place his travelling companions alighted to get a glass of "mint julep," yet they were not tipsy except for a slight inarticulateness of speech and earnestness in argument.[37]

"Spirit shops" were numerous everywhere, especially in the large cities. These were sometimes called "grog shops," the latter name designating the small grocers' and chandlers' shops which sold liquor as well as other staples. Many of these were situated on the corners of the streets, and were reputed to be kept chiefly by Irishmen. Fearon said that in 1818 there were 1,500 spirit shops in New York City, and that he was convinced that the quantity of malt liquors and spirits drunk by the inhabitants of New York much exceeded the amount consumed by the same number of English population. He ascribed the cause to the foreign birth of many of the inhabitants who brought habits of drinking from their European homes and now were better paid and able to indulge those tastes.[38]

It must not be imagined that the Americans themselves were blind to this national fault. Violent campaigns were carried on against it by the prototype of the modern prohibition movement, and English travellers commented frequently on the change in the public conscience that was gradually becoming noticeable, particularly in the last ten years of this period.[39] One writer attended a temperance lecture at an agricultural meeting in Stockbridge, Massachusetts, in 1834. The native orator spoke bitterly against dram-drinking, estimating that thirty hogsheads of spirits

[37] Hall, B., III, 71.
[38] Fearon, p. 289.
[39] Coke, I, 33; Tudor, II, 422; Fowler, p. 115; Vigne, I, 282-283.

of 150 gallons each were consumed annually in that one
town. This meant an allowance of two and a half gallons
per capita, and represented an outlay for liquor of $2,250.[40]
The change in manners in the East was commonly ascribed
to the influence of these organizations, which both natives
and foreigners rejoiced to see operating, however much they
objected to total abstinence.[41]

He who is at all familiar with the travel literature of the
time will remember in Mrs. Trollope's book the illustration
"Ancient and Modern Republics," in which the modern
type of republican, an American, is depicted sitting, with
his hat at a rakish angle, before a table upon which his
heels are reposing. In his limp hand he holds a glass from
which he has evidently just drained the "spirits." On the
wall beside him is a conspicuous advertisement of "Celebrated Chewing Tobacco." It is clear that many foreign
visitors considered that attitude peculiarly American, perhaps because much of the time of so many travellers was
spent in the taverns and other public places. "It was quite
common," we are told, "even in company to lean back in
the chair so as to let it stand on its hind legs, and when in
this position near a fire, they will sometimes place their feet
against the mantelpiece. Imagine a man sitting in this
manner with a cigar in his mouth and you have a complete
picture of American independence."[42] At an inn in central New York, in 1824, Howison was astonished to see that
each man occupied three or four chairs. "He sat upon
one, laid his legs upon another, whirled around a third,
and perhaps chewed the paint from the back of the
fourth."[43] This universal habit of lounging extended even

[40] Hall, B., II, 82.
[41] See, for instance, Alexander, II, 35.
[42] Candler, pp. 56-57; also Holmes, p. 342; Tudor, II, 28.
[43] Howison, p. 306.

to the Supreme Court and the state legislatures, to say nothing of the church. Nor were women exempt from the indictment, if we are to believe "The American Chesterfield," a curious little native publication which did its best to reform manners.[44]

In many other details of life were the Americans self-convicted in points of etiquette which must have jarred upon the sensibilities of the more refined stranger. It was difficult for the latter, for instance, to see a native American reaching across the table for his food, or using his own knife and fork to convey something to his plate, without venturing at least a mild remonstrance. Another habit which was not understood was that of yawning comfortably in the face of one's *vis-à-vis* in polite society. Abdy tells of an amusing experience in a Virginia stagecoach; an American opposite him yawned constantly; the narrator, supposing that the stranger was bored with the conversation, took the hint and desisted from talking. Further experience convinced him, however, that this expansion of the jaws was a national trait and that one could "yawn freely in the face of another person in America without committing a breach of good manners."[45]

We may expect to find in the tone of American interchange of ideas at this time a revelation of the enthusiasms of this hustling young democracy. Of conversation as a fine art, there was almost a total ignorance. There was no leisure class to cultivate it and no body of very wealthy people to stimulate interest in things not strictly utilitarian. Life was too full of politics, of business, of all the responsibilities incidental to a new country, to offer a place for less useful interests. One's vocabulary remained, or became, limited; a fact very noticeable to the Englishman

[44] See Hall, B., II, 406-408.
[45] Abdy, II, 272-273.

was that very few Americans read anything but the newspaper.

There seems to have been a conscious effort to avoid in general conversation any subject the discussion of which would stamp one as a pedant, or bore the rest of the company. This was more generally noticed to be true of the men than of the women; the latter have recorded against them statements ridiculous for pedantry. Miss Martineau tells of her encounters with some New England middle-aged women with "blue stocking" propensities. "A lady asked me many questions about my emotions at Niagara. . . . 'Did you not?' was her last inquiry, 'long to throw yourself down and mingle with your mother earth?' . . . Another asked me whether I did not think the sea might inspire vast and singular ideas. Another, an instructress of youth, in examining my ear-trumpet, wanted to know whether its length made any difference in its efficiency. On my answering 'None at all.' . . . 'O, certainly not,' said she, very deliberately, 'for sound, being a material substance, can only be overcome by a superior force.' The mistakes of unconscious ignorance should be passed over with a silent smile; but affectation should be exposed as a service to young society."[46]

As the Americans were not of a race of philosophers, and as their religious opinions were pretty well fixed and admitted of very little discussion, and because they had no interest in art and letters, their conversations dealt with local interests or with the all-absorbing subject of politics. Their manner of expression seemed to Englishmen to be simple and straightforward. One writer remarks, "Like a gently flowing limpid brook, their conversation has no turbulence, but shows everything at the bottom at a glance."[47] There was no bright and sparkling display of repartee,

[46] Martineau, II, 206-208.   [47] Candler, p. 92.

though the American was not without a certain native wit which was always thought by the Englishman to be unconsciously epigrammatic—one wonders sometimes how much of it was unconscious.[48] The speech generally gave the impression of being grave and earnest, and was devoted to the matter in hand. It was remarked that the Americans were habitually serious and silent, "even beyond English taciturnity," and to make them talk there was needed the stimulus of politics or liquor. Especially did brevity characterize the speech of the people in the Western country. They developed a laconic type of conversation that was so abbreviated that it was not always clear.[49] On the other hand, the Easterner, and especially the New Englander, became known for his "prosy but rich and droll" conversation. It was said that he "went back as near to the Deluge as the subject would admit and forward to the millennium, taking care to omit nothing of consequence in the interval."[50] Because of the narrowness of their range, the Americans were well-informed on what they talked about. Sometimes the absolute conviction and accuracy with which they were able to speak was disconcerting to an Englishman in an argument. For instance, Fearon had occasion to deplore the diffusion of knowledge in regard to the details of the War of 1812. His criticism extended even to the ladies, with whom, he ironically says, he could not converse without having his ears offended with the "refined and intellectual names of Commodore Hull, Captain Lawrence, and General Jackson."[51]

The tone of the American voice was agreed to be very

[48] D'Arusmont, p. 87; Martineau, II, 206; Hamilton, II, 179.
[49] Murray, I, 80; Hall, F., p. 272; Holmes, p. 362; Flint, pp. 288-289.
[50] Martineau, II, 204-205; Davis, J., p. 70.
[51] Fearon, p. 371; D'Arusmont, p. 87.

distinctive, though few strangers attempted to show in what respects it was so considered. Usually it was mentioned with condemnation, especially when the particular example under discussion was that of a New England woman. Her voice was described as being "between a whine and a twang," and was attributed to the general ill-health among women. Occasionally we find a hint of appreciation of the Southern dialect, which struck the English ear very pleasantly.[52]

A quality of American conversation most impressive to the Englishman was its scrupulous moral purity.[53] So great was the insistence upon this quality that more than one unsuspecting stranger found himself in a state of chagrin after making some remark which he considered perfectly innocent, but which met with surprised glances from his hearers. Candler says that while Walter Scott's poems would not be considered exceptionable in an English circle, there were several passages in "Marmion" and "The Lady of the Lake" which it would be unadvisable to read to American ladies. He himself, when reading aloud to a mixed audience, always omitted these. Many looked upon this as false delicacy and believed that American women would rise to a higher position of influence if they were not so scrupulously protected from everything that savored of evil. No one, however, seems to have regretted the fact that, because of this attitude, the conversation in public conveyances was absolutely unobjectionable, just as the behavior was usually decent and restrained. In all public places the general tone of the conversation was reported to be good-humored and civil, and to take rather for granted an identity of interest and intelligence.

[52] On the American voice, see Murray, C. A., II, 214; Hodgson, II, 27; De Roos, p. 31; Martineau, II, 200.
[53] Candler, pp. 100, 101, 482; Boardman, p. 176.

Many statements, however, testify to the prevailing profanity in American speech.[54] Even children were not exonerated, nor were the educated classes of adults excepted. This habit was particularly noticeable in the Western region. James Flint, whose interest lay chiefly in that locality, said that in his short stay in America he had heard twice as much profanity as during the whole period of his life in England. Virginians were evidently much given to swearing. They were compared to the Irish in that respect, just as the Kentuckians were said to resemble the latter in their love for strong drink.

Another charge brought against Americans was inquisitiveness.[55] Sometimes the traveller regarded this trait with indulgence, as he found that the natives were as willing to answer questions as to ask them, and that the stranger came off the gainer in that exchange. Sometimes he indulged his sense of humor and gave brief and vague replies to induce more questions, which were usually forthcoming. More often he resented the interference in his affairs and objected to the "routine of interrogations" which he must go through before his wants were satisfied. This failing does not seem to have been limited to one section of the country. We find mention of the tradition of it in New England, in the South, and in the West, though some authors confessed that they had not experienced it. Even if questions were not asked, a frank and eager curiosity in the affairs of strangers was betrayed. Perhaps it arose from a worthy desire for information—undoubtedly

[54] See, on American profanity, Holmes, pp. 362, 365; Hodgson, II, 259; Candler, p. 453; Murray, I, 158; Flint, p. 167; Melish, II, 208.

[55] For inquisitiveness, see Flint, p. 168; Weld, I, 234-235; Woods, p. 195; Hamilton, I, 209; Janson, pp. 196-197; Bradbury, Appendix, p. 313; De Roos, p. 63; Hodgson, II, 32-35; Candler, p. 483; Palmer, p. 178; Hall, F., pp. 36-37; Hamilton, I, 119-120; Shirreff, p. 275.

it did in many cases; but it was a source of annoyance to the stranger who, while carrying on a private conversation, sometimes found himself surrounded by a group of people, all obviously listening intently and making suggestions or comments as the spirit moved them.

It has been remarked that occasionally the English traveller was horrified to see a small boy smoking or drinking in the public-houses. This precocity was extended to other phases of life as well, and was one of the great mistakes in American policy, to the mind of the observer.[56] Because of the early marriages and the abundance of subsistence in the new republic, children played a very important economic part there, and represented a large proportion of the population. They were not relegated to the background, as in Europe, but were given a place, and that a prominent one, in the daily family life. A close connection was made by the stranger between the republican form of government and the unlimited liberty which was allowed the younger generation. The latter had a part in the family councils; they expressed their opinions freely and did not hesitate to contradict their elders. They were perfectly unabashed in conversation, having been introduced freely to all strangers. They were rarely punished at home, and strict discipline was not tolerated in the schools. By the conditions of life, independence was created in the child. Duncan speaks of the intelligence of American children and of their sense of responsibility. They learned to do things for themselves, and their independence was reflected in their characters. They matured very early; the boy quickly assumed the "gait, attire, and attitude of a man"; the girl ended her fragmentary and desultory education at an early age and was usually married before

[56] Faux, pp. 130-131, also p. 164; D'Arusmont, p. 310; Shirreff, p. 51; Abdy, I, 70-73, 217; Martineau, II, 271; Flint, pp. 170-171.

reaching the age of twenty. Shirreff gives several instances of juvenile politeness that he has experienced, but he is almost the only English traveller who has a good word for these sophisticated little beings who were notoriously given the centre of the stage and who often abused the privilege as a consequence. It was feared that respect for elders or for any other form of authority would soon be eliminated entirely from American life. Many of the defects in the native character were traced to this faulty education of the youth. On the other hand, lack of culture in the parents produced a corresponding disdain for accomplishments in the child. As he could not be punished in school, he learned to regard his teacher as an inferior and to disregard all law and order. The foreigner saw in this system of child-rearing a great menace to the future peace and happiness of the nation.

Days which were celebrated as legal holidays in America were always times full of interest to the foreign stranger, for he had then an opportunity to see the people in gala mood and to witness some of their distinctive customs. The great day was of course the Fourth of July.[57] This was observed at this time much as it was till a few years ago when the "safe and sane Fourth" began to be advocated. The celebration was remarked to be similar to that of the English King's birthday. It began before sunrise, and carried with it the usual hubbub of fire-crackers, cannon, and band music. There were parades, patriotic speeches, and banquets. Sometimes the traveller ended the day at the theatre, where he saw a patriotic play and listened to American airs played by an orchestra accompanied in its

[57] For Fourth of July celebrations, see Duncan, I, 47; Neilson, p. 214; Latrobe, II, 77; Tudor, I, 117-121; Finch, pp. 50-51; Melish, I, 42-43; Weld, I, 272-273; Howison, pp. 332-333; Coke, I, 128-129; Wilson, p. 27.

efforts by the beating of time from hundreds of feet. Fortunate, indeed, was he if his temper was not ruffled several times during the day, and if he was allowed to forget that the United States had once been English colonies and that they had thrown off a tyrannical yoke—references to which fact provoked a patriotic demonstration from all loyal Americans. Closely connected with this nation-wide celebration, both in time and significance, was the local interest in July 5th in New York. It commemorated the emancipation of all slaves in New York State, and was the particular holiday of all people of color, many of whom, according to Boardman, met with degrading treatment on this occasion.[58]

There is very little mention of an American Christmas and only casual notice of Thanksgiving. The English Christmas celebration was apparently almost unknown; most of the shops were open during the day, and only the Episcopalians seem to have gone to church.[59] As for Thanksgiving Day, very little notice seems to have been taken of it, probably because the observance of it had not yet spread beyond the limits of New England. One author observes that the Americans were too much engrossed with money-getting to take time to show their gratitude for their mercies.[60]

The social place of the Christmas jollification was largely taken by the observance of New Year's Day.[61] There are many accounts of the celebration of this festival. It was the day when ladies held their annual levee and all male

[58] Boardman, pp. 309-310; also Duncan, I, 59-60.

[59] Lambert, II, 108-109; Boardman, p. 331; Birkbeck, "Letters from Illinois," p. 24; Duncan, II, 278; Kendall, I, 287.

[60] Boardman, p. 330.

[61] For best descriptions of celebrations of New Year's Day, see Boardman, pp. 332-333; Lambert, II, 111; Hodgson, II, 113; Alexander, II, 316; Stuart, I, 273.

acquaintances and friends were expected to call. Nothing but a very serious reason was supposed to prevent this annual visit. Long-standing coolnesses were often atoned for in this way. Clergymen shared with the ladies the privilege of staying at home and receiving callers. Men whose acquaintance was numerous could of course spend very little time at each place; refreshments were served, of which they were supposed to partake, and the end of the day found more than one American gentleman in a befuddled condition of mind. Bakeshops served free cakes on this day, and bars offered free liquor to anyone who was inclined to accept their hospitality. The usual restraint was absent, and the foreigner probably saw the Americans more social, more easy in manners than on any other day in the year.

The traveller who wintered in the North or East witnessed an American custom which occasioned him great pleasure. This was the sleighing party, to which Americans were much addicted, and which the foreigner, if he had the opportunity, enjoyed fully.[62] Priest says that it was the chief amusement in winter, and that he never heard a woman speak of it but with rapture. North of Pennsylvania, said the traveller, this pleasure could usually be indulged in all winter, but farther south, the snow-fall was of such short duration that the most had to be made of every moment. Taverns were open all night for the reception of these parties of young men and women, who rode for miles around, stopping at every inn to have a dance. Sometimes a fiddler went with them in the sleigh. Hodgson in 1821 tells of a merry crowd that he joined to go to a country party ten miles out of New York City. He thus

[62] Lambert, II, 100-101; Duncan, II, 242; Priest, pp. 46-48; Finch, p. 33; Boardman, p. 339; Alexander, II, 316; Harris, p. 75; Neilson, pp. 132-133; Hodgson, II, 110-112.

describes Broadway during the sleighing season: "Broadway exhibits the gayest scene you can conceive. Painted sleighs, with scarlet cloth and buffalo skins, are dashing along in all directions at a prodigious speed; some with two horses abreast; others with four in hand. Every body seems to make the most of the snow while it lasts, and night does not put an end to the festivity. The horses have a string of bells round; and in these fine moonlight nights I hear them dashing away long after midnight."

Quite the opposite of this scene of merry-making was that of the American funeral, which deserves mention because of the universal comment it provoked.[63] It was the subject of much criticism. The English noticed with horror the practice of disposing of the dead within twenty-four hours, as well as the general air of indifference which seemed to them to mark the observance of the last rites. They complained of the practice of exhibiting the body to friends, and of having graveyards in the heart of the town, objecting to them as both unhealthful and depressing. Funerals were usually attended by walking processions, the friends of the deceased gathering in the home, the acquaintances joining them outside on the way to the grave. Notices of deaths were published in the papers together with a general invitation to friends to be present at the burial. Quakers and Free Masons always enjoyed the honor of having the longest funeral trains. Duncan tells of the funeral of a child which he witnessed. There were no men present except the father of the deceased. Almost everyone wore white and the mahogany coffin "was carried by white *ribbands* by four females." He ascribed this peculiar custom to the Methodists only.[64] The motley garb

[63] Lambert, II, 88-89; Power, II, 19; Duncan, II, 213; Blane, p. 12; Lambert, II, 181; Stuart, I, 133; Neilson, p. 261; Palmer, p. 284.   [64] Duncan, II, 314, also I, 104.

worn at funerals was often the cause of comment from strangers. There was very little mourning worn; large linen scarfs were provided for the clergyman, for the physician of the deceased, and for a few intimate friends who acted as pall-bearers. These were worn like a military belt, sloping across the body.[65]

The Americans were charged with indifference to this sad occasion and were much criticised on this score. Not only was little mourning worn, but it was intimated that very few evidences of grief were seen. Friends walked nonchalantly to the grave, often smoking a cigar en route. In short, the whole occasion as revealed by the Englishman lacked dignity and proper feeling, but at least, as even Fearon admitted, was free from evidences of hypocrisy.[66]

The importance of woman obviously reveals itself to the greatest degree in a newly-settled country. She is under such circumstances not only the creator of future population, but represents as well the influence which retards the downward trend in manners and morals which is likely to reveal itself gradually in isolated communities. The question of the status of American women in the period from 1785 to 1835 enjoys the rather unusual distinction of being one of the few questions on which Englishmen were agreed. They might differ in regard to almost any other phase of American life, but the position of woman was manifest, and the handwriting on the wall was never cryptic. The general facts in regard to her were the same, whether she represented the type of a potential "blue stocking" in New England, or a divinity south of the Delaware, or a pioneer helpmeet in the new West.

[65] Boardman, p. 66; Stuart, I, 134; Duncan, II, 311-314; Weston, pp. 70, 133-136.
[66] Fearon, p. 137.

The traveller found few astonishingly beautiful women among American types.[67] There was much prettiness, but the consensus of opinion was that there was little actual beauty of the type most admired by the Englishman. "I am speaking of the American ladies in general," says one writer, "when I remark that it is no injustice to them to maintain that where you will see twenty pretty girls, you will not see one really handsome woman."[68] It is a curious coincidence that several writers say that the prettiest women in America were seen in Baltimore.[69] The typical young woman seemed rather pale to eyes accustomed to look upon English roses. She did not look particularly healthy, nor did her delicate color survive her first years of girlhood. At the age of twenty-one or twenty-two, the American woman was destitute of bloom; at thirty, she was beginning to get old and to look forward to the future "when her reign of triumph will be vicariously restored in the person of her daughter."[70]

The gait was supposed to be distinctive but not particularly graceful. American girls did not stride like Englishwomen nor did they affect the mincing steps of a French belle, but they swung their arms too much to be quite approved by the observer.[71]

Many travellers speak of the delicate features, well-turned and classic in their purity.[72] The figure was almost invariably well-formed and slight—too slight to win the

[67] D'Arusmont, p. 24; Vigne, I, 130, also II, 244.
[68] Lambert, II, 323.
[69] Mrs. Trollope, I, 293; Coke, I, 75; Vigne, I, 130.
[70] For fading of American women, see Lambert, II, 92; Coke, I, 75; Abdy, I, 73; Hamilton, I, 32; Ferrall, p. 84; Candler, p. 69; Mrs. Trollope, I, 165; Murray, II, 213-214; Palmer, p. 152; Howison, p. 328.
[71] Mrs. Trollope, II, 135; Hamilton, I, 33; Candler, p. 71.
[72] Murray, II, 213-214; Hamilton, I, 32-33.

good opinion of some fastidious critics,[73]—and if the girl in question were from the city, displayed to advantage the French styles to which the Americans were most partial.[74] A criticism which one encounters frequently is the reproach of poor teeth among American women.[75] The cause of this condition was much argued; it was usually attributed to the hot food and to the sweets and preserves in which the Americans indulged to a startling degree. The use of salted food, too, bore its share of the blame. Many times we see a flat denial of this condition among women, and sometimes a statement to the effect that all Americans suffered from the same disability. Lambert says that the Americans themselves admitted that they were subject to a premature loss of teeth, and that the cause had even been discussed in the papers read before the American Philosophical Society. He believed that, as a whole, women were more likely to be exempt than were men.

The surmises made in regard to the early fading of American women, and the precarious state of their health, are extremely interesting to read.[76] Much of this physical delicacy was attributed to the sudden changes of climate, which "created a series of nervous complaints, consumption and debility, which in the states along the Atlantic carry off one-third of the population in the prime of life." The heat of the American summer was also supposed to rob

[73] Boardman, p. 13; Fowler, p. 212; Candler, p. 69; Hamilton, I, 32; Mrs. Trollope, II, 135; Lambert, II, 92.

[74] For fondness for French styles, see Fearon, p. 172; Hodgson, II, 109; Boardman, p. 13; Holmes, p. 348; Murray, I, 55; Candler, p. 69; Howison, p. 328; Hall, B., I, 156.

[75] Neilson, p. 308; Palmer, p. 152; Weld, I, 22-23; Lambert, II, 94; Hamilton, I, 33.

[76] Stuart, I, 131; Lambert, II, 82-83, 92; Fearon, p. 169; D'Arusmont, p. 314; Martineau, II, 264; Howison, p. 328; Alexander, II, 299.

the fair cheeks of their bloom. Too much use of stoves and a very inadequate amount of exercise played their part in this breaking-down process. Too much animal food in the diet; in fact, too great a variety of all sorts of food was urged as a reason for ill-health, and American women were admonished that the fashionable malady, dyspepsia, could be traced to the late suppers which they enjoyed so much. The charge of the lack of exercise was brought chiefly against the people of the Southern states, where the heat of the climate encouraged the tendency to have everything done for one by slaves. Here there existed the greatest apathy in regard to health, and women refused to be aware of the seriousness of the question.[77]

Then, too, the style of women's dress, particularly in the cities, was not conducive to health and vigor. Foreigners never ceased to be astonished at the light and flimsy attire which American women donned in winter.[78] The thinnest of gowns, satin shoes, and silk stockings were to be seen on the promenades of all the cities, even in the coldest weather, and provoked as much comment as they do today. This style of dress was held responsible for the large proportion of young women who succumbed to consumption, and for the general air of fragility which impressed the stranger. Duncan estimated that there were more than 500 deaths in New York in one year (about 1818), from consumption alone, and that the majority of these victims were young women. He describes the progress of a typical city girl proceeding to church through the snow, which penetrated her thin satin shoes. A black girl behind her carried a foot warmer at which the young lady toasted her

[77] Candler, pp. 67-68; Martineau, II, chap. II, sect. III.
[78] Neilson, p. 23; Alexander, II, 296; Hodgson, II, 109; Mrs. Trollope, II, 135.

toes during the service, after which she proceeded homeward in the same careless fashion.[79]

The accomplishments of the American girl were the natural result of the system of education by which she was reared. Very few observers would, I think, have agreed with Welby in his denunciation of the lack of education in useful female employments, of the frivolity and the general vacuity of mind which he says were the result of such a system.[80] Many, however, believed that the American woman could, and should, have a greater mental cultivation. Miss Martineau, as might be expected, made a special plea for more interests and more responsibilities of a public nature.[81] Some people believed that the esteem in which women were held, the fact that they bore "a high rate in the American market," and were scarce in proportion to the demand, acted as a deterrent to their best and most complete mental development; they were not obliged to resort to accomplishments to captivate.[82] Their education was undoubtedly incomplete; they attended a school or academy until they reached the age of twelve or fourteen, when their "book-learning" was generally conceded to be sufficient. Some few more fortunate ones protracted the process to include a smattering of French and a knowledge of music and dancing.[83] A girl was not encouraged, at any rate outside of New England, to study the classics or to penetrate into the mysteries of higher mathematics or science. This policy had the two-fold purpose of protecting the young mind from the corruption of the subject-matter of the classics, and of preventing anything like a pedantic

[79] Duncan, II, 291-292.
[80] Welby, p. 337.
[81] Martineau, II, 226 ff.
[82] See, for instance, Hall, F., p. 180.
[83] Candler, p. 71; Murray, II, 214-215; Vigne, II, 243-244.

and unbecoming display of learning. There were indeed "few occasions for a woman to make use of classical attainments in company."[84]

American women were known to be voracious readers, particularly of novels.[85] It is suggested that this fact may account for the general desire manifested by the young girls to be ethereal and delicate. The harmful effects of such reading were emphasized again and again both in foreign and in native literature. The annuals abounded in disquisitions on the subject, urging the moral and intellectual degradation which was sure to result from this wasteful occupation. A great many married women especially, who lived out their existence in boarding houses, were much given to reading, as well as to religious and social activity as an outlet for their energies.[86] Indeed, the feminine half of society was sometimes conceded to be much better educated than the masculine, owing to the absorption of the latter in business, and the resulting dearth of time to improve one's self intellectually.

The New England girls enjoyed the distinction of being considered the best educated of American women, not only in books but in domestic accomplishments as well. Especially was the former true of Boston women; they were thought to know more of literature and music than did their sisters of other localities. Hamilton says that New York women charged them with being dowdyish in dress, but that he considered their taste purer than that of their accusers.[87] Outside of New England, it must be admitted, travellers considered the average woman deficient in the management of household concerns, that is, in comparison

[84] Candler, p. 73.
[85] Fowler, p. 215; Candler, pp. 71-72.
[86] Martineau, II, 245 ff.
[87] Hamilton, I, 235.

with Englishwomen. This also was attributed to the interest of men in business and their consequent neglect of women, who sought entertainment in shopping, dress, and social frivolity.[88]

Many a stranger, travelling under new conditions and seeking shelter at a public or private house, was repelled by the coolness and apparent indifference of the women of the family.[89] Francis Hall called it "sulkiness" and accused American women of having water instead of blood in their veins,[90] but most strangers recognized in it a very creditable reserve which was largely made necessary by the manner of living. This came out strongly in the women of the lower classes and in most of the women of the Western territories, who were noted for their taciturnity.[91] On closer acquaintance, this reserve became transformed into an easy, affable, agreeable, manner, often accompanied by gaiety and talkativeness. Janson detested "the pertness of republican principles" even in the conversation of the country girls, and complained that they answered a familiar question from the other sex with the confidence of a French mademoiselle; but even he, one of the most critical observers of American women, attributed the fact to force of habit and education and not to any fault of morals.[92] Usually the feminine manners of social intercourse and family life were considered very charming; there was an artlessness, a liveliness, and a sweetness that were very appealing.[93] The American girl never concealed her ignorance on a subject of conversation, but frankly avowed it,

[88] Welby, p. 337; Fearon, p. 376; Fowler, p. 215.
[89] Hodgson, II, 253.
[90] Hall, F., p. 159.
[91] Candler, pp. 75-76; Alexander, II, 114-115.
[92] Janson, p. 87.
[93] D'Arusmont, p. 26; Vigne, II, 244.

and asked for information with absolute lack of embarrassment.

It is a significant fact that we never find in this travel literature under discussion, any aspersion cast upon the morals of the American woman. The standard of female virtue was high; evidence of this fact was overwhelming. Where vice existed, it was not flaunted in the eyes of the stranger. Stuart says that day or night there were apparently no light women in the streets, and that prostitutes could avoid unpleasant observation only by acting like decent women.[94] A general air of modesty accompanied the American girl both of the poorer working class and in the ranks of society. So strong was this impression that the charge of prudery was often brought against them. Fashionable women were conspicuous for the modesty of their dress, which was nevertheless often showy and costly, and of their manners.[95] The prevailing attitude toward waltzing is significant.[96] American young women were extremely fond of dancing, in which they indulged freely, and in which they excelled. It is true that to some eyes the gravity and seriousness with which they regarded the pastime were "almost pitiable." Quadrilles and cotillions were the favorite form of this amusement; the waltz gained headway but slowly because of the charge of indelicacy that was brought against it. These scruples prevailed longer in New England than in the South, where waltzing came to be very much in vogue.

The high standard of virtue seemed to the foreigner the

[94] Stuart, II, 131.

[95] D'Arusmont, p. 27; Murray, II, 216; Mrs. Trollope, I, 189-190; Vigne, II, 271-272.

[96] For American dancing, see Murray, II, 115-116; Lambert, II, 98-99; Winterbotham, I, 17; Hodgson, II, 4; Weld, I, 22; Hall, F., p. 181; D'Arusmont, p. 27; Alexander, II, 298.

more paradoxical because of the almost unlimited liberty and freedom of intercourse that existed between young people of the two sexes.[97] Usually boys and girls went to the same academy or to the same public school, after the latter became a feature of American life. Girls "came out" into society at a very early age and thereafter led a life of great liberty, as regards the other sex, until marriage. They were usually unattended by servants or elders, and walked, rode, and danced with male companions at their own pleasure and without any thought of impropriety. Certain arbitrary rules of conduct, however, prevailed to the astonishment and chagrin of the stranger. For instance, we are told that single ladies never accepted a gentleman's arm on the street lest they should be considered forward. "After sunset, or when they stand engaged," says one author, "they are less scrupulous."[98] Many a visitor, like the gallant De Roos, found the pleasure of an excursion with an American girl "damped" by his being obliged to walk in the gutter when the streets were crowded.[99]

Then, too, as regards the more formal intercourse, there were many things that affected the observer unpleasantly. There were many conflicting statements regarding the line of demarcation between the sexes in formal society. In many of the larger cities, women were not seen at formal dinner-parties, and at most other functions were relegated to one side of the room, where they discussed their own interests, leaving the men to enjoy theirs.[100] Basil Hall re-

[97] Duhring, p. 80; D'Arusmont, p. 28; De Roos, pp. 60-61; Latrobe, I, 35; Abdy, I, 69.
[98] Candler, pp. 70-71.
[99] De Roos, p. 61.
[100] Stuart, II, 308-309; Hamilton, I, 235; Kendall, I, 327; Weston, pp. 86-87.

gretted that thus women were prohibited from exercising to the full the influence they might exert over men, by participating more in the pleasures and amusements of the latter.[101] As Captain Hall drew most of his remarks from the absence of women at a cattle show near Boston, we are not obliged to take his strictures very seriously, but others mention the reserve and "icy propriety" that was evinced in mixed company, and the lack of social relations between the sexes.[102] Alexander, however, tells of an evening party which he attended in New York in the early thirties, where the sexes mingled freely, and he calls attention to the fact that isolation prevailed chiefly in the Western districts.[103] It was suggested, too, that American society had the same standards in that respect as did the provincial towns of Great Britain — it had not yet attained to the freedom of intercourse of the best London circles. The failure of women to participate in men's diversions was sometimes ascribed to the fact that owing to the scarcity of servants, the average American woman had little time to share in her husband's pleasures.[104]

The domestic burdens laid upon her were made heavier by the fact of the very early marriages and the number of women who entered the married state.[105] Marriage was considered a civil contract, more often performed by municipal authorities than by the clergyman, who was often invited as a mark of respect. It is significant of the early age at which this contract was binding that in the state of

[101] Hall, B., II, 150 ff.; Duhring, p. 75 ff.; Stuart, II, 308-309.
[102] Fowler, p. 215; Hall, F., pp. 180-181.
[103] Alexander, II, 298.
[104] Duhring, p. 78.
[105] For discussion of early marriages, see Flint, p. 165; Shirreff, p. 99; Mrs. Trollope, I. 166; Cooper, pp. 54-55; Wilson, Appendix, p. 105; Neilson, p. 225; Birkbeck, "Notes on a Journey," p. 86. See, also, Kendall, I, 288, and Weston, p. 223.

New York, in the thirties, Abdy says, consent of parents or guardians was not necessary provided the boy had reached fourteen years and the girl twelve years.[106] There was no practical difficulty or ban of public opinion to prevent this custom of early marriage. There was no fear of lack of subsistence for the future family, as any man with industry might hope to gain a competence and even wealth. Uniformity of wealth and social rank made most men equally eligible. Then, marriage presented at that time, as has been said, almost the only outlook for women. With the exception of a few teachers, dressmakers, and workers in the factories of the Eastern cities, women were dependent upon the men of the family for support. Therefore the young woman regarded marriage as a natural destiny and entered it as a matter of course, usually before she was twenty-two. It was not at all unusual for a woman to have a family of children before she was eighteen years of age. It was estimated that each marriage produced on an average six children, of whom four were reared.[107] A surprising number of travellers comment on the fact that marriage brought about almost invariably a change in even the most frivolous of women. They became more sober and serious, and took up, as a matter of course, the duties of domestic life.[108] The resulting absorption in this led to the much deplored division of the interests of husband and wife.

This, however, did not prevent a very apparent and very satisfying relation between the two. In the family group and in wider intercourse, the woman occupied a high if somewhat narrow niche. No man must occupy a chair while women were standing; in stage coaches and other public conveyances their comfort was considered before

[106] Abdy, I, 253.
[107] Winterbotham, p. 73.
[108] See, for instance, Hall, F., p. 182; D'Arusmont, p. 28.

that of anyone else.[109] Many an Englishman was astonished at the delay and inconvenience the presence of a woman might involve. Miss Martineau, who bitterly resented "the indulgence given American women as a substitute for justice," declared that the degree of consideration shown them was greater than what was rational or good for either men or women; that such treatment made women petulant and fault-finding.

Owing to the circumstances under which many women lived, especially in the more unsettled regions, they were hard-working drudges, but generally the effort was made to preserve them from unwomanly employment. In cases of emergency women were known to work in the fields, but public opinion did not encourage the practice. German and Irish emigrants persisted longest in it, in those parts in which they dwelt in considerable numbers, but the arrival of New Englanders among them usually banished women from the fields. Custom forbade that female duties should be much extended beyond the care of the domestic machinery.[110]

In the effort to summarize a few of these aspects of American life as revealed to us by those who visited our country with their eyes open, it may be well to reconstruct the type of domestic life which prevailed here at that time. It is true that the variations in the different parts of the country forbid anything but an imperfect generalization, but a composite picture may be of some value in bringing to a focus these various phases.

We find the typical family living in the country, and safely and comfortably ensconced in a frame house. This

[109] For deference to women, see Melish, II, 44-45; Neilson, p. 199; Hall, B., III, 71; Martineau, II, 227, 213; Abdy, II, 293.

[110] Neilson, p. 199; Kingdom, p. 12; Fearon, p. 221; Bradbury. Appendix, p. 303; Stuart, II, 172; Shirreff, p. 35.

dwelling was of course antedated by the two-room log house with a loft, an easily-built form of habitation, but one which at its best was clearly a makeshift. The house that succeeded it as quickly as possible was much more comfortable and capacious. It had the added advantages of floors and windows; the use of the latter was much limited' in unsettled regions in the earlier period by the great scarcity of glass for panes. In the towns, the wooden houses became more and more superseded by brick or stone buildings.[111] This was chiefly because of the great number of fires. Many of the wooden structures were made with chimneys of the same material, which proved a cheap but dangerous substitute for stone. The sound of the fire-alarm became so frequent, we are told, that the American citizen, unless he happened to belong to one of the volunteer fire companies, failed to regard it.[112] As the wooden buildings were destroyed, the tendency was to replace them in brick.

In this home lived a usually large and happy family. Besides the parents and the children, there were likely to be one or two old people who were dependent for their support. Especially did the care of an indigent woman fall to the lot of the nearest male relative. In the South, the number of people around the table of a wealthy family was likely to be augmented by a tutor, employed for the young people, especially the boys. If the group were of the working class, particularly in the North and East, it was likely to be diminished by the absence of some of the sons, who were bound out to learn various trades. They became under those conditions members of the employer's family.

The only professional servants were negroes and Eu-

[111] Holmes, p. 361; Priest, p. 171; Stuart, I, 26; Coke, I, 162; Wood, pp. 274-278.

[112] Stuart, I, 26; also Kendall, II, 259.

ropean emigrants, many of the latter, in the early days at least, the so-called "redemptioners." White servants often made part of the family life, eating and drinking with the members on terms of intimacy. This was almost always true if the home was in the country. The native laborer in the country districts was regarded, not as an inferior, but as a person to be treated with respect and consideration. Often he was the son of a neighbor, or an ambitious youth who needed money for his educational schemes. He received for his work, we are told, from eight dollars a month in winter to ten dollars in summer (1815) with food and lodging, and his hours were from sunrise to sunset.[113] Female domestic servants were called "helps." Throughout this period they were very scarce, and it was regarded as a great favor if they consented to help out the overburdened housewife.[114] They were seen more frequently in city homes than in the country.

The domestic economy of the South was of course quite different, owing to the presence of large numbers of slaves. The effect of this institution on Southern life remains to be traced in a subsequent chapter. It may be well, however, to say that in the typical Southern home, a less indolent form of life was lived than is sometimes supposed. To the responsibility of managing a large family of dependent slaves were added all the burdens entailed by isolation from schools and other evidences of civilization.

Owing to the uniform standard of wealth, the typical family was comfortably situated as regards food and other necessities, and was usually satisfied. It is true that long before 1835 there began to be seen evidences of great wealth in the Eastern cities—wealth made usually in the shipping trade. Life gradually became more luxurious, and the

[113] Abdy, I, 295; Stuart, I, 179.
[114] Alexander, II, 311; Martineau, I, 193 ff.

cleavage between capital and labor became more accentuated. Costly European importations decorated the homes of the rich; even the wealthy Quakers satisfied their love for beauty by indulging in the most expensive and beautiful furnishings for their houses.[115] But in the period with which we have to do, the typical American still lived in the country, where he grew his own food, and made many of his own tools, and wore clothing which had been spun, woven, and made for him by the women of his family.

We have already described the ineffectual winter costume of the city belle as she was presented to the eyes of the English visitor. Not all woman were dressed so foolishly, if we are to trust the statements of these same observers. Several noted the neatness and simplicity of the country girl's dress; it seems to have made a special impression in New England. One writer says (1808): "Their light hair is tastefully turned up behind in the modern style and fastened with a comb. Their dress is neat, simple and genteel, usually consisting of a printed cotton jacket with long sleeves, a petticoat of the same, with a colored cotton apron or pincloth without sleeves, tied tight and covering the lower part of the bosom. This seemed to be the prevailing dress in the country places."[116]

The dress of the men was more sober and conservative than that of the women, though a different state of affairs had prevailed in the preceding century.[117] This period witnessed the transition from breeches to pantaloons, and the accompanying abolition of wigs and powder and other frivolities of men's dress. James Flint says that in 1818 the garb of men in New York was much like that in Britain at the time, but that pantaloons were almost universal; the shorter small clothes were worn only by Quakers.[118] Pal-

[115] Palmer, p. 283; Alexander, II, 270. [117] Hamilton, II, 38.
[116] Lambert, II, 323. [118] Flint, p. 62.

mer says of the people of Philadelphia (1818), "The dress of both sexes is English, or closely bordering thereon, and all take a pride in being well-dressed and polite."[119] No class, whether men or women, could be identified by its costume, and it would have been extremely difficult in most cases to distinguish the mistress from the maid, or the employer from his clerk, as far as clothing was concerned.

It was not only in the public houses that strangers found a well-spread table, but in the private home as well. Two facts stand out in regard to American food: first, its universal abundance; second, the lack of thought and care displayed in the preparation of it. Food might vary in nature and in quality, but never in quantity. The natural resources, the fertility of the ground and the consequent ease with which food was produced, and the predominance of the agricultural class combined to make America a rich storehouse of provisions accessible to even the poorest in coin. From this provision the American drew always three good meals a day and sometimes four.[120] His breakfast, served about eight o'clock in the city and somewhat earlier if he lived in the country, included a great assortment of broiled fish, eggs, beefsteak, ham, sausages, hot bread, and coffee. Pork and corn meal in all forms were staple foods.[121] Buckwheat cakes were much in esteem in the North; their place was taken in the South by other forms of hot bread. Dinner came about six hours later and presented much the same array of foods. People had at their command in those times, as natural products free to all, luxuries which are now tasted only by the rich. Turkeys were abundant, the coast-line states abounded in oysters and terrapin, and canvas-back duck offered a novelty to

[119] Palmer, p. 283; Hall, B., I, 156.
[120] Candler, p. 78 ff.
[121] Parkinson, II, 331.

the English stranger, who looked forward to tasting this much-vaunted dish. The verdict in regard to it was unanimous.[122] Tea, which usually included supper, came at six or seven o'clock. A vast variety of foods more than compensated for some loss in substantial quality. Preserved fruits figured largely on the menu, and "oysters and sweet cakes, strawberries and cheese [were] placed side by side" with an astonishing indifference to the claims of digestion.[123]

In spite of all this display, it was often remarked that the Americans did not take their eating seriously enough to do it comfortably. The rapidity with which they dispatched their meals was proverbial, though the trait was not so apparent in the private home as in the inn dining-room. It is quite evident that they were not epicures. They ate to live; dining was part of the day's business. One traveller complained that they put too many kinds of food on their plates at one time, thereby betraying their indifference to flavor.[124] They did not linger over their wine, but drank it hastily and in moderate quantities. American cooking, too, was considered by Englishmen notoriously poor, and much of the dyspepsia was attributed to the heavy pastry and the fried food. In brief, the whole attitude of Americans toward their eating and drinking was a strictly utilitarian one, though they loaded their tables with all the luxuries afforded by their abundant resources.

Life was not all labor, even to the hard-working farmer's family. Work was often done in the country by declaring a kind of "frolic"; buildings were raised, corn

[122] For luxuries of the table, see Vigne, I, 125, 128; Stuart, II, 10; Tudor, I, 445; Candler, p. 81.
[123] Candler, p. 83.
[124] Candler, p. 81; Shirreff, p. 269.

husked, apples pared, and quilts provided for future winters by the joint efforts of the family and their neighbors. Not always were these "frolics" accessible to the traveller; occasionally there is mention of participation in one.[125] Hunting was the favorite pastime of the men;[126] it also yielded practical results for the table. Children were taught very early to use a gun, and many were remarkably proficient.

The social life in the cities was rather uniform; much the same kind of existence was passed in Boston and in Charleston. For instance, among fashionable people there were two periods of the day given over to calling: one lasting from twelve to two, when ladies either visited or received callers of both sexes; the other after the evening meal.[127] In Philadelphia and the cities farther south, the latter social hour was spent on the front steps of the houses in summer, and many a pretty picture has been drawn by foreign visitors of the group of white-frocked young women entertaining their callers in the cool evening air on the spotless marble steps of some dignified residence in Philadelphia or Washington.[128] Cards and billiards were popular aids to entertainment, and, judging from the frequent mention of concerts, the interest in them was very great. By eleven o'clock the guests at any function began to depart, and by twelve the streets were hardly disturbed by a footfall.[129] Palmer thus sums up the amusements of the commercial class of Philadelphia: "Their summer pastimes are excursions to various parts of the neighborhood,

[125] Parkinson, II, 331; Cobbett, Chap. XII; Bradbury, Appendix, p. 301; Ferrall, pp. 67-69; Holmes, p. 132, 358; Fearon, pp. 220-221; Weston, pp. 194-195, 196-197, 213-218.
[126] Coke, I, 120; Dalton, p. 58.
[127] Abdy, I, 69.
[128] See, for instance, Power, I, 243; Hodgson, II, 19.
[129] Power, I, 243; Weld, I, 252.

sometimes in carriages and often in steamboats up and down the Delaware, occasional visits to Peal's museum, the circus and vauxhall gardens; with the youths, fishing, bathing, cricket, quoits, etc.; in winter their amusements are the theatre, museum, billiards, sleighing, dancing and concerts; balls are not uncommon but masquerades are unheard of; the most splendid and genteel ball is on Washington's birth-night, which occurs sometime in February." [130]

Life in the communities of the West was much like that just described, though everything was on a more crude and less elegant plan. A description of society in Lexington, Kentucky, in 1806, reveals a state of affairs much like that in any large city in the East, except for the fact that it was colored by the more turbulent propensities of the men of the community and therefore lost much grace and elegance.[131] Even in those early days it was possible to live in luxury and elegance in the new West.

Whether the family was rich or poor, whether it lived in the country or in the city, the general feeling that existed within it was said to be the same. In the family life there was very little "surface sentiment." The lack of this was entailed not only by the hard-working existence that most people lived, but by the whole spirit of independence and self-reliance that permeated the family circle. Children relied very little on their mothers; even less on their fathers. The typical family, however, was a group of kindly, good-natured, tolerant people, very undemonstrative toward one another but maintaining a strong mutual affection and respect. This was, according to travellers, as conspicuous as their peaceful relations with the rest of society. "Private life," says Abdy, "resembles self-

[130] Palmer, pp. 283-284.
[131] Ashe, p. 192; Stuart, II, 271; Martineau, I, 201 ff.

government, compact in itself, inoffensive to others and tributary to the general union. . . . That respect for the feelings of others, which in mixed society induces mutual forbearance and forbids familiarity, is not, as in too many places, laid aside when it is most wanted. . . . There seems to be a sort of correspondence between the political institutions of the country and its family arrangements. . . . .

"I believe it is not so much the outward plenty, or the mutual freedom, or the simplicity of manners, or the incessant play of humor, which characterizes the whole people, as the sweet temper which is diffused like sunshine over the land. . . . I imagine that the practice of forbearance requisite in a republic is answerable for the pleasant peculiarity; . . . the respect for mutual rights which citizens have perpetually forced upon them abroad comes thence to be observed toward the weak and unresisting in the privacy of home." [132]

[132] Abdy, I, 70.

CHAPTER IV

THE CARE OF THE UNFORTUNATE

IN the care of the diseased, whether the affliction were physical, mental, or moral, America, at the time with which we are concerned, represented a kind of vast experiment station. In her desperate attempts to care for her rapidly increasing population she made, as a matter of course, mistakes which we are able to perceive now that years have elapsed, but which then stood for the most advanced knowledge of the day.

In the years before the Revolution, the care of the poor was a comparatively easy problem. If the aged or indigent could not be taken care of by their relatives, as was the custom, the duty of their support fell to the community, which paid their board with some private family. As the number of public poor increased, they were gathered into almshouses to facilitate the care of them. The first of these public homes was founded by the Friends in 1713, in Pennsylvania. The example was followed by other states, and by the beginning of the Revolution almshouses were a well-known institution. One of the first instances of mention of them by travellers is in 1799, when Isaac Weld visited what he called a "Bettering House" in Philadelphia. Here the poor were furnished with employment and were "comfortably lodged and dieted."[1]

In these places of refuge, which were sufficient for the

[1] Weld, I, 12-13.

THE CARE OF THE UNFORTUNATE 109

needs of the time, but which represented a very small financial burden on the taxpayer, the visitor saw a large and curiously assorted group of inmates. Orphan children found a home there, as there was no other place for them. The institution was seen to take the place of the hospital to the poor and aged of both sexes. Harmless lunatics always made part of the family and were allowed to wander about at large; if one became violent, he was kept caged like an animal, and treated as such.[2]

This comparatively simple condition of affairs was complicated from the first days of the new republic by the astonishing increase in pauperism. This was traced to several causes, of which the most serious was intemperance. The increase of the dramshop and the "corner grocery" was constant, and ominous for the future welfare of the United States. In 1809, an investigation by the Humane Society of New York revealed the presence of 1800 licensed dramshops in that city alone. In the First Annual Report of the American Temperance Society (Andover, 1828) quoted by Basil Hall, it was estimated that the number of paupers in the United States at that time was 200,000, whose support cost annually $10,000,000. The majority of these 200,000 were addicted to drink.[3]

In 1829, Cobbett made the statement that very few native Americans were paupers, but that the greater part were either Europeans in distress or free negroes. His own poor rates were trifling, amounting annually to only seven dollars upon a rent of six hundred.[4] Harriet Martineau supported the former statement by saying that pauperism was "confined to the ports, emigrants making their way back

[2] See Dalton, p. 57, for description of inmates of a Lancaster (Pa.) almshouse.
[3] Hall, B., II, 87-88.
[4] Cobbett, p. 224.

into the country, the families of intemperate or disabled men, and unconnected women who depended on their own exertions." She deplored the possibility of the curse of a legal charity, and looked with apprehension upon the "magnificent pauper asylum in Philadelphia, made to accommodate luxuriously 1200 persons."[5] It was this same "magnificent" institution that Thomas Brothers, a few years afterward, attacked so bitterly, quoting from the Pennsylvania papers to show the abuses that went on, and the cruel treatment of the inmates.[6] However, this was looked on as a model place of its kind, and a worthy example of Philadelphia's interest in benevolent concerns. No city in the world of the same population, it was said, had so many charitable societies as did the City of Brotherly Love. In 1832, it was estimated that there were upwards of thirty institutions and societies for the relief of the poor and orphans, besides more than 150 mutual benefit societies.

Out of the necessity for segregating certain classes of people in the almshouse grew the orphan asylum, the house of refuge, the public hospital, and the institution for the insane. It soon became apparent that the ordinary poorhouse was no place in which to bring up children. Lambert says [7] that in 1806, the Orphan Asylum Society of the City of New York was founded through the activities of the Ladies' Society for the Relief of Poor Widows with Small Children, "the first women's charitable organization in New York." After the movement was well-started, the state took a part in its support. One of the best-known and most frequently visited orphan asylums seems to have been that of Charleston, South Carolina. More than one

[5] Martineau, II, 289.
[6] Brothers, p. 246 ff.; Palmer, p. 275.
[7] Lambert, II, 78.

THE CARE OF THE UNFORTUNATE 111

English traveller mentions having seen it when his route lay through that city.[8]

The houses of refuge were founded for both boys and girls. According to Captain Hall, they offered a home for youthful delinquents who had either been in prison or who would "in the regular course of law be sent there."[9] The inmates, after a certain period of probation, were bound out to tradespeople, preferably in a part of the country where their previous history was unknown.[10] Hamilton says that they usually prospered in their new environment, and the institutions were invariably spoken of in high terms as having accomplished a great work of reformation.

In medicine and the care of the sick we have indeed travelled a long way since 1835. Consumption raged unchecked, especially among women. Then, too, it was not until the second decade of the century that the Americans were seen to combat successfully the dreadful scourge of yellow fever that devasted the coast cities practically every summer. At first it levelled its hardest blows at populous New York and Philadelphia, but later attacked the more Southern cities. New Orleans was said to have had 800 deaths from it in the summer of 1817, and 2190 in 1819. There grew up around this much-dreaded plague a literature which is highly illuminating in regard to the conditions of living at the time. English travellers from Weld to Ferrall give more or less full and vivid descriptions of the effects of the pestilence.[11]

Hospitals developed from the infirmaries which were a

[8] Stuart, II, 71; Lambert, II, 134-135; Neilson, p. 260.
[9] Hall, B., I, 24-25.
[10] Hamilton, I, 276-277.
[11] For remarks on the yellow fever, see Blane, p. 9 ff.; Hamilton, II, 212-214, 279-281; Weld, I, 4, 46; Hodgson, I, 50-54; Bernard, pp. 195-197, 260-261; D'Arusmont, pp. 354-355; Wansey, pp. 131-132; Ferrall, pp. 205, 213-214.

part of the charitable institutions. All through this period, and for many years afterward, the hospital was remarked to be the last resource of the penniless sick man. One's presence there marked one as an object of charity.[12] It is interesting to note that we find a survival of this attitude in certain rural districts even today. The Philadelphia hospital was originally a part of the almshouse. Weld again gives us our earliest description of this famous institution. In 1795, when he saw it, it was unsurpassed, he said, by any other institution of the kind in the world. It was still in process of building, though it had been founded in 1756. By 1793, it had sheltered 9000 patients suffering from disorders of either mind or body, "upwards of 6000 of whom were relieved or cured."[13] We have another description of it in 1821, a large convenient building "with spacious and airy walks, enclosed for the accommodation of the patients."[14] Tudor visited it in 1831 and spoke in high praise of its efficiency. It was, he says, appropriated equally to insane patients and surgical cases.[15] In 1833, there were 983 patients admitted, of whom 500 were foreigners. Those who could afford it paid three to six dollars a week, but its first object was the accommodation of the poor.[16] Other hospitals were visited by the stranger. There was a fine one in Boston, also one in New York, situated in the center of the city and possessing the advantages of a high elevation and extensive grounds,[17] but the Philadelphia institution is by far the most famous.

The treatment of the insane was, up to a late period, ill-judged and ignorantly cruel. The mentally unbalanced

[12] Coke, I, 38; Abdy, I, 41.
[13] Weld, I, 11-12.
[14] Dalton, p. 27.
[15] Tudor, I, 97; Palmer, p. 273 (1817); Coke, I, 38-39.
[16] Abdy, III, 136-137. [17] Hall, B., II, 133; Boardman, p. 92.

among the poor were kept in jail or in the almshouse; wealthier people usually employed an attendant or "boarded out" the patient. Instruments of torture were used in the belief that they acted as "tranquillizing" agents. Coke tells of seeing in an almshouse lunatic ward in Philadelphia "a man with a most forbidding countenance, feeding a poor girl who was chained to the wall and her hands confined in a strait waistcoat, but," he adds, "I was assured that such severe measures were but seldom, and blows never, had recourse to." [18] Insane asylums, as such, were very slow in coming. Cases of mental disturbance were, as has been said, taken care of in the general hospital, where a wing or a row of cells below the ground floor was set apart for them.[19] Gaillard Hunt says that the first real asylum in New York was established in 1839 when the insane were moved from Bellevue to Bloomingdale, and that the same year saw the establishment of the first asylum in Massachusetts. But Hamilton in 1830 visited an institution of this kind in New York,[20] and Abdy in 1833 saw in Boston a very interesting asylum the methods of which were astonishingly modern.[21] He says of it: "The principle on which the establishment is conducted differs very considerably, and from what I saw and heard, very successfully, from the methods usually pursued in the treatment of lunatics. No kind of deception, and if possible, no restraint, is exercised upon the patients, who are allowed every indulgence and gratification that are not incompatible with the object for which they are sent hither . . . with the aid of soothing language, occupation suited to their inclinations, proper exercise and appropriate medicines, an alleviation, if not a cure, of the malady is effected. . . . No one is confined, however vio-

[18] Coke, I, 39.
[19] Dalton, p. 27; Weld, I, 11.
[20] Hamilton, I, 276.
[21] Abdy, I, 98 ff.

lent and intractable, in irons or in solitude. No breach of promise, no attempt to mislead, is ever permitted. . . . Riding on horseback for both sexes is found very serviceable; gardening, or any other occupation that may interest or amuse, is employed with good effect; and as the house is open to visitors at all times, and the same courtesies are observed toward the inmates as are practiced in common life, a constant succession of objects presents itself, to give gentle exercise to the tastes and affections, and dispel the morbid illusions of the imagination. To gain his confidence, and imperceptibly lead him to the exercise of its disused energies and faculties . . . is all that the physician studies in the management of his patient.''[22]

In the early part of this period, a criminal class, as such, was conspicuously lacking in the United States. The population in the cities had not yet become congested, and while vice existed to a certain extent, the cases were more isolated and taken as a matter of course. In Pennsylvania and New York before the Revolution there had been sixteen crimes punishable by death.[23] The former colony in her penal code was again the instigator of much that was humane and broad-minded in policy. She was the first to do away with the death-penalty except for murder and treason, substituting labor and imprisonment. In 1796, New York followed her example, and gradually the death penalty came to be exacted only for the two crimes. Generally, lawlessness did not prevail to any extent. Dalton gives us a glimpse of the record of the Philadelphia police court for one night, which is significant of the conditions existing even as late as 1821.[24]

[22] Abdy, III, 137; also gives a description of the lunatic ward in the Philadelphia hospital.
[23] Hall, B., I, 63; Holmes, p. 415; Duncan, I, 230-231.
[24] Dalton, pp. 28-29.

"1. A black boy, twelve years old, found strolling in the streets at midnight, having no home—committed to be bound out as an apprentice.

2. A black girl, ten years old, found in the streets at midnight—committed as a runaway.

3. Two women, found drunk at eleven o'clock at night —were each sentenced to one month's imprisonment.

4. A man was bound over to court for leading a mob to resist the dog-killers.

5. Many boys were bound over to court for habitually disturbing the peace at the corners of streets during evenings.''

The prisons of America were at this time well worth visiting, as they were the scene of interesting sociological experiments, the results of which are apparent today in the same institutions. The term of imprisonment varied in length, as is the case today, but the manner of housing the prisoners, and the working out of the plans toward their reformation, presented a decided innovation.

Until the introduction of the penitentiary system with the reclamation of the convict as its aim, American prisons were unspeakable in their conditions and were veritable schools of crime. No discrimination was shown in housing the prisoners; the guilty of all ages and of all degrees of crime were herded together, and usually spent their days in idleness and vice. The best description of one of these early prisons is given us by the Englishman Kendall (1806), who visited in Connecticut a prison in an old copper mine.[25] He comments on the filthy and unhealthful living conditions, and especially on the disastrous moral effects of such imprisonment. In 1790, Pennsylvania instituted what was known as the penitentiary system, with separate cells for the convicts. Weld gives one of the early accounts of this

[25] Kendall, I, Chap. XXI.

institution, which he declared was probably better regulated than any other of its kind in the world. "As soon as a prisoner is committed to the prison," he says, "he is made to wash, his hair is shorn, and if not decently clothed, he is furnished with clean apparel; then he is shown into a solitary cell about 9 feet long and 4 wide, where he remains debarred from the sight of every living being except his gaoler . . . who is forbidden on any account to speak to him without there is absolute occasion. If a prisoner is at all refractory, or if the offence for which he is imprisoned is of a very atrocious nature, he is then confined in a cell secluded even from the light of heaven." The treatment of each prisoner was regulated during his term. "Solitary confinement in a dark cell is looked upon as the severest usage; next, solitary confinement in a cell with the admission of light; next, confinement in a cell where the prisoner is allowed to do some sort of work; lastly, labor in a company with others. The prisoners are obliged to bathe twice every week . . . and also to change their linen. Those in solitary confinement are kept upon bread and water, but those who labor are allowed broth, porridge, puddings and the like: meat is dispensed only in small quantities twice in the week. Their drink is water, on no pretense is any other beverage suffered to be brought into the prison. . . . Those who labor are employed in the particular trade to which they have been accustomed, provided it can be carried on in the prison; if not acquainted with any, something is soon found that they can do. . . . The women are kept totally apart from the men and are employed in a manner suitable to their sex. The laborers all eat together in one large apartment, and regularly, every Sunday, there is divine service at which all attend."[26] A brave attempt was made to render

[26] Weld, I, 13-19; Melish, I, 160-162; Hall, F., pp. 183-190.

this experiment successful, and once more Pennsylvania's example was followed by the other states, so that by 1821 fourteen of the latter had penitentiaries.[27] But unfortunately, the expected reformation in the criminal classes did not manifest itself, and other schemes were resorted to. From 1816-18 on, there were two rival systems, one being experimented with in the Philadelphia institution and the other in the state prison at Auburn, New York. All subsequently established prisons were managed according to one of these systems, and it was the result of one or both of these that was constantly being considered by the interested English traveller of the second and third decades of the century.

In 1818, the legislature of Pennsylvania changed from the old system previously described to that of solitary confinement. The prisoner neither saw nor heard a human being except his jailer, the chaplain or visiting clergyman, the inspectors, and other authorities of the institution. It was apparently some time before this could be put into operation. In 1819, when Dalton visited the penitentiary, the old system was still in use; he makes no mention of the new one.[28] Vigne in 1832 speaks of it as a new establishment and says the first warden was appointed in 1829.[29]

The principle on which this institution was founded, it was observed, was that reformation of the prisoner could be effected if by solitary confinement his thoughts were turned necessarily to himself and his guilt. By excluding him from the sight of his fellow-prisoners, the authorities believed they were doing him a great service; there was no danger that anyone would recognize him after his re-

[27] Duncan, I, 68.
[28] Dalton, pp. 24-25; see, also, Fearon, pp. 156-157.
[29] Vigne, I, 32.

lease, and he would therefore not be obliged to live down the disgrace of his prison life. "It was, in the first instance," Tudor says, "gravely determined, no doubt with good motives but with a most mistaken judgment, to condemn to solitary confinement without labor; the effect of which, leaving out of consideration the negative consequence of the loss of profit arising from their work, would have operated, I fear, more on the brain than on the heart. ... I am strongly inclined to believe that the supposed superior reformation of morals expected to be derived from the system would, in the majority of instances of persons confined for a series of years, terminate in self-murder or insanity."[30] It was exactly this result which is said to have forced the authorities to institute labor in the individual cells, thereby making the institution self-supporting. It was estimated that a prisoner who had two years or more to remain in confinement could earn sufficient to clear all his expenses from his admission till his discharge.[31]

The Auburn prison, which instituted the rival system, was begun in 1816.[32] In 1821, we are told by Dalton, it was not yet completed, but already housed 170 inmates. Before 1816, the New York State prison had been in New York City at Greenwich. It was a prison of the old type under the authority of a board of inspectors. Each convict worked, however, and received at his discharge, it was said, whatever sum had accrued to him during his imprisonment, over and above his expenses.[33] The first method of control adopted by the new institution was that of solitary confinement, as in Philadelphia, until the resulting preva-

[30] Tudor, I, 103-104.
[31] Vigne, I, 33-34.
[32] Tudor, I, 206; Coke, II, p. 1 ff.; Holmes, p. 420; Dalton, p. 92.
[33] Lambert, II. 67-68; see Palmer, p. 310 ff.

lence of insanity among the prisoners made a change imperative. The new system was destined to be known as the "beau ideal of what prison discipline should be" and to survive until the day of the Mutual Welfare League. The prisoners worked together but without communication of any kind, and were separated at night.[34] Tudor says that at the time of his visit in 1831, there were three representatives of the French government present in the town, sent there to inspect the prison as a model. At the time, it contained 700 men and only 30 women, a discrepancy in numbers on which the visitor comments, but adds that the jailer told him that he had "infinitely more trouble and vexation in keeping the thirty females in order and obedience, than with all the overwhelming majority of the more peaceable men whom he had in charge."[35]

Subsequent prisons in New York State were founded on the Auburn model; of these Sing Sing was agreed to be the most notable example.[36] Other states imitated either one or the other of these two great institutions, and we meet with many descriptions by travellers of prisons in Connecticut, Massachusetts, Vermont, Maryland, and Kentucky, which were modelled on these systems.[37] They all seem to have been more than self-supporting, which fact was much emphasized. Espionage was carried on by means of peephole in the walls of cells and workrooms, so that the prisoner never knew when he was under surveillance.[38] It was this last feature that Miss Martineau considered espe-

[34] This prison (Auburn) was visited by many travellers; Fowler, pp. 90-94; Stuart, I, 65 ff.; Coke, II, 1 ff.; Murray, I, 63 ff.; Howison, pp. 310-312.
[35] Tudor, I, 211.
[36] For accounts of Sing Sing, see Boardman, pp. 114-116; Abdy, I, 56-57; Hamilton, I, 167-179.
[37] Stuart, I, 77; Power, I, 114 ff.; Abdy, I, 90.
[38] Alexander, II, 264; Abdy, I, 269.

cially reprehensible when she visited the Auburn prison. She denounced it as "the deepest of insults," and a hindrance to self-respect in the morally infirm man. Most visitors, however, heartily approved the plan.[39]

Comparisons were constantly being made of the relative cost of English and American prisons, very much to the advantage of the American system. Basil Hall quotes the reports of the Boston Prison Discipline Society to show the astonishing cheapness of it. In England, in one year, 3699 convicts earned about $41,727. In the United States, 999 convicts earned $81,979. "Or, in other words," he says, "a little more than one-fourth part the number of convicts in the United States earn more than double the amount of nearly four times the number of convicts in England." He attributes this increase to the difference of discipline and of diet. American prisoners received more animal food than did the English. This was made necessary by the heavy labor they performed.[40] Another advantage which the American prisoner enjoyed after 1826 was an opportunity for free education, which, however, was not made compulsory.[41]

A feature of the penal code that was felt to be a grievous mistake was the ease with which pardons could be obtained in America. Seldom was a term of imprisonment completed. Pardons were granted on the principle that punishment was reformatory, and in the belief that the prisoner had reformed. The practice was so abused that complaints were heard from all sides. A life sentence was generally understood, one traveller says, to mean imprisonment for a shorter term than if a limited sentence of a few years had been imposed. "It is certain," says Basil Hall,

[39] Martineau, II, 286.
[40] Hall, B., I, 67-68.
[41] Ibid., I, 71.

"that at any rate the progress of prison reform was much delayed by this constant yielding to the temptation to be too merciful and that conviction and punishment were robbed of half their terrors for the offender."[42]

[42] On pardons, see Hall, B., I, 75; Martineau, II, 288; Abdy, I, 22-23; Duncan, I, 71.

CHAPTER V

SLAVERY

AMONG the forces that might make for the disintegration of this new union of states, the institution of slavery stood foremost in the minds of all thoughtful people in the early part of the nineteenth century. This curious anomaly of a large servile class in the midst of a population whose most cherished ideals had to do with freedom and equality, interested and puzzled the foreigner, and set him wondering just what the outcome would be.[1] A great deal was said and written about slavery in these years; no one seems to have taken it lightly, though the question had by no means assumed the menacing proportions that it assumed a few years later.

The Northern states had either developed a personal conscience in regard to the matter or had begun to realize the utter lack of profit for themselves in slave-holding; they had not yet reached the point of trying to influence the South; in short, slavery was still a local matter. At the close of the Revolution, the New England and other Northern States either abolished the institution outright, as was the case in Massachusetts, New Hampshire, and Vermont, or passed laws for its gradual abolition. They decreed that

[1] Flower, p. 96; Duncan, II, 251-252; Blane, p. 201; Shirreff, pp. 311-312; Tudor, II, 71. See Moore, T., "Epistle to Lord Viscount Forbes" (Poems Relating to America).

"after a certain day in a certain year slavery should be prohibited; that men and women who were slaves on that day should remain so, but that children born thereafter of slave parents should be free on attaining a certain age." In 1817, New York passed a law providing that on July 4, 1827, slavery should cease in the state.

Even after his emancipation in the North, the negro had his influence on the economy of that part of the country. We have seen in a previous chapter that domestic service of various kinds was considered humiliating because it was usually performed by the negro race and therefore carried with it the taint of degradation. As for his personal treatment, there were many observers whose testimony shows that to all practical purposes, the negro was still in bondage. "They are subjected to the most grinding and humiliating of all slaveries," said Hamilton in 1834, "that of universal and unconquerable prejudice. The whip indeed has been removed from the back of the Negro but the chains are still on his limbs, and he bears the brand of degradation on his forehead."[2] That the limitations of the negro's power arose from prejudice rather than from legislative enactment is true, though it must be admitted that even the anti-slave states guarded their prerogatives jealously and limited the political rights of the negro as much as possible, chiefly from the conception of his intellectual and moral inferiority. The education of the free black in the North, even to those who were benevolently interested, seemed rather a hopeless and futile task. Hamilton says that while there were Americans who testified to the fact that the negroes often revealed themselves as apt pupils, it was admitted that there was no point to be gained in educating them, as the future held no promise for them

[2] Hamilton, I, 93. Also Fearon, pp. 58-59; Holmes, p. 334; Abdy, III, 206-207.

and their education only helped to aggravate their sense of exclusion from the rights of white citizens.³

This attitude of superiority toward the unfortunate freedman aroused the indignation of many English visitors in whom this kind of prejudice was to a large extent lacking. They urged justice at least toward these beings who were "protected as citizens when the public service required their security, but not otherwise treated as such."⁴ Very few Englishmen would have gone as far as Abdy and Candler, who could see no harm in the amalgamation of the two races. The former, who came here as companion to an English government inspector of prisons, had as his chief interest the welfare of the negro, and believed that objection to intermarriage was narrow-minded and unjust.⁵ Candler affirmed confidently that the union sooner or later would certainly take place. "Much as the whites at present may dislike the idea," he said, "it will contribute to their mutual advantage. The notion that the species will be deteriorated by the union is ridiculous. Physical reasons may be given for believing directly the reverse. The sooner this union takes place the better, for a caste in society is a dangerous evil."⁶ Though one might not, however, be in favor of the intermarriage of the negro and the white, there were numbers of people who resented the personal indignities heaped upon the helpless freedman in the states where he had been set at liberty. Fearon rejoiced at the absence of negroes in Connecticut and Rhode Island, not from personal prejudice but because he hated all forms of oppression, and the sights

---

³ Hamilton, I, 90-92. See, also, Holmes, pp. 331, 334.

⁴ Candler, Chap. XXI (entire), p. 280 ff; Martineau, I, 145; D'Arusmont, pp. 52-53, denies degraded condition of the Northern negro.

⁵ Abdy, I, 156-162.   ⁶ Candler, p. 298.

he had witnessed among the free negroes of New York and
New Jersey made him reluctant to see any more cruelties.[7]
Boardman (1833) tells of the interference with the negroes'
Fifth of July celebration in New York. The fact
that impressed him the most in the treatment of the free
blacks was that they were not permitted to be buried in
the same cemeteries as the whites, "as if the distinction
were to be perpetuated forever."[8] Abdy went, in Boston,
to hear a public lecture on slavery; he says that there were
at that time (1833) fewer free blacks in Boston than in
New York, but they were not better treated. They had
difficulty in gaining a livelihood; with the exception of one
or two employed as printers, one blacksmith, and one shoemaker,
there were no colored mechanics in the city.[9]

In the South, the attitude toward the negro was more
easily to be understood by the foreigner. The whites in
the slave states were in the peculiar position of having to
cope with a part of the population that was seemingly
indispensable and that nevertheless represented a drain
upon the life of the community. That the Southerner was
sincere in his belief that the slave was necessary for existence
in the South was believed by English visitors; that
he usually considered the institution a great evil and a
menace to the best interests of his state and country is just
as evident.[10] What, then, was he to do? asked the observer.
Often his whole fortune was tied up in his slaves
and his land; the former were necessary if he was to get
income from the latter. Slavery prevented the introduction
of any other class of laborers, and the lack of these in
turn made it necessary that the unsatisfactory institution

[7] Fearon, p. 97, pp. 167-168; also Kendall, I, 141.
[8] Boardman, p. 311.
[9] Abdy, I, 121-122.
[10] Murray, II, 204; Power, II, 80.

should be preserved. A deadlock was thus produced. Besides, few white laborers could endure the hard life on the rice, sugar, or cotton plantation in the Southern climate.[11] It was argued that the cessation of slavery would put a stop to the cultivation of both rice and sugar in the United States. Hamilton says that during all his tour through the country he never talked with an American on the subject of slavery without the latter's at once admitting the magnitude of the evil. "The planters," he says, "uniformly speak of it as a noxious exhalation by which their whole atmosphere is poisoned. 'Yet what is to be done?' they ask. 'You express yourself shocked by the existence of slavery, have you formed any plan for its abolition? . . . At all events, do not suppose that we maintain slavery in our territory from choice. Far from it. We regard those states where this curse is unknown with envy. We would gladly become as they are, but *cannot.*'"[12] It was easy for the Northern states to free their slaves; there was no vital reason for keeping them; in fact they were a drain upon Northern resources and their emancipation involved no particular sacrifice, but in the South, circumstances were quite different. The planters there would have welcomed a solution of the problem that "substituted bad labor for good, and an unsound population for a healthy one."[13]

It was noticed that there was a great deal of fear, too, mingled in the attitude of the Southerner toward his slaves. Memories of atrocities in Jamaica and San Domingo, and unpleasant experiences in individual cases, made him be-

[11] Janson, p. 358; Lambert, II, 170; Hamilton, II, 227-229; Hall, B., III, 188; Neilson, p. 326.

[12] Hamilton, II, 225; also D'Arusmont, pp. 52-53.

[13] Hall, F., Appendix, p. 251; Hall, B., III, 159; Finch, pp. 236, 240.

lieve that the blacks must be kept wholly under his control if they were to be restrained at all.[14] In Northern books written since the Civil War, this danger is minimized, but to the planter and his family it seemed very real, and constituted the primary reason for the stringent laws that governed slaves in the Southern states. This severity extended to legislation against the free negro, who seemed a serious menace because of his half-assimilated ideas of freedom and equality, his smattering of education, and his consequent influence on the enslaved population. It was the fear of a possible negro insurrection that prompted the following law, quoted by English travellers from the Georgia statute books, but representing a type of legislation that prevailed in all the states:—"Any slave or free person of color or any other person, circulating papers or bringing into this state, or aiding in any manner in bringing into the state, papers for the purpose of exciting to insurrection, conspiracy or resistance among the slaves or free persons of color, against owners, or the citizens, is to be punished with death."[15] Harriet Martineau says that upon the vaguest suspicion people travelling through the country were fined, flogged, or imprisoned on the charge of trying to arouse an insurrection. "It was declared by some liberal-minded gentlemen of South Carolina after the publication of Dr. Channing's work on Slavery that if Dr. Channing were to enter South Carolina with a body-guard of 20,000 men, he could not come out alive."[16] Committees of Vigilance throughout the South helped to enforce laws

[14] For surmises as to slave insurrections, see Alexander, II, 19; Janson, p. 361; Bristed, p. 149; Holmes, p. 239; Candler, p. 270; Ferrall, p. 196; Melish, I, 377; Blane, p. 208 ff., 214 ff.; Duncan, II, 332; Hall, B., III, 242.
[15] Stuart, II, 86; Hall, B., III, 254.
[16] Martineau, II, 133-134.

against the spread of anti-slavery doctrines, in spite of the theoretical freedom of speech set forth in all the state constitutions.

Sedulously did the slave owner protect his negroes from the disturbing influence of education. Many travellers mention the fact that in most of the Southern states, teaching a slave or free negro to read or write was punished by imprisonment and a fine not exceeding $500, if the offender were white, by fines and whipping if he were a slave or freedman.[17] A law which prevailed in the Carolinas, and which aroused a great deal of comment from foreigners, contained the following clause: "And whereas cruelty is not only highly unbecoming in those who profess themselves Christians, but is odious in the eyes of all men who have any sense of virtue or humanity, therefore, to restrain and prevent barbarity from being exercised toward slaves, be it enacted, That any person wilfully murdering a slave shall forfeit 700 pounds currency, and if any person shall on a sudden heat or passion or by undue correction kill his own slave or slave of another person he shall forfeit 350 pounds currency." This law one author characterizes as "an exquisite specimen of that legislative cant and cruelty with which the governments of all nations from time to time edify their country and mankind."[18] A slave-owner could not torture his negroes under penalty of $200 fine,[19] and in some places premeditated murder carried with it loss of right to hold any office, civil or military, in the state. These enactments, theoretically at least, protected the person of the slave—in other respects he was but a chattel of his master. It was no-

[17] See, for instance, Ferrall, p. 197; Hall, B., III, 254; Stuart, II, 85-86; Martineau, II, 131.
[18] Hall, F., Appendix, pp. 253-254.
[19] Martineau, II, 131 (note).

ticed that he had no right to benefit of trial by jury, and that his evidence was never accepted against a white person, though he could testify against one of his own color without oath.[20]

But it was the free blacks in the South who were seen to be limited by the most severe restrictions of law. It has before been intimated that they were looked upon with dread by the average Southerner. It was this fear that had finally induced the slave states to consent to the prohibition of importation of slaves, to take effect Jan. 1, 1808. For the four preceding years, merchants were preparing for it, and such large importations took place that the market was glutted. Lambert gives the following informatin concerning the numbers imported into Charleston alone:[21]

1804	5,386
1805	6,790
1806	11,458
1807	15,676
	39,310

By 1808, the states that had formerly objected to the abolition of the foreign trade were quite willing to agree to it, it was said, as the practice of permitting great numbers of freedmen from the West Indies to pour into the coast cities of the United States, was dangerous because of their influence on the native slaves. Many accounts are given of the threatened insurrection in Charleston in May, 1822, which led to hasty and severe legislation on the part of South Carolina. In the investigation that took place, it was found that aid had been sought in San Domingo, and that letters had been carried back and forth by free negroes

[20] Hall, F., Appendix, p. 253.   [21] Lambert, II, 165.

on the ships visiting Charleston. A new law was therefore put into effect that as soon as a ship entered a port of South Carolina with a free negro on board, the latter should be seized. "The sheriff must board the vessel, drag the negro to the jail and keep him there till the ship had cleared out and was ready to sail. Then the [ship] master must pay all costs of detention and carry the man away, or he would become liable to a fine of $1000 or imprisonment for two months and the negro would be sold as a slave." [22] It was noted that in 1829 Georgia made laws to the same effect, subjecting to a forty days' quarantine any ship which should enter her ports having on board a free negro employed as steward, mariner, or in any other capacity.

Observers tell how desperately each state tried to keep the free colored people outside her boundaries.[23] In Virginia, a master who freed slaves had to remove them at once from the state, and no negro set free in another part of the country was allowed on Virginia territory. The latter enactment was also in force in Louisiana, in South Carolina, and in Delaware. In the last-mentioned state, if an offender were seized, he was made to pay a fine; failing this, he was sold into bondage. By fines and imprisonments for vagrancy and other minor offenses, Maryland tried to discourage freedmen from settling within her borders. In some states, Tennessee, for instance, freedom papers must be registered—any free negro or mulatto in any of the slave-holding states might be sold into slavery if he could not prove his freedom by documentary evidence. He was of course not allowed to be taught to read or to write. Attempts at schools were broken up and teachers and pupils flogged. In some states, freedmen

[22] Stuart, II, 72; Neilson, pp. 294-295.
[23] Stuart, II, 80; D'Arusmont, p. 383.

could not assemble in numbers greater than seven, could not have their own churches, or could not buy or sell in places outside the community in which they lived. Municipalities followed the example of the state in restraining this despised class. James Stuart says that the City Council of Savannah, about 1830, passed a law imposing a tax of $100 on free persons of color coming to that city.[24] In Charleston, a military police seized every man of color on the street after dark; if he were without a pass, he was punished.[25] In any city in the South, it was said, he was fair game for kidnappers, who on the slightest provocation, and often without any excuse at all, seized him and sold him into slavery. Despised in the North, and hated and feared in the South, the free negro enjoyed no enviable existence. The question of what to do with him became an extremely embarrassing one throughout the country— a question which was not satisfactorily answered by the Civil War.

The attempt to solve this problem led to the adoption of a radical scheme for the removal of this undesirable class, which was rapidly increasing, and which it was evident could never be amalgamated with the white race. This was colonization, that is, transporting the free negro to some other part of the country or to some distant land, thereby both removing the menace of his presence and letting him develop according to his own nature. Travellers tell us much about this movement.[26] There was some discussion, they say, as to whether a tract of Western ter-

[24] Stuart, II, 80.
[25] Hall, F., pp. 254-255; Holmes, p. 329; Finch, p. 329; Alexander, II, 25-26.
[26] For general discussion of colonization, see Duncan, II, 261; Abdy, I, 125 ff.; Mackenzie, pp. 207-210; Hodgson, I, 15-17; Stuart, II, 43 ff.; Boardman, p. 247 ff.

ritory might not be set aside for the freedman's use with advantage, but this idea was soon shown to be wholly impracticable. Not only would there be danger of the negro's refusing to remain in the West, but it was also very evident that he was unfitted to perform the strenuous labor that was called for in beginning a new life there. There seemed to be a peculiar fitness in returning him to Africa, his native country, and the experiment took that direction. Many prominent citizens of slave states were promoters of the movement, out of which grew an organization called "The American Society for the Colonization of the Free People of Color of the United States." It is said to have met at first with opposition from the very class for whose benefit the movement was initiated. The free blacks, Englishmen said, had no confidence in their benefactors and imagined that they were to be decoyed to sea, to be sold ultimately to the Spanish colonies.[27] Moreover, they did not wish to leave the United States and begged that lands be given them in the far West. But the whites were obdurate, and as the exile was to be purely voluntary on the part of the negroes, the scheme of colonization might have failed for lack of experimentative material had not Georgia come to the rescue with some confiscated slaves that had been smuggled into her territory contrary to the law of 1807. These she was accustomed to sell for the benefit of the state. In 1830, James Stuart, who investigated the question of colonization during a visit to Washington, found that in the fourteen years since the society was founded, it had expended the relatively small sum of 27,000 pounds sterling, yet had succeeded in establisting a flourishing colony of 2000 emancipated slaves. By that time auxiliary societies had been founded in various parts of the United States, and an annual conven-

[27] Hodgson, I, 17; Abdy, I, 127-128.

tion was held in Washington. For seven pounds, ten shillings the society was enabled, Stuart says, not only to "secure the freedom of a slave and pay his passage to Liberia, but constitute him a freeholder of 30 acres of fertile land." He also says that Henry Clay, in addressing the auxiliary society of Kentucky in 1829, regretted that the means were inadequate to accommodate all who were willing and anxious to go, though the expense of transportation and subsistence during the voyage was reduced to $20. He estimated that one million dollars applied annually during a period of sixty or seventy years for the purposes of the society, would eventually rid the country of the whole colored population.[28]

On this movement English writers took sides. Those who were avowedly philanthropic and whose first interest was the welfare of the negro, bitterly opposed it. "The American helots," said Abdy, "are goaded with prejudice and proscription into 'voluntary' exile, and are shipped off by their Christian brethren for a distant shore to struggle with a tropical sun, a barbarous people and a pestilential climate. All this is done that the increase of the black population may be kept down to that exact point which shall quiet the fears and secure the profits of the slaveholder; while the New Englander lends his aid to this cruel policy and talks about abolishing slavery with the same self-complacent inconsistency with which the philanthropist sweetens his tea with free-labor sugar, while he lulls his cares with the fumes of slave-grown tobacco. . . . To say that these people are 'willing' emigrants to Africa is to acknowledge that they are driven by injustice and cruelty from America."[29]

Even those who took a more charitable view of the scheme, and who thought the founders "well-meaning"

[28] Stuart, II, 43-44. [29] Abdy, I, 127-128.

and truly benevolent, still regarded the whole idea as visionary and chimerical, and rather calculated to perpetuate than to extinguish slavery.[30] This feeling was heightened by the prevalent opinion that the blacks preferred to stay in the United States. Some few visitors were willing to take the word of the Society that the scheme was practicable, and to leave the result to the future.[31]

As a matter of fact, most visiting Englishmen lost sight of the real object of the Society, which was simply to remove the free negro from the United States. The organization was frankly not for the abolition of slavery nor for the amelioration of the condition of the negro. There was no hatred of the blacks in the attitude of the founders of the Society, though there may have been lack of broad outlook and of humanitarianism. They simply wished to rid themselves and the country of a people whom *The African Repository*, the official paper of the organization, characterized in its first number as follows: " . . . a class among us introduced by violence, notoriously ignorant, degraded and miserable, mentally diseased, broken-spirited, acted upon by no motives to honorable exertions, scarcely reached in their debasement by the heavenly light."[32] In dealing with the problem, the Americans, Northern and Southern, were overcome by a sense of utter helplessness; this seemed the only way open to them—a fact which few casual visitors understood or appreciated.

Regarding the personal treatment of the slaves by their owners, there is much said that is contradictory and confusing. The truth is that there were good masters and

[30] Duncan, II, 261; Boardman, p. 249; Tudor, II, 77.
[31] D'Arusmont, p. 51; Hodgson, I, 16.
[32] See "African Repository," I, 68.

bad, and slaves happy and unhappy in their condition. Many travellers, under the influence of the hospitality dispensed to them by Southerners, sought to make light of the personal indignities suffered by the negro, though they almost universally disapproved of slavery as an institution.[33] Many, on the other hand, repeated shocking stories which they had heard of the great cruelty with which the slaves were treated. Though very few of these atrocities were actually witnessed by the visitor, it is probable that such barbarities did sometimes occur.[34] For instance, Lambert tells us, "A lady at Sullivan's Island (S. C.) is said to have assisted her husband in whipping their negro to such a degree that his back was completely raw; not thinking he had been sufficiently punished, they applied a pickle of *pepper and salt* to his wounds, and the miserable wretch died a few hours after in the most excruciating tortures." The first volume of *The American Museum* gave an account of a Virginia slave who for some offense was imprisoned in a cage hung from the branches of a lofty tree and left to die of hunger and thirst, the birds of prey meanwhile feeding upon his quivering flesh. This was a favorite story among travellers.[35] Southern state laws exacted penalties for maiming a slave or otherwise cruelly using him, cutting out the tongue, dismembering, and other tortures of various kinds. These atrocities must therefore have been common enough, it was said, to call for legislation concerning them.[36] Hodgson mentions the frequent shooting of slaves for attempted escape. He tells of a conversation with a young planter not yet twenty-two

---

[33] See, for instance, Hall, B., III, 77 ff.

[34] Lambert, II, 172; Janson, p. 376; Fearon, pp. 239-240; Davis, J., pp. 100-101; Martineau, II, 113; Faux, p. 73.

[35] This story was first told by Crevecœur. See, Bristed, p. 425.

[36] Hall, F., p. 254; Wilson, C. H., Appendix, p. 97.

years old, "whose general manners bespoke mildness rather than the contrary," yet to the Englishman's surprise he had within a year deliberately shot one of his slaves for running away. No notice was taken of the murder. Another planter made a "frolic" for his friends to hunt two runaway negroes.[37] There are frequent accounts of the burning of slaves for rebellion or murder. No English traveller seems to have actually witnessed such executions, although they were public, but they were usually careful to give authority for the statement that such things did happen.[38] The worst atrocities were said to take place near the coast-line where the negroes were employed on the rice and sugar plantations. Here their labor was perforce of the most wearing kind and their food of the poorest, as the plantation did not of course feed those who lived on it. It was estimated that in the rice swamps the stock of negroes had to be replaced every seven years, so high was the mortality. Even in these places, however, it was to the interest of the owner to treat his slaves as humanely as possible.[39] On the inland plantations, particularly on those where the slaves were handed down from one generation to another, a quite different state of affairs was seen to prevail.[40] The health and happiness of the servile class were usually considered; the master assumed a patriarchal relation to them, and they, in their turn, regarded him and his family with affection and devotion. Especially did the domestic slaves usually enjoy the best

[37] Hodgson, I, 186; also 189.

[38] Melish, I, 31; Lambert, II, 173; Hodgson, I, 188; Abdy, I, 385-388; Neilson, pp. 290-291; Martineau, I, 374.

[39] See account of life on a South Carolina plantation, Hodgson, I, 45-46; Neilson, p. 289.

[40] Murray, I, 120-122; Hall, B., III, 224 ff., also 172 ff.; Martineau, II, 107; Mrs. Trollope, II, 49-50.

of treatment—everywhere throughout the slave states their lot seemed to the foreigner the most enviable.[41]

No matter how fortunate a slave might be, there was one factor in his existence that, to the mind of the on-looker, must prevent his feeling anything but degraded,—that was the consciousness that he, at best, was but a slave, the property of another human being, and could be bought and sold as such.[42] That this fact determined the negro's psychology and contributed largely to his personal degradation, is very evident. No matter how high his personal ideals were, he could never rise above the fact that he was a chattel. No matter what attachments he had formed, he was liable to be separated at any moment from those he loved, and sold into another part of the country.[43] This was the fear that, by tradition, haunted every slave north of Louisiana—a fear so great that many negroes, travellers said, took refuge in suicide as a lesser evil.[44] It stood to reason that the more Southern states, because they worked their slaves so exhaustingly, required frequent replenishment of their stock. After the abolition of the African slave trade, though a certain amount of illegal traffic was carried on for many years, the more Southern coast-line states had to depend on their Northern neighbors, Virginia, Delaware, Maryland, North Carolina, Kentucky, and Tennessee, to recruit their supply of laborers, as their own condition precluded the breeding of sufficient negroes.[45] The interstate slave trade thus became a thriving business in many localities. This was the subject of much interesting comment. Take the case of Virginia, for instance.

[41] See Hall, F., p. 256; Finch, p. 238; Hodgson, I, 25-26; Neilson, p. 289.
[42] Candler, p. 268; Hall, B., III, 183-184; Mrs. Trollope, II, 50.
[43] Boardman, p. 245; Mrs. Trollope, II, 50; Hodgson, I, 194.
[44] See, for instance, Hodgson, I, 195.
[45] Alexander, II, 25; Candler, p. 277; Hall, B., III, 196.

She was said to pride herself on her reputation for humane treatment of the negroes.[46] Her agriculture, carried on by slave labor, declined steadily for many years. Abdy quotes an article in *The American Quarterly Review* of 1832 which said that the whole agricultural produce of the state at that time did not exceed in value the exports of eighty or ninety years before, when the state contained not one-sixth of its population and when not one-third of the surface was occupied.[47] In this predicament, she and her sister states who were suffering the same embarrassment, bred great numbers of slaves. Some of these were hired out in the cities as servants in private families and in hotels.[48] We are told by Lambert: "Those who are unable to give 500 or 600 dollars for a slave, which is the usual price of a good one, generally hire them by the month or year of people who are in the habit of keeping a number of slaves for that purpose. Many persons obtain a handsome living by letting out their slaves for 6 to 10 dollars per month. They also send them out to sell oysters, fruit, millinery, etc., or as carmen and porters. The slaves who are brought up to any trade or profession are let out as journeymen, and many of them are so extremely clever and expert that they are considered worth two or three thousand dollars."[49]

The other alternative to which Virginia especially resorted to fill her empty treasury was the internal slave trade, with what profit may be estimated by the fact that in 1829 the annual revenue from it was said to be a million and a half dollars. By 1836, according to *The Virginia Times*, it had leaped to $24,000,000. Eighty thousand slaves were taken out of the state in that year by mas-

[46] See Birkbeck, "Notes on a Journey," pp. 21-22; D'Arusmont, p. 382; Palmer, p. 153; Candler, p. 269; Bristed, p. 425.

[47] See Abdy, II, 247.

[48] Boardman, p. 245; Lambert, II, 163-164; Hodgson, II, 86-88; Stuart, II, 125.   [49] Lambert, II, 164.

ters settling in other parts of the country; 40,000 were sold to dealers.[50] The numbers were swelled by the plantation incorrigibles who were sold "down the river" at high prices with fictitious recommendations, and by the kidnapped free blacks who had fallen a prey to the avaricious dealer.[51]

At certain seasons of the year the roads and the steamboats were filled with large companies of slaves on their way to be "sold South." They were bought by regular dealers or agents, who drove them in gangs chained together. It was the sight of these groups of unfortunates that aroused the greatest indignation and sympathy in the English visitor and called forth many a protest. "In God's name," cries one, "let this unhallowed traffic be put a stop to. Let not men's eyes be shocked with a sight so atrocious!"[52] If there was a sadder spectacle to English eyes than this, it was that of the slave market where human beings were exposed for sale.[53] Foreigners were always shocked to witness this kind of transaction, and the sight of a slave-auction often changed their whole attitude toward the institution. From the many accounts of such sales, one has been chosen as typical. "There are slave-auctions almost every day in the New Orleans Exchange. I was frequently present at these, and the man who wants an excuse for misanthropy will nowhere discover better reason for hating and despising his species. The usual process differs in nothing from that of selling a horse. The poor object of traffic is mounted on a table, intending purchasers

[50] See *Niles' Register*, LI, 83.
[51] Hodgson, I, 195; Alexander, II, 25-26.
[52] Hamilton, II, 222 (quotation); Melish, II, 95; Hall, B., III, 197; Palmer, pp. 142-143.
[53] For accounts of slave auctions, see Ferrall, p. 193 ff.; Birkbeck, "Notes on a Journey," p. 21; Abdy, III, 13; Hodgson, I, 55; Hall, B., III, 143-145, also 35 ff.; Tudor, II, 68; Hamilton, II, 216 ff.; Harris, W. T., p. 49; Stuart, II, 74; Neilson, pp. 284-288.

examine his points and put questions as to his age, health, etc. The auctioneer dilates on his value, enumerates his accomplishments, and when the hammer at length falls, protests in the usual phrase that poor Sambo has been absolutely thrown away. When a woman is sold, he usually puts his audience in good humor by a few indecent jokes.''[54]

The general effect of this treatment was seen to be to reduce the negro to the status of a brute. The degradation of his position was manifest to the sympathetic visitor.[55] He could claim no rights; even the few he was supposed to have were purely theoretical. It was no wonder, Englishmen said, that he had no incentive to labor or to live for anything beyond the passing moment. He was often not allowed to marry, but was encouraged to form loose relations with the women of his people. Manifestly, few uplifting influences entered his life, even in the home where he was kindly treated. His religion was looked upon as a mere fabric of superstition and emotionalism. We cannot wonder that the constant complaint of the foreigner was that practically nothing was done for the benefit of the negro. Granted that slavery was a necessary evil, the United States had done nothing to improve the condition of the victims of that institution.[56] Many Englishmen believed that the negroes were capable of being raised even to the intellectual and moral status of the white man, and refused to see any difference except in the color of the skin.[57] ''Does a man's complexion alter his intellect?''

[54] Hamilton, II, 216.

[55] Tudor, I, 55-56; Priest, pp. 188-189, 191; Candler, pp. 266, 268, 301; Neilson, p. 293; Murray, I, 124; Lambert, II, 173-175.

[56] Candler, p. 264; Hamilton, II, 219 ff.

[57] Davis, John, p. 94, also pp. 99-100; Abdy, I, 44-45; Mrs. Trollope, II, 55; D'Arusmont, p. 54; Hall, B., I, 30; Blane, pp. 219-220.

asks Blane indignantly. "Do the abilities of a European whose color has been changed by a residence in Africa, of necessity deteriorate? That the mass of the Blacks are at present inferior in ability to the Whites cannot be denied, but why?—because they are kept enslaved both in mind and body, because every obstacle is thrown in the way of those who wish to learn reading and writing, and because in some of the slave states it is contrary to law to instruct them. How then can it be expected that any marks of genius should appear when their minds are under the domination of ignorance and their bodies under that of the lash?" Many travellers went so far as to insist that the more intelligent of the white population agreed with them; that it was only the vulgar who regarded the "accidental distinction" of color as a symbol of the inferiority of the negro.[58] It was believed that fear of the increasing numbers of blacks and of their "advancing intelligence," prompted the contemptuous and cruel treatment of them.[59]

But to the mind of the European it was not the influence of slavery on the negro himself that was most to be feared; it was the evidences of degeneration in the life of the people who owned him. The appalling effect of slavery on the whites was first set forth in the days immediately after the Revolution in Jefferson's "Notes on Virginia." His attitude toward this evil was quoted repeatedly by native Americans and by foreigners, numbers of whom regarded the work as an authority. Though Jefferson considered the negro unfit at that time for freedom, he felt deeply the unhappy influence that slavery exerted in the new republic. His opinion, though rather well-known, should perhaps be quoted: "The whole commerce between master and slave is a perpetual exercise of the most boisterous passions; the

[58] Hall, B., III, 190-191; D'Arusmont, p. 54.
[59] Abdy, I, 45.

most unremitting despotism on the one part and the most degrading submission on the other. Our children see this and learn to imitate it. . . . The parent storms, the child looks on, catches the lineaments of wrath, puts on the same airs in the circle of younger slaves, gives a loose to his worst passions and thus nursed, educated and daily exercised in tyranny, cannot but be stamped with its odious peculiarities. The man must indeed be a prodigy who can retain his manners and morals undepraved by such circumstances. . . .

"With the morals of the people, their industry also is destroyed. For in a warm climate, no man will labour for himself who can make another labour for him. This is so true that of the proprietors of slaves, a very small proportion indeed are ever seen to labour. I tremble for my country when I reflect that God is just, that his justice cannot sleep forever . . . ." [60]

These views of Jefferson's were corroborated by those who were not affected by the institution and who could thus view the matter impartially. It was asserted by travellers that the farther South one went, the more languid and inactive-looking did the people become. They laid the blame, not on the climate, but on slavery.[61] Candler says too that he could tell at once when he had passed from Pennsylvania into Maryland, so great was the change in the appearance of the country. Instead of the neat farms and substantial houses with gardens which he had just left, he saw on all sides slovenly, ill-built dwellings with negro huts little better than pig-sties. The roads were bad and there were no bridges over the streams; there was no attractive village life, few churches and those very poor,—in short, no signs of the busy, progressive existence that he had seen

[60] Jefferson, "Notes on Virginia" (1788 ed.), pp. 172-173; quoted by Blane, pp. 206-207; also by Melish, I, 239 ff.

[61] Stuart, II, 60; Candler, p. 249 ff.; Hamilton, II, 159.

in Pennsylvania. Harriet Martineau tells of what South Carolina should be, with its rich soil, full streams, fertile bottoms, fine trees, etc., and what it was under the influence of slavery, with its roads nearly impassable, its lands exhausted, and its villages and towns rude in character.[62] Even the conveyances that one met on the roads of the South proclaimed that one was among a slave-holding population. Whereas in the Northern states, it was said, there could usually be seen great numbers of fine fat horses drawing stout, well-made wagons, in the South no such thing was to be met with. Sometimes a traveller saw a ragged black boy or girl driving an ill-assorted team of a cow and a mule which was pulling a wretchedly-constructed wagon, and he was quite likely to declare that this was the typical conveyance of the slave-holding state.[63]

Slavery was said to act as a check to the building of towns and villages because it prevented demand for labor and merchandise.[64] A man's slaves were fed and clothed in the coarsest and cheapest manner; they lived of course on the master's plantation; they sold and bought nothing. All industries were carried on by slaves within the limits of the plantation. The deadening economic effect of such a system was obvious.

There is no doubt that slavery was considered a cause of deterioration in the morale of the community. Even if there had been only the effect of the loss of industry which Jefferson deplored, the situation would have been seen to be serious enough. Accustomed to look upon all labor as the office of a servile class, the slave-holder came to despise work.[65] There were foreigners who considered that this resulted ultimately for the good of the country, as it produced a leisure class with time enough to give serious attention

[62] Martineau, I, 75. [63] See Sutcliffe, p. 99. [64] Blane, p. 202.
[65] Duncan, II, 259; Bristed, p. 388; Candler, pp. 252-254.

to politics and statecraft. Note, they said, the services to the country of such men as Washington and Jefferson, both of whom belonged to slave-holding families. But this advantage was, in the minds of most people, more than offset by the decline in personal morality in the South. It was regretted that children were brought up in close intercourse with a race that possessed no standards of decency by which to regulate actions or conversation. Over this servile class they had unlimited opportunity for tyranny and injustice which was seldom punished by their elders.[66] Travellers even found a reason for the greater amount of swearing that one noticed in the South in the constant "lording it over slaves."[67] The undeniable habit of miscegenation between the races, and the sanction given it, were producing, it was feared, a class of young men with unbridled passions and lax views of right and wrong; it was also producing a race of long-suffering white women whose personal virtue and purity were conceded, perhaps by contrast, to be above the average.[68] Slavery produced an inability to comprehend human rights, and a torpor and indifference to the sight of human suffering. Several travellers intimate that women slave-holders were at times more cruel than men, and even little children ordered or inflicted punishment on slaves who had angered them. It was this insensibility to the rights of the negro as a human being that it was feared

The problem of freeing the land from the grasp of this would eventually produce a race of self-centred, tyrannical, despotic people.[69]

[66] Birkbeck, "Letters from Illinois," p. 72; Martineau, II, 128-129; Flint, J., p. 142.
[67] See Stuart, II, 61.
[68] Duncan, II, 259; Sutcliffe, p. 53; Candler, p. 267; Martineau, II, 120; Holmes, p. 327.
[69] Martineau, II, 129; Neilson, p. 292.

octopus which threatened to destroy it, was, as has been said before, regarded with hopeless pessimism by most Americans, especially those in the slave states. Foreign visitors were more sanguine; they were eager to give advice on the subject, though they confessed themselves dismayed by the conditions which they witnessed. Some Englishmen expressed impatience with the hopeless attitude of the Americans. If the policy of the United States continued to be to keep her negroes in constant degradation and ignorance, how were they ever to attain to that grade of intelligence which would mark them as fit for personal liberty? If America sincerely wished to free her slaves, she was thus defeating her own ends. That something should be done at once was the general opinion. "The disease is deeply rooted," said Murray, "its ramifications extend even to the vitals of the body-politic, and the remedies to be applied are proportionately difficult and dangerous; but they must be applied, and that too at no distant date, or the gangrene will have spread beyond the reach of medicine."[70] Birkbeck, who abhorred slavery, warned the country that ". . . a remedy, mild as the case will admit, must be applied by a wise and strong legislature; or some dreadful eruption will bring about a cure, arising out of the evil itself."[71]

Very few believed that a sudden and general emancipation would improve matters. "I look upon slaves," said one Englishman, "as public securities, and I am of opinion that a legislature's enacting laws for their emancipation is as flagrant a piece of injustice as would be the cancelling of the public debt. Slave-holders are only share-holders, and philanthropists should never talk of liberating slaves more than cancelling public securities, without being pre-

[70] Murray, II, 203-204.
[71] Birkbeck, "Letters from Illinois," p. 72.

pared to indemnify those persons who unfortunately have their capital invested in this species of property.'"[72] The evil to be feared from emancipation was not confined by observers to the pecuniary loss. No man could foresee the consequences of suddenly freeing these vast numbers of ignorant, emotional, and easily-influenced human beings. In some states they outnumbered the whites, upon whom they might reasonably be supposed to take vengeance if the opportunity were offered.[73] This side of the question, however, did not occupy the mind of the foreigner so much as it did that of the American slave-owner, with whom it was a very serious consideration. Most travellers were rather inclined to look at the whole problem from the point of view of the negroes.

To the latter as well, a general emancipation, it was said, would bring ruin.[74] They were obviously unfit for freedom. For generations they had been governed by a superior will; every act had been ordered for them; no incentive except the lash had stimulated them to industry. The result of freedom on this undeveloped, demoralized class would be to leave them helpless and bewildered. How could they be expected to resume at once the duties and responsibilities of citizens? It would be cruelty to free them, especially those who were fortunate enough to have kind masters. In short, from the point of view of both master and slave, immediate manumission was seen to be impracticable, and the question was looked upon as the ''most profitless of all possible subjects of conversation.''

What plan then was to be adopted, and how was the government to steer a middle course between slavery and

[72] Ferrall, p. 203; also Hall, B., III, 160-161; Duncan, II, 253.

[73] Brothers, Thos., p. 196; Janson, p. 358; Neilson, p. 297.

[74] Bristed, pp. 388-392; Brothers, p. 196; Hall, B., III, 160-161, also 204; Duncan, II, 253.

freedom? It is evident that the Americans themselves tried desperately to solve the problem of making their burden as light as possible. "Almost every gentleman I met with in the South," says one traveller, "had some project or other for mitigating the national oppression arising from this incubus, as they frequently called it, or believed he had discovered some nostrum for removing a great portion of its bad effects."[75] *Niles' Weekly Register* for some time urged upon the American people a scheme for the annual expatriation of certain numbers of young female negroes to check the increasing black population. This aroused the ire of philanthropic Englishmen. The plan was designated as "an atrocious suggestion which involves so much inhumanity in the expedient recommended, and so much demoralization in the results, that we are at a loss to decide which most deserves our reprobation, the writer of such an article, or the people to whom it is addressed."[76]

One suggestion offered by observing Englishmen was the gradual education of the negro in the uses of liberty.[77] This scheme would be rendered easier by the fact that the importation of African slaves was stopped, and the negroes now spoke a common language and were brought up under more unified conditions. By the gradual spread of education, each generation would take a slightly higher place in the scale of society than the preceding one had enjoyed.

Closely connected with this idea was the expedient of reducing the ranks of the slaves by legislation, or by what one author calls "timely expedients."[78] Emancipation by degrees had worked well in other places; why would it not

[75] Hall, B., III, 204.
[76] Abdy, I, 49.
[77] Duncan, II, 254; Tudor, II, 74-75; Candler, p. 264; Hall, B., III, 233.
[78] Tudor, II, 74-75; Candler, p. 271; Duncan, II, 256; Hodgson, I, 198-199.

succeed throughout the United States? Were there no instances of its practicability in the history of the South American provinces, "none in the gradual revolutions of society in Great Britain herself?" The method used by the Northern states was urged as an example to be followed by slave-owners, sometimes without an adequate appreciation of the difference between Northern and Southern conditions.

Murray says that the only proposal which ever assumed definite shape before the legislature was that made by Mr. King in the Senate in 1825. It was to the effect that "as soon as that portion of the funding debt for the payment of which the public land was pledged, should be paid off, the whole remaining public land with the moneys arising from future sales thereof, should form a fund for the gradual extinction of slavery by the purchase and emancipation of slaves, their removal to other regions, etc." This plan is supposed to have been favored by Chief Justice Marshall, himself a citizen of a slave-holding state. "Why," asks the Englishman, "now that the debt has been liquidated, has the above proposal never been revived or discussed?"[79]

We have thus seen that slavery in America was to the Englishman an evil which could not long endure without danger to the country. Something must be done about it, or the United States must expect to face not only economic ruin, but the contempt of the other civilized nations. Moral enlightenment was the chief desideratum for the governing class. When the United States should sacrifice her hopes of immediate gain, in other words, overcome her cupidity, and should regard her black population in the light of human beings, her first steps would be taken toward freeing herself of the evil.

[79] Murray, II, 204-205.

CHAPTER VI

AGRICULTURE, MANUFACTURE AND INDUSTRY

AGRICULTURE is obviously the most necessary and popular occupation of the settlers of a new country. It is only after the food supply of a family or a community is assured that the members turn to the satisfying of other needs less imperative in their demands. At the close of the Revolution and for a great many years afterward, the necessity for agricultural labor made the inhabitants of the United States oblivious to the interests of any other means of livelihood, and retarded the growth of the manufacture of articles which the Americans for a long time imported cheerfully from other parts of the world.

A convention was held in Philadelphia in 1787 to inquire on what principles a commercial system for the United States was to be founded. In the resolutions adopted, agriculture was designated as the spring of American commerce and the parent of American manufactures. Almost fifty years later, an English traveller notices that this attitude towards the land remains unchanged. "The possession of land is the aim of all action, generally speaking, and the cure of all social evils among men in the United States. If a man is disappointed in politics or love, he goes and buys land. If he disgraces himself, he betakes himself to a lot in the West. If the demand for any article of manufacture slackens, the operatives drop into the unsettled lands. If a citizen's neighbors rise above him in the towns, he betakes himself where he can be monarch of all he surveys. An artisan works that he may die on land of his own. He is frugal that he may enable his son to be a land-owner. Farmers' daughters go into factories that they may clear off the mortgage from their fathers' farms, that they may be independent landowners again."[1]

The interest in tilling the soil was heightened by the generous policy of the new government in regard to the sale of public lands. Ouseley gives us the best English account of this. About 1800, the land system went into effect, a system which was much admired by foreigners. All new public lands were surveyed accurately by the government; they were then divided into townships of thirty-six square miles, and sub-divided into sections of 640 acres each. One section in each township was reserved from sale for the support of education; the rest was sold to whoever wished to buy. Until 1820, credit was given on purchases of public lands, but so many people bought on speculation that they soon owed the government great sums of money. It was therefore considered advisable to substitute a cash payment, at the same time reducing the minimum price of the land from $2.00 to $1.25 an acre.[2]

In connection with the holding of land, it was noted that the system of rents in use in England was little employed. Every American wanted his own farm, and though he might for a time consent to work on shares the surplus acres of his more fortunate neighbor, his aim was invariably a place of his own which he could hand down to his descendants. If poverty forced him to work on shares, he received two-thirds of the produce if he provided the labor-

[1] Martineau, I, 292.
[2] Ouseley, p. 135 ff.; Birkbeck, "Notes on a Journey," pp. 70-71; Holmes, p. 148.

AGRICULTURE, MANUFACTURE AND INDUSTRY

ing animals and the seed, and one-third if the owner took that responsibility.[3]

Nothing was more evident to the foreigner than the general esteem in which the farmer was held and the important part he played in public life. He represented the most influential class of society, and unless he had bought rashly, and were "land poor," his condition was one of substantial comfort and comparative prosperity.[4] Thomas Cooper gives us a description of an ideal farm in Pennsylvania in 1795. The possessions of the progressive owner included, besides 300 acres and house and barns, a fish pond, a distillery, an icehouse, a smokery for hams and bacon, a saw mill, and a grist mill. "This," Cooper says, "is a tolerably fair though a favorable specimen."[5]

It was not without reason that much advice was given the prospective emigrant in regard to the wisdom of choosing the life of a farmer in the new world. Land, in the natural order of events, steadily increased in value without effort on the part of the owner, who might then by industry add a double profit.[6] Lieut. Francis Hall applied to the American farmer the quotation: "O fortunatos nimium sua si bona norint,"[7] while Frances Wright gushingly exclaimed, "I have seen those who have raised their voice in the senate of their country, and whose hands have fought her battles, walking beside the team and minutely directing every operation of husbandry with the soil upon their garments and their countenances bronzed by the meridian sun. And how proudly does such a man tread his paternal fields, his ample domains improving under his hand; his

---

[3] Shirreff, p. 340.
[4] Ibid., p. 72; also Stuart, I, 170.
[5] Cooper, p. 123 ff.
[6] Ibid., p. 71.
[7] Hall, F., p. 21.

garners full to overflowing; his table replenished with guests, and with a numerous offspring whose nerves are braced by exercise and their minds invigorated by liberty."[8]

But we must not forget, as the enthusiastic traveller sometimes did, that this ideal picture had another side. It was evident to most strangers that in a sense the position of the American farmer was no sinecure. In the first place, there was the scarcity of labor, which has already been emphasized. It is true that if the farmer were fortunate enough to get a native American to work for him, he had a laborer on whom he could depend. Cobbett says that the Americans were the best workers he ever saw. "They mow four acres of oats, wheat, rye or barley in a day, and, with a cradle, lay it so smooth in the swarths, that it is tied up in sheaves with the greatest neatness and ease. They mow two acres and a half of grass in a day. And they do the work well."[9] Added to this speed and thoroughness was the astonishing versatility of the average native laborer. He could do almost everything on a farm, from wood-chopping to shoe-making.

Because of the scarcity of help, the farmer and his family were forced to become accustomed to the hardest kind of manual labor.[10] They were also obliged to exist without many of the things which they had previously come to regard as the necessities of life and which were as yet unobtainable. J. Flint points out that in the management of his farm, the owner was much hampered by lack of improved machinery; his utensils were crude and homemade, and he constantly resorted to makeshifts.[11] Many travel-

[8] D'Arusmont, p. 138.
[9] Cobbett, p. 190.
[10] See Parkinson, pp. 26-30.
[11] Flint, p. 123; also Fearon, p. 222.

AGRICULTURE, MANUFACTURE AND INDUSTRY 153

lers commented on the lack of neatness and trimness of American farms. "Even in Pennsylvania and among the Quakers, too," we are told, "there is a sort of out-of-doors slovenliness which is never, hardly, seen in England. You see bits of wood, timber, boards, chips lying about here and there, and pigs and cattle trampling about in a sort of confusion which would make an English farmer fret himself to death, but which is here seen with great placidness." [12] This condition was due in many cases to circumstances rather than to any inherent slovenliness in the owner.

The difference in the soil of the various sections of the country was not at first so evident as it became later. The natural fertility of the land unexhausted by frequent planting, produced abundant harvests for the first settlers. The test of the ground came when a rotation of crops had affected its productivity. Often this promise of rich soil led the pioneer astray. Timothy Dwight warned his fellow countrymen against overestimating the value of land because it was covered with a thick layer of vegetable mould. He reminded them of the many sections of the country where this false promise had given way to eventual sterility, and of the continued disappointment which had accompanied the trend of settlement toward the West.[13] Shirreff says that the peculiarity of Indian corn, which was capable of being grown for several years on the same land without application of fertilizer, helped too, to give rise to unfounded hopes in regard to the fertility of the soil.[14]

It was universally conceded by travellers that in the Eastern districts where labor was more available and where estates numbered fewer acres, the land on the whole was

[12] Cobbett, p. 189 (quotation); Weld, I, 113-114; Martineau, I, 338; Holmes, p. 174.
[13] Quoted by Stuart, I, 174-175.
[14] Shirreff, p. 394.

better cared for and consequently more productive. In the West, where profits were low, very little money was put back into the land. It was not until the vast tracts of Western territory were broken up into units more available for satisfactory cultivation that fertilization and rotation of crops became understood.

Throughout the New England states, there was seen to be little farming on a large scale. Each state seems to have had as its object the feeding of its own population, with little regard for exportation to other countries. Melish tells us a great deal about New England land. He says that Rhode Island in 1812 was not producing enough grain for home consumption. Most of the New England farms, however, were at this time well-cultivated and produced the usual grain-stuffs needed by the family, as well as the fruits and vegetables.[15] New Hampshire fed herself only; Vermont, having a more generally productive soil than her neighbor, exported (1806-11) quantities of food-stuffs over the border to Canada as well as to the larger New England cities reached by river routes. Connecticut had a great deal of good land within her boundaries, and was admirably adapted to grazing. Farms ranged here in size from fifty to 500 acres.[16]

Fowler, who devotes his entire book to New York, tells us how diversified this state is in soil and climate; some travellers were inclined to prefer the eastern parts of the state where the climate was more temperate, but many praised the fertile valleys of the central and western parts.[17] Even before the building of the Erie Canal, New York took one of the two leading places among the states;

---

[15] Melish, I, 78, 99, 104.
[16] Melish, I, 124-126; Palmer, p. 179; Kendall, I, 311; Candler, p. 12.
[17] Fowler, p. 180.

with Pennsylvania she monopolized a great deal of the wealth; she possessed good roads and many waterways, was rather thickly settled, and became known as generally prosperous and progressive. In 1832, Shirreff says, a New York State Agricultural Society was formed, which petitioned the legislature the next year for a grant for an agricultural school.[18] Long Island shared New York's prosperity. In 1795, it was already laid out in farms of a general fertility, and was noted, travellers said, for its fruit, particularly its apples.[19] The crops raised by the New York farmer, it was noticed by Stuart, were much the same as those grown in Great Britain, with the addition of corn, or maize, as it was often called. This staple article of diet was raised at the rate of thirty to forty bushels and sometimes as much as 150 bushels an acre. Wheat seems to have been the most valuable of the crops.[20]

The same was true in Pennsylvania, which represented for a long time the most advanced state of agriculture in the country. Weld says that the south-eastern part was better cultivated when he saw it (1795-1797), than any other part of America. Here practically everyone who cultivated land owned his farm, whereas in the northern parts large tracts were still in the hands of speculators. Farming in Pennsylvania, according to Weld, was done with an eye to profit only. There were few gardens, as the labor they entailed did not balance the small profits to be gained from them. Vegetables were therefore scarce and of the poorest and coarsest quality. Indeed, there were many who saw infinite possibilities in Pennsylvania as an agricultural state, and regretted the lack of intensive farming

[18] Shirreff, p. 59 ff.
[19] Neilson, p. 123; also 129; Shirreff, pp. 14-15.
[20] Stuart, I, 170-171.

in many sections of her territory.[21] If from twenty to twenty-five bushels of wheat and from twenty-five to thirty of corn could be raised per acre without much labor, what results might a little more care and industry not bring? Faux says in 1820 that though the land in Pennsylvania was of the best quality and the best farming in the United States was done there, the average production of wheat was only sixteen bushels per acre, and that crops were very subject to the Hessian fly and to mildew. The price of machinery was so high about that time that many farmers were hindered by lack of proper implements.[22] The tract of land through which ran the thoroughfare from Philadelphia to Pittsburg was called "The Great Valley." Fearon remarked that it shared in the general fertility, and abounded in "substantial barns, fine private dwellings, excellent breed and condition of live stock and superior cultivation."[23]

Delaware and New Jersey were, according to Melish, similar in their agriculture to Pennsylvania and New York. They raised the usual grain stuffs, vegetables, and fruit. Both of these states raised quantities of wheat, of which flour was made for the export trade.[24]

Melish also tells us that a change became apparent as one went into the Southern states. The soil of Maryland was of varied character but the greater portion of it was poor — in the east low and sandy, with many swamps. There were some fertile spots in the interior.[25] Virginia was said to present the worst example of lack of economy in farming. As early as 1795 her fields were exhausted

[21] Weld, I, 112-113; Melish, I, 174; Flint, p. 82; Holmes, p. 175.
[22] Faux, p. 100; Welby, p. 323.
[23] Fearon, p. 181; Power, I, 326.
[24] Melish, I, 181.
[25] Ibid., I, 188.

through the continued cultivation of tobacco. It was not that the tobacco plant required an extraordinary amount of nutriment, explained one observing Englishman, but the peculiar mode of cultivating it, that brought about this condition. It was necessary for the laborers to be walking about among the plants from the moment they were set out. The soil thus remained exposed to the sun and became hard and beaten down and unproductive. Then, too, the same piece of land was worked year after year without change of crops, except perhaps an occasional planting of Indian corn, and became totally exhausted. It was then allowed to grow over and often became covered with woods of a stunted growth.[26] In 1824, Hodgson had a conversation with some members of an agricultural society in Virginia, in the course of which he was informed that the injurious effects of such a system of tobacco growing were becoming too obvious to be ignored, and that many were relinquishing the culture of the plant.[27]

Cultivation of cotton in the Southern states united the production of a very useful and profitable commodity with a number of other advantages obvious both to the Southern planter and to the visitor. In the first place, the price that cotton brought was invariably high. As an article of export either to the manufactories of the North or to foreign countries, it was always in demand. It gave occupation to the slaves of the estate during several months of the year, which was a desideratum, and it occupied people of all ages, even children of eight or nine. Then, too, it would grow almost anywhere, provided the climate were warm enough. Thirty-six degrees latitude was considered the northern limit for the growing of a superior grade of cot-

[26] Martineau, I, 299; Weld, I, 151-152; Tudor, I, 451-452.
[27] Hodgson, I, 33.

ton.[28] It seems to have flourished in all of the Southern states irrespective of the quality of the land. In these states, it was observed that any great amount of fertility was limited to the river bottoms;[29] along the coast the land was likely to be swampy and sandy. Melish says that much of the extent of Georgia was covered with pine barrens which yielded only such products as tar and turpentine.[30] Alabama possessed rich alluvial lands which became the Mecca of thousands from the impoverished neighboring states when that territory ceased to belong to the Indian reserves. It was estimated about 1835 by Tyrone Power, that no fewer than 10,000 families had left the Carolinas and Georgia during the course of one season for Alabama.[31]

The conditions which made Louisiana an unhealthy state in which to live, rendered her an ideal location for the cultivation of her two great staples of commerce, cotton and sugar. Of the former, Tudor says, New Orleans alone exported in a single year (1829-30) over 350,000 bales. The traffic in sugar was equally extensive. In a report of an agricultural society of Baton Rouge, which the traveller quotes, it was stated that "the entire amount of sugar produced in Lousiana in 1828 was 88,878 hogsheads of 1,000 lbs. each, that the number of sugar plantations was about 700 and the capital invested in them about $45,-000,000." One field hand on a well-regulated estate could cultivate five acres, with a result of 5,000 pounds of sugar worth five and a half cents a pound and 125 gallons of

[28] Bradbury, p. 277; Holmes, p. 178. See Tudor, II, 87, for table of cotton growing, 1829-1830; also Hall, B., III, 218 ff., for description of a visit to a Sea Island cotton plantation.
[29] Lambert, II, 205.
[30] Melish, I, 34.
[31] Power, II, 123.

molasses at eighteen cents a gallon. Money invested in a sugar plantation always paid a high rate of interest.[32]

Travellers call attention to the fact that the value of the Western lands depended on many circumstances, such as "distance from towns, the convenience of shipping produce, . . . the quality of the land, its water privilege and the permanency of those streams."[33] Even in these Western districts, the observer noticed that the population was not stable, but extended itself constantly toward the Rocky Mountains. "On the road, every emigrant tells you he is going to Ohio," said Fearon, "when you arrive in Ohio, its inhabitants are 'moving' to Missouri or Alabama; thus it is that the point for final settlement is forever receding as you advance."[34] It is difficult to say whether this was the cause or the effect of the type of people who settled the land. Many of these took up their abode on government soil with no intention of buying it. "The first clearers or squatters as they were called," Melish tells us, "look out a situation where they can find it, and clear and cultivate a piece of land. A second class come after them who have got a little money, and they buy up the *improvements* of the first settlers, and add to them, but without buying the land. A third and last class generally come for permanent settlement, and buy both land and improvements. When this last class have made a settlement, the country rapidly improves and assumes the appearance of extended cultivation."[35]

The richness of the river bottoms west of the Alleghanies was seen to be the cause of the enormous amount of emigration thither, though they were known to be wet and un-

[32] Tudor, II, 84-87; Holmes, p. 150.
[33] Fearon, p. 235; Shirreff, p. 397.
[34] Fearon, p. 234.
[35] Melish, II, 119.

favorable to health.³⁶ On the higher lands, more health was to be enjoyed but less produce was raised. Here great numbers of sheep and cattle were pastured. The chief products of the Western lands were wheat and Indian corn, which were raised in quantities large enough not only to supply the needs of the population but to export down the watercourses to the southern or the foreign trade. Sometimes the farmer himself took his produce down the river in the spring to New Orleans, sold it, and returned on horseback to his farm hundreds of miles away. Unless one were able thus to find a market elsewhere for one's produce, profits from agriculture in the West were likely to be exceeding small. In a region where every man was a landholder, there was no demand for the agricultural produce of one's neighbors. According to Fearon the average price which the Eastern farmer received for his wheat was about $1.00 a bushel, and for corn forty to seventy-five cents, depending on locality.³⁷ In Maryland in 1817, Palmer says, wheat was selling at the high price of $1.40 a bushel, but this was unusual.³⁸ In the West, prices were always lower; wheat sometimes reached seventy-five cents and corn twenty-five cents.³⁹ Hodgson says that in Kentucky and Ohio about 1820, all that the farmer could get for his wheat was twenty-five to thirty-three cents, and for Indian corn twelve and a half cents. Birkbeck estimated the price of grain in this same territory at seventy-five cents for wheat and forty cents for corn, but Hodgson says he was too optimistic.⁴⁰

Certain parts of the Western land, Kentucky and Tennessee for instance, were especially desirable from the

---

³⁶ Flint, pp. 118-119; Melish, II, 192.
³⁷ Fearon, p. 199.
³⁸ Palmer, p. 40.
³⁹ Flint, p. 117; Janson, p. 445.
⁴⁰ Hodgson, II, 66-67, 78.

AGRICULTURE, MANUFACTURE AND INDUSTRY 161

point of climate; Melish pointed out that they were warm enough to permit the cultivation of cotton and tobacco and still far enough north to escape the enervating heat of the more Southern states.[41] Faux maintained that the richest land in the Western country was near Birkbeck's settlement on the banks of the Wabash.[42] Harmony, Indiana, the scene of Rapp's communistic experiment, was also a place of "prodigious richness." The first grade of land in the Illinois district, Palmer said, was "inexhaustible in fecundity," as it had been cultivated annually without manure for more than a century. He found in this region six different kinds of soil suitable for every type of agricultural interest.[43] The subject of the American prairie in the Middle West interested many visitors; it was so different from anything else of the sort that travellers had seen in other countries, and even different from the far western lands.[44] The prairies were invariably rich and easily cultivated, were usually well-watered, and thus presented a place of settlement attractive to the emigrant as well as satisfying to the aesthetic sense of the casual visitor. Many surmises were made by those who looked upon this unusual land formation, as to its origin. The theory which was generally held was that the whole of the region over which prairie land extended had once been submerged.

A feature of rural life in America which deserves mention here because of the general comment it caused, was the distinctive kind of fence with which the farmer surrounded his acres. The earliest form of barrier was the so-called "snake" or "worm" fence which extended in

[41] Melish, II, 192-193; also Janson, pp. 443-444.
[42] Faux, p. 282; also p. 248.
[43] Palmer, p. 412; Holmes, p. 242.
[44] See, for instance, Latrobe, II, 160-162; Wilson, C. H., Appendix, p. 111; Shirreff, p. 243 ff.

zigzag lines over all the cleared sections of the country. It was put together carelessly, Ferrall says, consisting of "bars about eight or nine feet in length laid zigzag on each other alternately."[45] It was constructed with sublime disregard of the waste of the land occupied by its wanderings; it was only when the ground became something to be surveyed carefully and cultivated economically that other forms of barrier took the place of the primitive fence. It was superseded by the stone wall, especially in New England, where the latter form served a double purpose, as it incidentally afforded a use for the stones that too often encumbered the ground.[46] Sometimes this kind of wall, it was noticed, was surmounted by two or three rails. The "ne plus ultra" of the west country farmer was the post and rail fence. Ferrall gives us a description of one: "[It] is constructed of posts, six feet in length, sunk in the ground to the depth of about a foot, and at eight or ten feet distance; the rails are then laid into mortices cut into the posts at intervals of about thirteen or fourteen inches."[47] Live hedges were rarely seen; they invariably were said not to thrive well; in the South, however, one occasionally saw a privet or cypress hedge which was much more pleasing to the eye than were the wooden fences.[48] Thorn hedges were sometimes seen in the North on well-kept farms near the larger cities. Shirreff mentions having seen them near Boston and Philadelphia.[49]

The price of land in the United States depended of course on local circumstances. It was said to range from twenty-

[45] Ferrall, p. 63; Dalton, p. 41; Neilson, p. 108; Janson, p. 391.
[46] Martineau, I, 295; Stuart, I, 166; Kendall, II, 184; Candler, p. 12; Shirreff, p. 43; Neilson, p. 107.
[47] Ferrall, pp. 63-64; also Woods, J., p. 198.
[48] Cooper, p. 127; Holmes, p. 175.
[49] Shirreff, pp. 24, 43.

five cents an acre to $110 a foot.[50] Land in the more promising towns was usually conceded to be very dear, much dearer than in the best parts of London, we are told by Fearon.[51] Farms near cities were accordingly high-priced whether in the East or in the West. In 1817 and 1818, Fearon and Palmer say that farm land is selling for about $100 an acre near Pittsburg, Hagerstown (Maryland), Cincinnati, and on Long Island.[52] At this time the price of farms in Pennsylvania was considered to be low. Welby remarks on this fact, and says that a farm of 200 acres only six miles from Philadelphia, part of which was good grazing ground and the remainder of good quality, and including a good newly-erected brick house, was sold for $5,000.[53] In 1835, Shirreff says, land in the best condition in the neighborhood of Philadelphia brought from $100 to $120 an acre.[54] Even in 1818, however, the farms in the Great Valley of Pennsylvania brought the high price of $200 an acre, as the soil was unusually fertile. One traveller remarked that even at this price it was cheaper than the fifty-cent and the dollar-and-a-half lands in some other parts of the Eastern states.[55]

Western prices also were affected by proximity to cities. About 1810, the land around Lexington, Kentucky, was selling for $200 an acre, "the most beautiful tract I ever saw," says the enthusiastic observer.[56] In other parts of this state, however, very good farms could be bought at the same time for less than $12 an acre.

[50] Martineau, I, 335-336.
[51] Fearon, p. 200; Bradbury, p. 299.
[52] Fearon, p. 70, also p. 199; Palmer, p. 85.
[53] Welby, p. 323; Faux, p. 100.
[54] Shirreff, p. 26.
[55] Fearon, p. 181.
[56] Melish, II, 189-190.

As well as one may judge from the fragmentary remarks of travellers, it would seem that the average price of farm land throughout our fifty-year period ranged from $2 to $5 an acre for uncleared territory anywhere throughout the country, and from $20 to $50 for average well-cleared land with improvements. Thomas Cooper says that in 1795, hilly, unimproved land near Harrisburg, Pennsylvania, was selling at 20 to 30 shillings an acre, which was the average price, it would seem.[57] Almost twenty-five years later, good uncleared land in Ohio was selling for $2 to $5 an acre.[58] From coincidences of statements like these, it is evident that the price of uncleared land did not show any great variation. About 1820, farms in Virginia, in Connecticut, and in Pennsylvania were selling at an average of $30 an acre.[59] Ten years later, Fowler says that in Dutchess County, New York, a very fertile tract of country ranged from $30 to $60.[60] Prices of cleared land in the West seem to have been a little below this average. The term "improved" did not connote the same degree of excellence here as it did in the East. The buildings were chiefly log huts, and much of the land on even the superior farms had not been cleared. Consequently the prices ranged from about $8 to $30 an acre, sometimes $40 if the land were near a city or a watercourse.[61]

There was in this period a vital connection between the agriculture of the United States and the development of her manufactures. To just what extent importation of foreign goods should be encouraged, and how much America should manufacture for herself was a question which in

[57] Cooper, p. 123.
[58] Palmer, p. 85.
[59] See Fearon, p. 199; Palmer, p. 36, also p. 179.
[60] Fowler, pp. 180-181.   [61] Fearon, p. 216; Palmer, p. 85.

the early days of settlement did not of course arise. The only business of the pioneer was perforce agriculture, which he performed as well as he could with the only implements at his disposal, either those he had brought with him from England or what he had fashioned rudely for himself. Not only was it cheaper to import necessities, but it was in most cases the only way to obtain them. Often, too, Wansey tells us, a mechanic who came to the United States to engage in some kind of industry contracted the land-fever and forsook the loom for the plough.[62] As time went on, and the land became more and more occupied, a definite attitude toward manufacture in the United States necessarily shaped itself. Many good Americans believed that to encourage the increase of factories in the United States was to foster a demoralizing element in American life. Among those who so believed was Jefferson who, in "Notes on Virginia," strongly expressed the opinion that a purely agricultural class was the only one that could keep its morals uncorrupted. "While we have land to labour then," he said, "let us never wish to see our citizens occupied at a work-bench, or twirling a distaff. Carpenters, masons, and smiths are wanted in husbandry; but for the general operations let our workshops remain in Europe. It is better to carry provisions and material to workmen there than to bring them to the provisions and materials, and with them their manners and principles. The loss by the transportation of commodities across the Atlantic will be made up in happiness and permanence of government. The mobs of great cities add just so much to the support of pure government as sores do to the strength of the human body."[63] Though Jefferson is said by Bristed to have

[62] Wansey, p. 196; Bristed, p. 53; Holmes, p. 202.
[63] Jefferson, T., p. 175, "Notes on Virginia" (1788 edition); Bristed, p. 55.

changed his opinion later, his argument represents the chief objections to domestic manufactures, among native Americans and many travellers as well. The prevailing attitude was seen to be, however, toward the encouragement of manufactures, especially after the exclusion forced upon America by the Long Embargo of 1807-9 and by the War of 1812, showed how self-sufficient the country could be in this respect. By this time, Americans had seen that they were able to do without English goods if it were necessary, and many native products had become seemingly indispensable. There were some complaints that this home market compelled Americans to pay 100 per cent more for goods of an inferior quality,[64] but it became a matter of patriotism to use these products of native manufacture. Later, the United States was driven to the encouragement of factories because of the congestion of the land, particularly in the East. Miss Martineau tells of the insufficiency of the soil in New England to support its population. Many of the farms were heavily mortgaged and members of the family turned involuntarily to work in the factories to secure the ready money needed. The largest proportion of factory girls in New England was furnished by country families.[65]

A phase of American industry interesting to the foreigner was the domestic manufacture which went on in practically every American home and on every American farm in the early days of our period.[66] If a saw mill or a grist mill, for instance, were not available to the progressive farmer who had logs to be sawed or wheat to be ground, he contrived some means of improvising such conveniences. Members of the family had to be clothed; there-

[64] Bristed, p. 57.
[65] Martineau, I, 294-295.
[66] See Melish, I, 99, 103, 115, 118; D'Arusmont, p. 285.

fore the resources of cotton available to the Southerner in his own fields and to the Northerner at a small price, were drawn upon by the women of the family. Wool and flax, too, were generally at hand when needed. It was said that so general was the knowledge of spinning and weaving that there were even great surplus quantities of coarse tow cloth to be exported from the country districts of some of the states. The product of these domestic looms was always substantial and good. Hodgson said as late as 1820 that domestic manufacture was carried on all over the country to a surprising extent.[67] In New York state, many small farmers could not have existed without it; in Pennsylvania it was still more general, "the importation of Irish linen having been most seriously checked by the greatly increased cultivation and manufacture of flax in the immediate vicinity of Philadelphia." In Virginia, North Carolina, and Georgia, the same combination of agriculture and manufacture was noticed.[68] The planters often supplied all their needs by the work of slaves on their own estates. Weld says of the Virginians, "Amongst their slaves are found taylors, shoemakers, carpenters, smiths, turners, wheelwrights, weavers, tanners, etc. I have seen patterns of excellent coarse woolen cloth made in the country by slaves, and a variety of cotton manufactures, amongst the rest good nankeen."[69] Bradbury says that in the West also flax was grown, many had a cotton patch, and few were without sheep. Some of the women wove their own goods, others entrusted it to a professional weaver. He also says that domestic manufacture of wool was much facilitated by the carding machines which were to be seen in every part of the United States, some proprietors owning two or three.[70] In short, so great was the necessity for domestic

[67] Hodgson, II, 71.
[68] Melish, I, 32-33.
[69] Weld, I, 147.
[70] Bradbury, pp. 303-304.

manufacture throughout the nation that in 1812 it was estimated by Melish from "information received from every state and from more than 60 places," that probably about two-thirds of the clothing and house and table linen of the inhabitants of the United States who did not reside in sea ports, was made in this way.[71]

From the point of view of the progressive American, the future of his country's manufactures outside the home seemed one of great promise; the English merchant, however, suffered increasing apprehension for a most profitable part of the export trade of Great Britain. English travellers tried to reassure the people at home that America could never become a serious rival in manufacture. In 1794, Priest wrote to a friend in England that importation of British goods would continue to be necessary for an indefinite time. The United States had so few inhabitants and so much land uncultivated that it was not to their interest to engage in manufacture. When the country became sufficiently populous, it would be much easier to conquer and settle South America than to "go through the drudgery of fabrication."[72] If manufacture could take a firm footing anywhere, Priest said, it would be in New England, but the people of that district preferred to emigrate to the West rather than engage in a laborious trade. That this hope of the English was unfounded was proved by the subsequent history of manufacture in the United States, and admitted by later travellers, one of whom in 1812 says that the opinion that the Americans had an overwhelming predilection for agriculture was more specious than solid, that he himself investigated the matter as he had a personal interest in it, and was now quite convinced that internal manufacture would in all probability be eventually substituted for foreign commerce.[73] In 1824,

[71] Melish, I, 395-396.   [72] Priest, pp. 83-84.   [73] Melish, I, 83.

Hodgson confessed that the array of manufactures at an exhibit near Boston required all his philanthropy "to suppress the rising apprehension of an English merchant."[74]

The natural features of New England made that part of the country admirably adapted to the growth of manufacture. Observers commented on the fact that she had plenty of poor land, but fine situations for mills, also an extended coast line for the exportation of her manufactured products.[75] Besides these natural advantages, she had a surplus population to provide the labor for her factories. Women were especially plentiful, as has been said; the factories employed much energy which otherwise would have been wasted. The high price of labor, too, compelled the constant employment of ingenuity and skill in the invention of aids to cheaper and better manufacture, such devices as carding machines, for instance, and particular kinds of nails and screws, in the making of which the Americans were considered very clever.[76]

Much is told us of manufactures by Melish, who was primarily interested in trade.[77] He says that Rhode Island was the first state to become known for her cotton mills. Her earliest attempt at establishing this branch of manufacture was in 1791; this was followed by another in 1795. Two factories were built in Massachusetts in 1803 and 1804, and during the three succeeding years, ten more in Rhode Island and one in Connecticut, making fifteen mills before 1808, which produced about 300,000 pounds of yarn a year. By the end of 1810 there were said to be eighty-seven cotton factories in New England. Morse's "Universal Gazetteer" says that in 1821 there were more than one

[74] Hodgson, II, 7.
[75] See Martineau, II, 40-41, 137.
[76] Power, II, 18; Shirreff, p. 46; Candler, p. 435; Melish, I, 83.
[77] See Melish, I, 78, also 394.

hundred cotton factories in Rhode Island and the adjacent parts of Connecticut and Massachusetts, and that ten vessels were constantly employed at Providence, in the exportation of cotton goods.[78]

Lowell, Massachusetts, became the best known manufacturing city in the United States, and was visited by many observers. This town, situated at the confluence of the Merrimac and Concord rivers, possessed a water power which made it an ideal place for factories.[79] It was named for Francis Lowell, we are told, who introduced the manufacture of cotton into the country. Miss Martineau tells that in 1818 it possessed only a small satinet mill employing about twenty hands. In 1825, a corporation was formed, which increased steadily in wealth and influence until in 1832 the capital invested represented over $6,000,000. It employed 5,000 people, of whom 3,800 were women and girls. Over 20,000 bales of raw cotton produced in one year 25,000,000 yards of goods. Thousands of yards of woolen cloth were produced in Lowell as well, and sixty-eight carpet looms were constantly at work. Murray says that in 1834 when he visited this town, it was employing annually 7,000 persons, and turning out 40,000,000 yards of cotton goods of which one-fourth was printed.[80] American designs and colors were supposed to be unusually good.[81]

A sight interesting to the visitor to these mills was the appearance of the women operatives. Many travellers mention the fact that they looked attractive and prosperous. They were paid, besides their board, an average of $2 to $3 a week for seventy hours' work; this was considered a large

[78] Quoted by Hodgson, II, 130.
[79] See Shirreff, p. 44; Martineau, II, 42; Vigne, II, 236-237.
[80] Murray, I, 78-79.
[81] Hodgson, II, 8; Power, II, 18.

sum for female labor. This accounted, it was said, for their well-dressed appearance; most of them were able as well to save quite a sum annually.[82] Their day's labor lasted from daylight till dark, with a half-hour's intermission for breakfast and for dinner. They slept in houses provided by their employers; sometimes many in one room, to the distress of strangers who visited their quarters.[83] Shirreff tells of seeing a crowd of Lowell operatives going home from work on a Saturday afternoon: "All were clean, neat and fashionably attired, with reticules hanging on their arms and calashes on their heads. They commonly walked arm in arm without displaying levity. Their general appearance and deportment was such that few British gentlemen in the middle ranks of life need have been ashamed of leading any one of them to a tea party." [84] In regard to the prevailing purity of morals of these young women, it was said that the cause lay in the strict supervision and high standards set by the mill-owners, and in the class of people to which the girls belonged. Many of them were in the factories because they had too much pride to enter domestic service. Was it strange, then, thought the traveller, that these women could not stoop to immorality? Generally, they represented an intelligent class; sometimes factory owners built a church in the community and provided lyceums and libraries for their operatives.[85]

The circumstance most favorable to cotton manufacture was the low price of raw material, on which Melish comments; cotton could be obtained very cheaply by water carriage in most parts of the United States. In Ohio, the expense of bringing it from Mississippi (1825) was only

[82] Shirreff, p. 45; Martineau, II, 58; Hall, B., II, 135-136.
[83] Martineau, II, 139.
[84] Shirreff, p. 45.
[85] Martineau, II, 58, 138.

one and one-half cents per pound; in New England, the price seldom reached twenty cents, in 1812 it was as low as twelve or thirteen cents.[86] Another advantage was that British cotton goods, to secure the manufacturer any profit, had to be priced high because of the carriage charges, import duties, and other expenses. Thus a happy combination of circumstances favored the increase of this branch of manufacture in the United States.

New England abounded in other factory industries, many of which were visited by the traveller. Paper mills were seen in Rhode Island and Massachusetts;[87] factories for the production of sheet-iron, steel, nails, anchors, sailcloth, and other necessities for shipping, multiplied near the coast. Hartford, Connecticut, was known as a manufacturing town, its woolen mills being famous throughout the country.[88] The boot and shoe trade was a distinctive part of New England production. This was carried on at first in the homes, chiefly in the spare moments of the women and children. It grew to be so valuable, we are told, that in 1831 the value of boots and shoes made at Lynn, Massachusetts, was nearly a million dollars annually. Here, 3,500 people were employed in the making of about 1,500,000 pairs.[89] In short, so vital was the interest in industry in New England that in 1824, when Hodgson went with some friends to an exhibition of domestic manufactures at Brighton, Massachusetts, he says it would have been difficult to mention any article that was omitted, "from a tawdry rosy-cheeked wax doll to the most substantial fabrics of woolen and cotton."[90] The Governor of Ohio,

[86] Melish, I, 84; Hodgson, II, 8.
[87] Wansey, p. 34; Melish, I, 78.
[88] Wansey, p. 261.
[89] Martineau, II, 44-45; also Kendall, III, 21.
[90] Hodgson, II, p. 7.

AGRICULTURE, MANUFACTURE AND INDUSTRY 173

he says, was present to inspect the manufactures with a view to encouraging the introduction of them into his own state.

The Middle Atlantic States were more given up to agriculture, but nevertheless produced great numbers of useful manufactured commodities. Thomas Cooper remarked in 1795 that the extensive production of military supplies enabled the United States to derive from their own resources everything from ships of war to the buckles on the soldiers' shoes.[91] The manufacture of firearms was carried on in Pennsylvania, chiefly at Lancaster, and was very lucrative. The American rifles were not so handsome as the European variety, Englishmen said, but were excellent in quality.[92] The flour mills throughout the state were a great curiosity to visitors. Those on the Brandywine River were especially celebrated.[93] Weld comments on the sight of thirteen mills built close together along this watercourse, some for flour, the others for stone-cutting and wood-sawing. Pennsylvania was indeed one of the greatest manufacturing states in the Union. In 1810, by Melish's account there were thirty iron furnaces within her boundaries, besides manufactories turning out furniture and agricultural implements, all kinds of leather goods, woolen goods, and a variety of other articles such as glass, china, liquors, powder, shot, etc.[94]

Pittsburg, Fearon says, was bombastically called by the Americans "Birmingham" because of its numerous factories, most of which originated during the War of 1812. An influential citizen of the town furnished the English-

[91] Cooper, p. 220.
[92] Melish, I, 111; Priest, pp. 59, 85; Dalton, p. 58; Weld, I, 117; Coke, I, 115-116.
[93] Priest, p. 21; Weld, I, 34; Cooper, p. 134.
[94] Melish, I, 174; see also Vigne, I, 97.

man with a list of manufactures for 1817. It summarized the employment of 1280 workmen in forty-one different types of industry and represented a value of $1,896,396.[95] We have evidence that even before the war, Pittsburg had made rapid progress in industry. A list of the occupations engaged in there in 1810 represented sixty-one different kinds of work, with an annual value of over $1,000,000 yearly; that is, Melish estimates, an average of over $200 a year for every man, woman, and child.[96]

When we turn to New York State, we marvel at the variety of important productions. In 1810, they included "articles of glass, ashes, ironware of various descriptions, leather of all kinds, hats, carriages, paper and printing, pottery-ware, umbrellas, mathematical and musical instruments"; they amounted to $17,000,000.[97] Howison in 1821 or 1822 visited a cotton mill at Utica; here again one was impressed with the bright and healthy look of the operatives, who were as usual mostly women and children. "Many of the females were reading the Bible, and others sat sewing, during the intervals of leisure which their respective occupations afforded them."[98] The shoe trade of New York State was, about 1830, more valuable, we are told, than the total commerce of Georgia.[99] The manufacture of silk flourished to some extent. One farmer on Cayuga Lake told James Stuart that he was selling silk to the amount of about $600 a year.[100] The central part of the state was noted for its salt-works, as it boasted "the strongest saline water yet discovered in the world." Forty

---

[95] Fearon, p. 197; also given by Flint, pp. 84-85.
[96] Melish, II, 55-56; see also Hulme, p. 37.
[97] Melish, I, 137.
[98] Howison, p. 318.
[99] Martineau, II, 44-45.
[100] Stuart, I, 177; see, also, Kendall, I, 251.

AGRICULTURE, MANUFACTURE AND INDUSTRY   175

gallons of water yielded a bushel of pure salt, Fowler says. In 1830, there were one hundred salt factories at Salina and twenty-five at Syracuse, all of them state property, and rented out according to custom.[101] A small group of industries sprang up around New York and Brooklyn, the latter of which had numerous tanneries, distilleries, and cotton and linen manufactories.[102]

After Pittsburg, Cincinnati was the most important manufacturing town on the Ohio River. "The professions exercised," said Melish, "are nearly as numerous as at Pittsburg."[103] Cincinnati's location was particularly favorable to manufacture and the export trade, and the rapidly increasing population of the town and of the surrounding country called for more and more luxuries as time went on.

Kentucky was the center of the hemp industry, as it was suitable for slave labor. In Lexington, her chief city, this particular branch of manufacture brought the state $500,000 in 1810.[104] At that time there were also eight cotton mills, three woolen manufactories, and an oil cloth factory in the town, besides a number of smaller enterprises.

The South throughout this period had no particular interest in manufactures, except those of the domestic sort that were carried on on the plantation. A traveller speaks of his pleasure in hearing the sound of mill stones in a country district of Georgia, the grist mills moved by water power being the only type that the Southerner saw frequently.[105] Slave labor was not satisfactory in manufac-

[101] See Fowler, pp. 87-88; Maude, John (p. 43), says state rent was four cents for every bushel of salt made.
[102] Wansey, pp. 68, 70; Fowler, p. 25; Neilson, pp. 32-33.
[103] Melish, II, 127; Palmer, pp. 72-74.
[104] Melish, II, 187-188; Fearon, p. 245.
[105] Melish, I, 38.

ture; the blacks were not by nature fitted for this kind of work, and there was no other laboring class in the South. Miss Martineau saw one factory at Richmond, Virginia, worked by black labor. The quality of the work was good, "to the surprise of those who tried the experiment."[106] This difference in attitude toward industry, revealed by the two parts of the country, was destined to account for much of the economic struggle that arose later between the North and South.

It is thus apparent that manufacture, in the Northern states at least, showed a disposition to take its stand beside agriculture as one of the two leading occupations of the American people. In 1810, a point of time midway in this period, the report of the Secretary of the Treasury of the United States, quoted by a traveller, puts the total of American manufactures at more than $120,000,000 annually, and "it is not improbable," he says, "that the raw material used and the provisions and other articles consumed by the manufacturers, creates a home market for agricultural purposes not very inferior to that which arises from foreign demand."[107]

Mining was an occupation in which the first settlers were not interested. They lived on the top of the soil, many without even the necessity of digging a well. The presence of such useful commodities as salt, iron, coal, etc., was indicated at times on the surface of the earth and led, Bradbury says, to the first attempts to penetrate below the soil.[108] Weld says that valuable mines of iron and copper were discovered in Virginia before 1795, but were just beginning to be worked at that date.[109] Wansey, about the same time, visited a new copper mine near Paterson,

[106] Martineau, I, 300.
[107] Quoted by Melish, I, 397.
[108] Bradbury, pp. 55, 88, 161.
[109] Weld, I, 210.

AGRICULTURE, MANUFACTURE AND INDUSTRY 177

N. J.[110] Several travellers tell of the discovery of gold in 1800 in the sand and gravel of the North Carolina watercourses;[111] after 1814, this state furnished the government mint with "great quantities" of the precious metal. A succession of gold mines was also discovered in Virginia, South Carolina, and Georgia; in 1830, the mint was receiving the output of all of these states. Of the gold coined in that year by the government, about $446,000 of the total $643,000 was native metal.

Throughout all the Western country, including western Pennsylvania, there were great possibilities of salt, coal, iron, lead, and nitre. Missouri especially abounded in lead; coal was believed, with truth, to be very abundant; caverns in the rocks yielded great quantities of saltpetre; in short, the mining possibilities of the West seemed to foreigners as unlimited as the prospects for agriculture and manufacture.[112]

Trades and mechanic arts flourished in the same proportion. Even in the sections patently agricultural there seems never to have been a lack of masons, carpenters, smiths, and mechanics of all sorts. Yankee ingenuity was an acknowledged trait, and many a native American combined several trades with his primary vocation.[113] His endeavor to do so provoked sometimes a complaint from the traveller who required his services. James Flint tells of the incapacity of the average Western mechanic. He says that almost every well-finished article in the West was imported.[114] The country west of the Alleghanies offered

---

[110] Wansey, p. 187.
[111] For gold in North Carolina, see Alexander, II, 116 ff.; Vigne, I, 221 ff.; Janson, p. 365. See Ouseley, Chap. XVII.
[112] Bradbury, pp. 259, 291; Holmes, p. 226.
[113] See Melish, I, 83.
[114] Flint, pp. 196-197.

a fine field for mechanic arts, and there is no doubt that the great competition in the Eastern states, which many travellers emphasize, did a great deal to send that class of people westward. Staple trades like shoemaking and tailoring were glutted, Fearon says, while the labor which produced the finer arts—goldbeating, gilding, carving, etc., was in its prime about the middle of this period.[115]

It is interesting in the light of present conditions to know what were the average wages of a mechanic.[116] Melish tells us that in 1810 in Pittsburg, where labor was considered well-paid, carpenters received $1 a day; cabinet-makers, being paid by the piece, averaged slightly more than that. Smiths and tanners worked for $12 a month and board. Shoemakers received ninety-four cents for making a pair of shoes and $2.50 for a pair of boots. Shipwrights were very well paid, they received $1.50 a day. Other mechanics received $1 and unskilled laborers seventy-five cents. A few years later (1818), James Flint says that in Cincinnati journeymen mechanics received $1.75 to $2 a day. Their board cost about $3 a week; thus they were able to dress well and in some cases to keep a horse.[117]

That there was a certain amount of discontent and dissatisfaction with laboring conditions is apparent. Fearon gives some instances of grumbling that he has heard—once in Pittsburg chiefly among mechanics of foreign birth, and once in New York City.[118] We read of one notable strike. This was in New York City in 1833, when the carpenters struck for an increase of one shilling a day on their wages, and secured it after a two weeks' demonstra-

[115] Fearon, pp. 25, 29 ff.
[116] Melish, II, 56; Wansey, p. 80; Flint, p. 150; Neilson, p. 6.
[117] Flint, p. 150.
[118] Fearon, pp. 25, 207; Abdy, I, 30.

AGRICULTURE, MANUFACTURE AND INDUSTRY 179

tion.[119] Any dissatisfaction, however, that arose among the laboring classes, was likely to be on the point of hours rather than of wages. Under the influence of Frances Wright, afterward Madame D'Arusmont, and others, the working classes of New York City were, about 1830, organized into bodies for the monopoly of political power. These socialistic organizations were of several different kinds, depending on the interests of the members, who were called "Workies," and who united in attacks on prevailing conditions of society. The "agrarians," for instance, Ferrall says, tried to bring about legislation to the effect that no one should be allowed to hold more than a certain quantity of land, and that at given intervals of time, there should be an equal division of property.[120]

The future of the mechanic arts was well summed up by the traveler Latrobe, who visited America in 1832-33. " . . . whether it is in the fine arts that America is to distinguish herself or not, there can be no doubt that in the mechanic arts she will attain great excellence. Of that, everything gives promise, and the very circumstances that would seem to be against her in her cultivation of the former, are highly conducive to her advance and perfection in the latter. Travel where you will through the middle and eastern states, you will see tokens of a busy spirit of emulative industry, boldness of design and conception in every branch of mechanics, from the lowest to the highest, which must command admiration. To this the absence of monopolies, the incessant call for exertion and emulation, the vastness of the public works are all favorable. . . . The steam-vessel contains abundant proof of this mechanical talent in every part of its details. From the

[119] Abdy, I, 30 ff.; II, 308-309; Shirreff, p. 401.
[120] For the best account of these, see Ferrall, p. 327 ff.; also Abdy, II, 311.

bridges, water works, railroads, docks, and public works of every description, down through the countless number of aids to human comfort to the very mouse-trap, you detect the prevalence of this same busy ingenuity and talent. And there is no reason to believe it will not increase with the growth of the country.'' [121]

[121] Latrobe, II, 68.

CHAPTER VII

TRADE AND FINANCE

As a result of her productive agriculture and manufactures, the United States had a great deal of surplus goods to export to all parts of the world as an offset to her enormous imports. She was peculiarly fitted to become a great commercial market, not only because of these conditions of production, but because of the extended coast line, the good harbors, and the facilities for inland transportation. To all these circumstances was added the great advance made by the Americans in the art of ship-building.[1] This was carried on in every American port, and even as far inland as Pittsburg, 2300 miles from the ocean, the vessels passing by way of the Ohio and Mississippi Rivers.[2] Though the price of labor was high, the Americans, it was said, could build ships cheaply because of the wealth of material at their disposal. The best woods were cedar and live-oak, the latter of which was exported from the Southern states to the coast towns.[3] Travellers describe these ships as being long and sharp, and lighter and faster than the British boats, which they superseded to such an extent that even English merchants refused to send their produce from their home ports in anything but American ships.[4]

[1] De Roos, pp. 43-44; Cooper, p. 211; Bristed, p. 39; Melish, I, 184.
[2] Ashe, p. 26; Janson, p. 438.
[3] Wansey, pp. 230-231; Priest, pp. 86-87.
[4] See Blane, p. 347 ff., for a very good account of American ships.

They were never loaded heavily, and therefore completed a sea-voyage much more quickly than did the English boats. Like the later steam-vessels on the inland waters, they were finished remarkably well, and the comfort, and even elegance, of their furnishings impressed travellers very much. Enthusiastic Englishmen compared them to Cleopatra's barge, or to the royal yachts of their own country.[5]

Into every American port which had any connection with the back country, poured streams of export material, the overflow of American activity. Owing to the United States' policy of unrestricted export trade, any one was able to send anything he wished to any harbor in the world.[6] Observers saw going out from the ports of Boston, Salem, Providence, and New York, great shipments of manufactured commodities: paper, glass, iron, leather, soap, candles, spirits, hats, shoes, and cotton and woolen goods.[7] Farther South, flour and other agricultural products from Pennsylvania, New Jersey, and Delaware were shipped with the manufactured iron, paper, and lumber.[8] The chief articles of agricultural export from the United States were wheat, flour, rice, Indian corn, beans, peas, potatoes, beef, tallow, hides, butter, cheese, pork, tobacco, cotton, and indigo. It was estimated by Bristed that the amount of vegetable food alone exported in one year (1803), was valued at $14,080,000—a little less than half of the total amount of agricultural export. This, in turn, represented three-quarters of the whole domestic export. Much of this came from the vast area of the Middle West by way of New Orleans, while the South contributed great quantities

[5] Blane, p. 351; Candler, p. 435.
[6] Flint, p. 205; Cooper, p. 213; Blane, p. 346.
[7] See Melish, I, 78, 90, 99-100, 115, 126.
[8] Melish, I, 181, 185.

TRADE AND FINANCE   183

of raw cotton, tobacco, and rice, both to the North and to foreign ports.[9]

It was noticed that harbors that had not easy connection with inland resources became neglected for those that had. Newport was cited as an example of this; her harbor was one of the finest along the coast and she was in most other respects eminently fitted for a promising commercial career, but she had no adequate means of receiving export goods from the inland districts, and therefore became neglected and impoverished.[10] The same was seen to be true to a less degree of Boston, which never attained to the commercial importance of New York, Philadelphia, and Baltimore, because of the lack of navigable rivers in her vicinity.[11]

In 1784, a traveller tells us, the exports from the United States amounted to $4,000,000, the imports to $18,000,000; by 1790, the former had increased to $6,000,000 while the imports were now valued at $17,260,000.[12] An examination of Bristed's statistics reveals the fact that, beginning with 1791, the export trade increased steadily. By 1816 it had reached $81,920,452, in spite of two setbacks during the Long Embargo and the second war with Great Britain.[13] In 1825, according to Harriet Martineau, the exports represented a value of $3,000,000 more than the imports, which were estimated at $96,000,000; while by 1835, the imports were $126,000,000 as against $104,000,000 in exports.[14] It

[9] Melish, I, 276; Palmer, p. 74; Bristed, pp. 23-24. Bristed bases his figures on Timothy Pitkin's "Statistical View of the United States" (revised edition, 1817); see Pitkin, pp. 123, 146.
[10] Hodgson, II, 132; Power, II, 22-23.
[11] Weld, I, 55-56; Melish, I, 90.
[12] Bristed, p. 40.
[13] Bristed, p. 40. (*State Papers*, Doc. #4, 16th Congress, 1st session, Vol. I).
[14] Martineau, II, 64-65.

may thus be seen that however rapidly manufacture and agriculture developed in the United States, the demand for foreign commodities seemed to persist as well. As wealth increased in the new republic, the demand for luxuries grew correspondingly, and importations of that kind supplanted more or less the shiploads of necessities that had formerly entered American ports.

It was said that there was no known harbor of the world in which American ships could not be found, and from which they did not bear rich cargoes to their home cities. Coffee, rum, and sugar came from the West Indies, and from the East Indies, tea, muslins, and calicoes.[15] Luxuries and curiosities from India and China appeared in New England homes as a matter of course. Indeed, the traffic with China became a fixed and important part of American commerce. The United States not only sent her own products to China but did all the carrying from Great Britain to that country, as well.[16] "The return cargoes," says a traveller, "consist of teas, silks, nankeens, shawls, japanned cabinet goods, china, coloured blinds, screens, papers, ivory and mother-of-pearl trinkets, fancy stationery and an endless catalogue of articles under the class of useful and ornamental bagatelles which all find a ready sale at a considerable profit, as well for the store keepers as for the importers."[17]

The Americans were seen to carry on more trade with Great Britain than with any other country. From her they exported chiefly manufactured articles of a practical nature; commodities which they themselves had not yet found time nor facilities for producing, as for instance, certain kinds of woolen, cotton, and linen goods, hardware,

[15] Weld, I, 54.
[16] Wansey, p. 230; Candler, pp. 436-437; Boardman, p. 348 ff.
[17] Boardman, p. 349.

cutlery, hosiery, and earthenware.[18] Most of these were carried in American ships. Isaac Holmes says that in 1823 there were ten American ships to one English merchantman.[19] Another English observer primarily interested in commerce explains why so much of the carrying was done by American vessels exclusively. Goods transported in this way from England to the United States were 8 to 10% cheaper and those from America to Great Britain 10 to 20% cheaper than if they had been carried in English vessels. The reason lay in the high rate of insurance which Great Britain was obliged to pay on her shipping because of her continued participation in war.[20]. Priest says that in 1791 the imports to the United States from England alone amounted to over $19,000,000, chiefly in manufactured articles.[21] In this same year, another traveller tells us, of the $17,500,000 worth of exports from the United States, about one-half went to Great Britain.[22] Bristed estimates that, judging from the figures of the years 1802, 1803, and 1804, the trade between the United States and England was greater than that between the former country and all the rest of the world.[23] The importation of raw cotton into Great Britain was an important feature of the trade; so great was the increase of traffic in this commodity, it was said, especially after the peace of 1815, that in one period of four years' duration (1819-1823), the number of bales was more than doubled, increasing from 204,831 to

[18] Melish, I, 442; Weld, I, 54.
[19] Holmes, p. 234.
[20] Melish, I, 443.
[21] Priest, p. 27.
[22] See table in front of Wansey's book. Government report gives exports at $19,012,041 (*State Papers*, Doc. #4, 16th Congress, 1st session, Vol. I).
[23] Verified by Pitkin, pp. 192-193; Bristed, p. 41.

449,255.[24] Subsequent tables of statistics given by English travellers bear the same testimony to the importance of the trade with Great Britain, and show that it increased proportionally all through this period. One account of 1830 puts the exports from England to America in that year at over $22,000,000 and the imports at $24,000,000, which was more than double the trade with France, which stood second on the list.[25]

No discussion of the commerce of the United States, as Englishmen saw it, would be complete without some mention of the Long Embargo and its effects. Jefferson's act provided for the entire suspension of shipping, except the coasting trade, for an indefinite period of time. The restriction was removed in 1809, but its effects were felt long afterward. It had been confidently expected, it was said, that the embargo would increase American manufacture by the stoppage of foreign importation, but the distress and financial loss that it caused offset whatever good it may have done in that direction. The traveller Lambert tells of two visits to New York in November, 1807, and in April, 1808, and of the contrast the city presented on these two occasions. In 1807, New York was a scene of bustling and cheerful activity. "But on my return . . . the following April," he says, "what a contrast was presented to my view! . . . The port indeed was full of shipping; but they were dismantled and laid up. Their decks were cleared, their hatches fastened down, and scarcely a sailor was to be found on board. Not a box, bale, cask, barrel or package was to be seen upon the wharfs. Many of the counting houses were shut up, or advertised to be let, and the few solitary merchants, clerks, porters and laborers that were to be seen, were walking about with their hands in their pockets, . . . the grass had begun to grow upon the wharfs.

[24] Hodgson, II, Appendix, 361.   [25] Tudor, II, 384.

... In short, the scene was so gloomy and so forlorn that had it been the month of September instead of April, I should verily have thought that a malignant fever was raging in the place; so desolating were the effects of the embargo, which, in the short space of five months, had deprived the first commercial city in the States of all its life, bustle, and activity; caused above one hundred and twenty bankruptcies; and completely annihilated its foreign commerce!" [26]

In 1792, according to Wansey, Massachusetts stood fourth on the list of exporting states, ranking below Pennsylvania, New York, and Maryland with an export trade of $2,389,922.[27] Melish says that by 1805 she had exceeded at least two of these, Pennsylvania and Maryland, with a trade valued at more than $19,000,000.[28] In the same year, the duty paid upon imports into Boston amounted to $6,408,000; those into Salem, to $1,034,498, as against $12,862,020 and $7,777,965 in New York and Philadelphia respectively.[29] The commercial history of Salem is very picturesque. When Miss Martineau visited it in 1832, it had a population of 14,000, and more wealth in proportion, she says, than probably any other town in the world. "The enterprising merchants of Salem are hoping to appropriate a large share of the whale fishery, and their ships are penetrating the northern ice. They are favorite customers in the Russian ports, and are familiar with the Swedish and Norwegian coasts. They have nearly as much commerce with Bremen as with Liverpool. They speak of Fayal and the other Azores as if they were close at hand.

[26] Lambert, II, 62-65, also 294-295; Bristed, p. 37; also Kendall, III, 277, 293.
[27] See tables in front of Wansey's book.
[28] Melish, I, 115, 153, 190.
[29] Lambert, II, 490-491; also Kendall, II, 261.

The fruits of the Mediterranean countries are on every table. They have a large acquaintance at Cairo. They know Napoleon's grave at St. Helena and have wild tales to tell of Mosambique and Madagascar, and stores of ivory to show from there. They speak of the power of the King of Muscat, and are sensible of the riches of the southeast coast of Arabia. . . . The merchants doubt whether Australia will be able to surmount the disadvantage of a deficiency of navigable rivers. They have hopes of Van Diemen's Land, think well of Singapore and acknowledge great expectations for New Zealand. Anybody will give you anecdotes from Canton and descriptions of the Society and Sandwich Islands. They often slip up the western coasts of their two continents; bring furs from the back regions of their own wide land; glance up at the Andes on their return; double Cape Horn; touch at the ports of Brazil and Guiana; look about them in the West Indies, feeling there almost at home; and land some fair morning at Salem and walk home as if they had done nothing very remarkable.''[30]

The commercial history of the other states was, as in the case of Massachusetts, the development of their principal seaports, or the harbors to which they were accessible. As Pennsylvania surpassed the other states in her export trade immediately after the Revolution, Philadelphia was at that time looked upon as the first port in the Union. Its wharves offered a safe navigation, Priest says, for vessels of a thousand tons burden.[31] In 1792, a total of 420,000 barrels of flour was shipped from this port. Into it came not only the produce of the greater part of the territory east of the Alleghanies, but that of New Jersey and Dela-

[30] Martineau, II, 67-69; Hall, B., II, 141.
[31] Priest, p. 26; Palmer, p. 257.

ware as well. In 1793, according to Priest, 1414 vessels of different sizes entered her harbor to trade.[32]

Because of her superior natural advantages, New York quickly surpassed Philadelphia as a trading port. It is difficult to say whether her imports or exports were more important. Strangers saw on her wharves produce, both agricultural and manufactured, from the New England states, from New Jersey, and from her own prosperous and hustling counties. She was the center of the import trade of cotton from the Southern states; her harbors were full of shipping, the greater part of it in the coasting trade.[33] Melish says that her exports amounted in 1805 to over $23,500,000; her imports to $25,000,000.[34] The revenue brought into the country by duties paid at this port is variously estimated at one-fifth, one-fourth, or even (in 1822) two-thirds of the whole amount of duties in the United States.[35]

Norfolk was, early in the history of the country, the largest commercial town in Virginia, and carried on a flourishing trade with the West Indies. Weld says it would have been greater if an unfortunate policy of the Virginia legislature during the Revolution had not alienated the trade from Great Britain. The state had declared that all merchants owing debts to England might liquidate those obligations by paying that amount toward the prosecution of the war against the British. After peace was declared, the British were of course not satisfied with this form of payment, and accused the Virginians of bad faith. An effort was finally made to reinstate them in the good graces

[32] Priest, p. 27; Holmes, p. 223.
[33] Holmes, p. 223; Murray, I, 52; Melish, I, 60-61.
[34] Melish, I, 60.
[35] Palmer, p. 301; D'Arusmont, p. 280; Lambert, II, 75; Holmes, p. 223; Neilson, p. 39.

of England by paying the money, but the British continued to be reluctant to trade with that particular state.[36] Melish says, however, that the exports of Virginia in 1805 were valued at $5,606,620, and the imports at nearly as much—half of the latter were from Great Britain.[37]

There seems to have been a curious reason given for the neglect of Annapolis as a trading port, in favor of Baltimore. Annapolis had an ideal situation, a healthful climate, and above all, a fine harbor. "But," says Priest, "unfortunately these advantages were rendered abortive by the bite of a small insect; the worms are so troublesome in those waters that a vessel lying in this harbor during the summer months will be as full of holes as a honey-comb." Baltimore was apparently free from this pest because of the large proportion of fresh water in her harbors; accordingly, she drew all the trade from her rival. At the time when Priest wrote, Annapolis had only one square-rigged vessel belonging to her port, while Baltimore had several hundreds.[38] In 1805, Melish says, the exports and imports of Maryland, practically all of which passed through Baltimore, were valued at more than $10,000,000 each.[39]

Wilmington, North Carolina; Charleston, South Carolina; and Savannah, Georgia, represented the three mediums of commerce in their respective states; in regard to the first, very little is said;[40] the other two were world-famous ports. Through Charleston went an enormous trade, chiefly in cotton. Before the Revolution, South Carolina had a very promising commerce which fell off

[36] Weld, I, 170-171.
[37] Melish, I, 239.
[38] Priest, pp. 15-16.
[39] Melish, I, 190.
[40] Lambert, II, 491.

greatly during the war, according to Lambert, as the labor of the slaves had to be turned from raising cotton and tobacco to the domestic manufacture of goods hitherto imported from Great Britain. After the war, her agriculture and trade increased rapidly. "In 1801, 1274 ships entered the port of Charleston, of which 875 belonged to that port; the rest were chiefly British vessels." [41] In 1805, by Melish's report, the exports of the state amounted to $9,060,525, with probably as much more through the medium of the Northern ports; the average of tariff duties at Charleston for four years ending in 1805 was $3,031,639. This traveller also says that Savannah, Georgia, in 1810, employed "thirteen regular ships to Britain, fifteen packet brigs and schooners to New York; two or three to Philadelphia, Baltimore, and Boston; two or three sloops to Charleston, and four or five vessels to the West Indies." [42] Besides a considerable amount of rice, Georgia exported the famous "Sea Island" cotton, the finest in the country. Savannah was the only shipping port in the state; her exports early in the century averaged over $2,000,000 annually, besides what was carried in her coasting trade.

Most of the surplus produce of the West went down the Mississippi to New Orleans, though some of it was said to be transported to Philadelphia and Baltimore by way of Pittsburg, over which route there was likewise imported to the Western towns a great deal of East Indian and European goods.[43] As certain places near the Ohio were settled by emigrants from New England, they partook of the commercial spirit of the older settlements, and maintained a flourishing trade.[44]

[41] Lambert, II, 212-214, 347; Melish, I, 283; Tudor, II, 519; Neilson, p. 329. [42] Melish, I, 26-27.
[43] Melish, II, 194; Palmer, p. 74.
[44] See Melish, II, 102, also 234.

The promise shown by the city of New Orleans has perhaps been elsewhere sufficiently emphasized. Ashe pointed out that she received exports from the region of the upper Missouri, from the western part of Pennsylvania, from Kentucky, Ohio, Illinois, and Indiana, from the territory west of the Mississippi drained by the White, the Red, and the Black Rivers, from New Mexico, Florida, and Georgia. This same traveller remarked in 1806: "the city is a depot of all the various wealth and productions of countries extending from it for two to three thousand miles in many directions. . . . Besides becoming the necessary depot of such extravagant wealth, it has strong advantages from its own situation; it stands on the very bank of the most perfect course of freshwater navigation in the world; it is but 100 miles from the sea, within a few days' sail of Mexico, of the French, Spanish and British Islands in the West Indies, and lies open to, and trades with Russia, Sweden, Denmark, Hamburgh, United Provinces, Great Britain, Austria, Netherlands, Germany, France, Spain, Portugal, Italy, Morocco, and several parts of Africa, China, and various Asiatic countries, and the north-west coast of North, and the East coast of South America."[45]

The importance to the central American government of all this wealth of commerce, especially that of the import trade, was seen to be very great. The United States had two chief sources of revenue, the sale of the public lands and the duties on imports. She was therefore compelled to face the question of a protective tariff early in her history. The attitude of Englishmen may be easily surmised.[46]

[45] Ashe, pp. 338-339.
[46] For English attitude toward the tariff, see Martineau, II, 46 ff.; Tudor, II, 459; Hamilton, I, 190-191, 197, 199-202; Hodgson, II, 72 ff.; Vigne, II, 238-239; Hall, B., II, 101-106; Candler, p. 436; Boardman, pp. 215-216.

They rose against the tariff to a man, and deplored generally the unnatural interest in domestic manufactures on the part of the Americans. The United States had such a great extent of territory; they were increasing so rapidly in wealth and population—"why trammel industry with artificial restrictions?" They should "refrain from counteracting the beneficence of nature, and tranquilly enjoy the many blessings . . . placed within their reach." No good was to be gained by leading American industry by roads which it would not have followed naturally, especially when such a course involved enriching one part of the country at the expense of another. Why should America anticipate a state of independence of other countries when it was well-known that the welfare of any nation was only promoted by intercourse and a reciprocity of advantages? Then too, it must be remembered that a high duty encourages smuggling, which would be a simple matter on America's extensive coast-line, and the moral effects of which would be appalling.

Holmes says that after the peace of 1815, great shiploads of English goods flooded the American market, and were sold at auction at very high prices. This utterly crippled the domestic manufacture of certain kinds, especially that of cotton and woolen goods.[47] Then began a struggle on the part of native manufacturers to bring about a higher duty on imported goods, for home protection. Fearon gives in full an example of the kind of petition that was sent to Congress repeatedly by manufacturing communities. This one is from the people of Oneida County, New York, to the Senate (Jan. 7, 1818), urging the imposition of a higher tariff. It disclaims any attempt to introduce any general system of manufactures into the United States, but merely emphasizes the need of encourag-

[47] Holmes, p. 192.

ing and protecting those that already exist.[48] This type of petition was answered by protests from the agricultural societies of the various states, especially those in the South, which accused the manufacturers of trying to solicit a monopoly. Faux gives an example of one from Virginia.[49] Thus the struggle continued, a source of great interest to foreigners, some of whom, Tudor, for instance, warned the Americans that therein lay the seeds of discord and of ultimate separation.[50]

There was also to be considered the question of England's prohibition of American importations. Was England too generous in her policy, and should she impose a duty on raw cotton, for instance, especially if it were carried in American ships? Many loyal Englishmen believed that the mother-country was far too careless of her own profit in her dealings with the shrewd Yankees. Others held quite the opposite opinion. "If we persist in refusing to admit her corn into Great Britain," says one traveller, "she must of necessity limit her importation of our manufactures; for her consumption is bounded by her means of payment, and by that alone. Had our Government been sufficiently alive to this consideration, they would surely have paused before they crushed an incipient trade, and dried up a new source of payment, by the imposition of a duty of 6 d. per pound on the importation of raw wool."[51]

The question of free trade or protection was indeed a puzzling one. It was obvious that all the interests of the country could not be served, and the dilemma thus created within this period was not to be avoided in spite of heroic efforts to do so.

[48] Fearon, pp. 296-298. [49] Faux, p. 117.
[50] Tudor, II, 459; Vigne, I, 258; Hall, B., II, 102-103.
[51] Hodgson, II, 73; Ferrall, pp. 336-337.

TRADE AND FINANCE

The whole financial administration of the United States aroused, as a system, the greatest admiration from observers. It brought about such satisfactory results in increase of revenues and in efficiency at so small an expense.[52] "There can be little doubt," said the traveller Ouseley, "that both theoretically and practically, it is the cheapest government that could be established in a country of such extent in the present day." It has already been remarked that the absence of heavy taxes and tithes contributed largely to the popularity of the United States as an objective point in emigration. So light was the excise in the early days of the republic, Wansey said, that the whole internal revenue did not make more than one-seventh of the national income. The few impositions were those that were absolutely necessary for the maintenance of schools, the keeping up of roads, etc. It is curious to see how small the expenses of the central government were. Even as late as 1831, the total for the year was estimated by Ouseley at only $30,967,201, one-half of which went toward the payment of the public debt. The expense of the whole judiciary of the country at that time was reckoned at only $395,866. The post-office was intended to pay for itself and practically did so, Ouseley says; turnpikes were kept up by tolls which were relatively high, owing to the scattered settlement of the population; in short, the Federal burden that fell upon the citizens of the United States might perhaps be estimated at one dollar per person, annually, aside from the money that went toward the public debt.[53] One of the greatest sources of expense was the army, which although it numbered only 6000, Ouseley says in 1832, cost

[52] Ouseley, p. 68 (quotation); Cooper, p. 210; Wansey, p. 176.
[53] Ouseley, p. 176. See Ouseley generally for information concerning the financial affairs of the United States. His work was based on government documents. Holmes, p. 121.

$4,200,000 annually. The traveller quotes General Bernard in the statement that this great item was partly accounted for by the fact that the American soldier was a volunteer and demanded the high wages paid to all labor at this time. The sum included, too, a large amount annually voted for the manufacture of muskets and small arms and of artillery, and for the expense of raising fortifications, etc.[54] To the navy was devoted a sum averaging $2,500,000 a year, the greater part of which went into building new war-vessels.[55] It was maintained that both army and navy could be doubled in number without much added outlay of money.[56] Another expense was the sum paid to the Indian tribes, a total which, about 1830, amounted to approximately one-twentieth of the whole American budget.[57] In spite of these expenses, the United States at this time, it was said, was saving money every year. Holmes says that as late as 1823, the government receipts amounted to $2,000,000 more than the expenditures.[58] In 1832, the expenses amounted to $13,000,000 exclusive of the public debt, while the country's revenue was estimated at over $30,000,000, of which $26,000,000 was from the customs, $3,000,000 from the public lands, $490,000 from bank dividends, and $110,000 from incidental receipts. In this last class was included such income as that derived from "spirits distilled in the United States, . . . postage on letters, taxes on patents . . . snuff manufactured in the United States, sugar refined here, sales at auction, licenses to retail wines and distilled spirits, carriages for the conveyance of persons, stamped paper, direct taxes."[59] The

[54] Ouseley, p. 118; Holmes, p. 118; Hamilton, II, 58.
[55] Holmes, p. 118.
[56] Ouseley, pp. 118-119.
[57] Ibid., p. 120.
[58] Holmes, p. 116.
[59] See Ouseley, pp. 176-177. Tudor, II, 478, gives the same table.

form of revenue was criticised by many foreigners as being insecure and inefficient, and too susceptible to loss in value in case of adverse circumstances, a protracted foreign war, for example. Revenue from imports was characterized too as "internal taxation," in fact if not in name, for one-half of the amount collected was from British goods, not luxuries but necessities, so that the population of America was in reality helping to pay the taxes of Great Britain as well as defraying the expenses of their own.[60]

Bristed says that the cost of the Revolution was about $135,000,000, of which half was paid during the war by taxes levied at the time.[61] When the Federal government assumed the state debts, the whole financial burden which lay upon the country amounted to over $75,000,000, which by 1812 had been reduced to about $45,000,000. The second war with Great Britain increased it to over $121,000,000.[62] How rapidly it was being paid off during the twenty years from 1815 to 1835, may be inferred from a table given by an English traveller for the ten years 1821 to 1830 inclusive. About $2,000,000 was paid each year on the interest and an average of $6,000,000 to $7,000,000 on the principal. In 1824, over $11,000,000 was paid on the latter, and, in 1832, the last date in our period for which English travellers give us any figures, the debt was reduced to about $24,000,000.[63] "The national debt," says Ferrall in that year, "will be totally extinguished in four years, when this country will present a curious spectacle for the serious consideration of European nations.

[60] Bristed, p. 57; Fearon, p. 384; Neilson, p. 220; Holmes, p. 120.
[61] Bristed, p. 72. See also Coxe, Tench, p. 496. See Pitkin, pp. 307-309.
[62] Lambert, II, 494; Bristed, pp. 74, 76.
[63] Ouseley, pp. 176-177, 204; Bristed, p. 72; Holmes, p. 116; Tudor, II, 480; Ferrall, p. 238.

During the space of fifty-six years, two successful wars have been carried on—one for the establishment, and the other for the maintenance of national independence, and a large amount of public works and improvements has been effected; yet after the expiration of four years from this time, there will not only be no public debt, but the revenue arising from protecting tariff duties alone will amount to more than the expenditure by upwards of 10,000,000 dollars.'' He adds that the president has suggested that the surplus revenue should be divided among the states in proportion to their representation.[64]

Several English travellers explain the currency system of the country. This was provided for in 1786 on the basis of the decimal system. Theoretically, eight coins were put out in three metals, but the copper cent and half-cent were not issued until 1792 and the gold coin until 1800, when the mint was established in the new Federal city. That the new system of coinage was much needed is very evident. Scarcely three of the states, we are told, agreed as to the value of a dollar. "In South Carolina [it was] four shillings and eight pence, at New York eight shillings, and in the New England states, six shillings." Priest says that in spite of the superiority of the new system, the government had great difficulty in persuading the people to abandon their old currency of pounds, shillings, and pence for practical use.[65]

At the close of the Revolution, the country was flooded with paper money which was issued both by the Government and by the separate states, and which circulated side by side with a varied assortment of foreign coins of all

[64] Ferrall, p. 234.

[65] On currency system of the United States, see Melish, II, 451-453; Palmer, pp. 264-265; Shirreff, Preface, iii; Wansey, p. 154; Neilson, p. 140; Priest, pp. 63-65; Woods, pp. 187-188.

denominations. This paper money was an inconvenience, to say the least. Great was the stranger's discomfiture to find that the notes which he had bought in a certain town decreased in value the farther he went from the place. Fearon said that if he had understood the system when he landed in America, he could nearly have paid his expenses by buying in one place the notes of that to which he was going.[66] In 1818-20, the paper of Western banks was 30% under par in the East, according to James Flint.[67] The notes of unchartered banks especially were often bought in a distant town at from 10 to 40% discount.[68] Very little specie was seen. Isaac Holmes states that sometimes a bank which was circulating notes for millions of dollars would possess not more than $200,000 in real money. In 1828, the whole amount of gold and silver coined in the United States since the establishment of the Government was only about $23,000,000. Money was especially rare in the West, where a system of barter necessarily took its place.[69] Blane says that nowhere was the state of affairs worse than in Kentucky, after the close of the War of 1812. By the flooding of the state with paper money, and the subsequent contracting of the currency to specie on the part of the Federal government, hundreds of people were ruined. In 1822, paper in Kentucky was only half the value of specie. "No such thing as a silver coin of any kind was to be seen in circulation, and notes of 4, $6¼$ and $12½$ cents formed a substitute for copper." As anyone was at liberty to issue these and other promissory notes below the value of a dollar, worthless money flooded the country.[70]

[66] Fearon, p. 233; Duncan, II, 309.
[67] Flint, p. 136.
[68] Fearon, pp. 232-233.
[69] Holmes, p. 211, also p. 213; Candler, p. 442; Blane, p. 256; Brothers, p. 63. [70] Blane, pp. 256-257; Faux, p. 119.

To avoid the use of this valueless paper, the people resorted to the curious scheme of cutting a silver or a Spanish gold dollar into quarters or eighths and using the parts for small change. Many travellers speak of having been obliged to resort to this "cut money," as it was called. The custom was liable to abuse, of course, as unscrupulous people often cut a dollar into five or nine parts and passed the pieces off as fourths and eighths.[71]

Most of the comments on the banking system made by travellers during these years, reveal the lack of organization and the general confusion that prevailed. Several observers give us the history of the United States Bank, which came into existence in 1791 with a charter which was to extend over a period of twenty years.[72] The first differences between the Federalists and the Democrats had to do with the bank system. Owing to the outbreak of the war with Great Britain, and the unpopularity of the Federalists at the time the charter expired, the latter was not renewed, and the United States Bank ceased to exist. Vigne says that in three years the loss to the country was estimated at not less than $46,000,000. In 1816, the second bank was incorporated at Philadelphia, with a twenty-year charter and a capital of $35,000,000. Seventy thousand shares were subscribed by the government, about one-fifth of the whole. It was the beautiful, white marble building of this institution that many observers commented on. It was copied from the Parthenon, with a Doric portico, and Ionic pillars brought from Italy.

It is difficult to trace after this the rapid increase in banks. In 1818, James Flint remarked that even in Ken-

[71] For "cut money," see Fearon, p. 232; Flint, pp. 130-131; Blane, p. 257.

[72] For United States bank, see Martineau, II, 76-85; Vigne, I, 46 ff., 54; Coke, I, 50-51; Tudor, I, 89-90.

tucky, there were two branches of the United States bank, thirteen of the Kentucky bank, and fifty independent institutions, some of which were not in active operation. In Ohio, he says, there were thirty chartered banks, and a few others which had not yet "obtained that pernicious distinction."[73] Dalton explains the difference between chartered and unchartered banks. The chartered banks were in the hands of stockholders, who thus became proportionately responsible to the community for the debts of the bank; in an unchartered bank, everything rested on the credit of the proprietor.[74] So intense did the "bank mania" become that riots occurred sometimes at sales of stock.[75] "Institutions have been suffered to multiply until almost every village has its bank," says one traveller in 1821.[76] Of course the majority were doomed to destruction, and their money was refused in all government transactions. According to James Flint, the paper of only two of all the banks in Indiana, Ohio, Kentucky, and Tennessee was accepted in 1820 in payment for public lands.[77] Hodgson says that, because of the bank mania, more than one-half of the city of Richmond and one-third of Baltimore were mortgaged in 1820, as real estate had fallen 50 to 75%.[78]

By 1832, we are told, the United States Bank had established branch institutions in twenty-two of the principal commercial cities in the Union.[79] Several years before 1836, the time of the expiration of the charter, rumor stated

[73] Flint, p. 133; Fearon, p. 282.
[74] Dalton, p. 61.
[75] Brothers, p. 54.
[76] Dalton, p. 60.
[77] Flint, p. 219.
[78] Hodgson, II, 85.
[79] Coke, I, 51; Vigne, I, 54.

that the latter would not be renewed. Most of the observers who touched upon this matter analyzed Jackson's reasons for vetoing the renewal. He objected on the grounds that the bank was a monopoly, that it had failed to establish a uniform and sound currency, and that a large proportion of those owning and managing it were foreigners, who, in case of war, could turn the funds to the advantage of their own country. The government deposits were withdrawn from the Bank of the United States in 1833, and it was proposed to establish a national institution, founded on the credit of the government and its revenues.[80]

[80] Tudor, II, 461-462; Abdy, II, 128; Martineau, II, 84-85; Coke, I, 51-52.

CHAPTER VIII

EDUCATION AND LITERATURE

THE general diffusion of education in America filled every citizen of the United States with pride, and offered to the visitor the clue to much that was distinctive in American life. Contrary to the policy that prevailed in most European nations, the government here took a hand, immediately after the settlement of the country, and, through its wise ruling, it was brought about that the English traveller, as he passed through the various states, saw practically no native American of school age or over who could not at least read and write and "cast accounts."[1] This universality of education was looked upon as one of the most promising indications of the future prosperity and stability of the Union. "The wise men of the United States," we are told, "know that the maintenance of their liberties greatly depends upon having an enlightened population who are capable of appreciating the advantages they enjoy; for despotism is more strongly supported by ignorance than by armed thousands."[2] It was not until near the end of our period that universal education became a problem, owing to the thousands of foreign emigrants that annually entered American ports. In the thirties, the traveller Abdy noticed a quite different state of affairs from that which

[1] For comments on the universality of education, see Vigne, II, 71-72; Holmes, p. 382; Duncan, I, 110; Bristed, pp. 318-319; Blane, p. 480; Hodgson, I, 144-145 (also note); Murray, II, 201.
[2] Blane, pp. 480-481.

prevailed in earlier days. As he quotes from the "American Annals of Education," one is forced to believe him, pessimist though he usually is, when he says that in 1833, there were more than a million free white children in the United States left without an education. More than this, another million of youth between the ages of fifteen and twenty had no chance to acquire anything beyond the most rudimentary instruction.[3]

In the promotion of public education, New England was always far in advance of the other sections of the country, perhaps, as it was suggested, because of the greater democracy of her colonial institutions.[4] In 1800, the towns were authorized to raise money by taxation to build and furnish schoolhouses. Before that time, it was said, the work had gone on in the basements of churches, or in any other place that was convenient. Usually there were two terms a year; one in the summer, taught by a young woman, who had usually small children and girls in her classes, as the boys and young men were employed at that time in agricultural labor; another throughout the winter, usually taught by a young man. The curriculum was more extensive than in the summer session and offered to both boys and girls instruction in "reading, writing, arithmetic, English grammar, geography, the Constitution of the United States, the Constitution of Massachusetts, and the dictionary."

This early system, travellers tell us, was extended in Massachusetts to include the whole progress of a child's education from four to seventeen years of age, or until he entered college. We are told by Stuart that in 1829 there were sixty-eight free schools in Boston alone, at which there

[3] Abdy, II, 333.
[4] D'Arusmont, p. 306; Hamilton, I, 217-220; Boardman, p. 294; Rich, p. 80; see p. 76 ff. for history of American public schools; Shirreff, p. 53.

were taught (besides reading, writing, and arithmetic) bookkeeping, ancient and modern languages, grammar, mathematics, navigation, geography, history, logic, political economy, rhetoric, and moral and natural philosophy. Shirreff criticises this statement of Stuart's and says that it refers to the grammar schools only. The teachers for this higher instruction were required to be college graduates.[5] In 1831, Tudor estimates that there were 10,000 children in the public schools of Boston alone;[6] out of a population of 60,000 in Massachusetts, about this time, according to Stuart, there were only 400 beyond the age of childhood who could neither read nor write.[7] In 1828, the school tax in the state was said to be about $3.50 upon every thousand of income, an imposition which fell heavily upon no one; least of all, upon the poor. Some Englishmen wondered that the latter did not consider themselves objects of charity under the system, but this consideration seems to have had little weight in New England, where free education was accepted as one of the prerogatives of the American citizen.[8]

It is impossible to take up in detail. the progress of the establishment of free schools in all of the states. The trend of education, like that of the settlement of the country, was gradually westward, and the problems of Massachusetts were repeated with local variations in all of the states. Connecticut's educational fund came from the interest on money from sales of land in New Connecticut, a great tract of land in northern Ohio. There was a close

[5] Stuart, I, 206-207; also Shirreff, pp. 53-54.
[6] Tudor, I, 373.
[7] Stuart, I, 206, says 60,000 (in 1829); this is probably a misprint for 600,000, as the census report gives the population of Massachusetts in 1830 as 603,359.
[8] See Hall, B., II, 165-166; also Rich, p. 77.

connection in this state between the educational and ecclesiastical systems, which is said to have entailed complications all through this period.[9] New York made brave efforts for a free school system, especially during the governorship of DeWitt Clinton, but she was seen to be encumbered with a large board of Regents of the University of the State of New York. The public school system was not fully established till 1821.[10] New Jersey and Delaware were more backward still. Both states possessed plenty of academies, but were deplorably deficient in elementary free schools.[11] Pennsylvania was still struggling with her educational problems in 1835, when a traveller observed that though she was one of the wealthiest and most populous states in the Union, she had done less for the education of her people than had many of the inferior states. The situation was said to be complicated here by the high price paid for child labor in the factories, and the consequent indifference to the claims of education on the part of the poorer classes.[12] Maryland's schools were, for the most part, private institutions, or the kind established by benevolent or ecclesiastical societies.[13] In Virginia, there were two colleges, Melish says, one of which, William and Mary, was highly endowed; also several academies, but the education of the masses was neglected.[14] One Englishman, in 1834, made inquiries concerning the public schools of Richmond. He found there were none, "but then, there were capital races. The training that was denied to the children was

[9] For Connecticut's schools, see Blane, p. 472 ff.; Hamilton, I, 216; Duncan, I, 109; Kendall, I, 106-107, also Chap. XXVIII.

[10] For New York school system, see Dalton, p. 96; Boardman, p. 69; Abdy, I, 9, also 26-27.

[11] Melish, I, 146, 181.

[12] Abdy, III, 157.

[13] Melish, I, 190.

[14] Melish, I, 241-242.

given to the horses." Virginia had, just at this time, given over to one college one-third of the money she had granted for schools, and the provision had aroused little or no opposition.¹⁵ The case was the same in North Carolina, the inhabitants of which had granted half of her money to academies. In Georgia, a great deal of attention was said to be paid to the school system. The college at Athens was well endowed, provision was made for an academy in every county, and there were some good common schools, but there was admitted to be still room for inprovement. South Carolina, too, had a college at Columbia, and several other colleges and academies throughout the state. The towns, especially Charleston, were rather well supplied with schools, but those in the country districts were very poor. In 1832, the state was reported to have educated in her free schools only 8,390 children. Melish says in justification of all the Southern states that the population was too thin to admit of the establishment of such schools as existed in the North.¹⁶

In the West, the difficulty of administering the public lands donated to education was increased by the natural obstacles to concerted action. Here, too, Melish intimates that the mistake was made of beginning at the top rather than at the bottom, of encouraging the founding of colleges at the expense of elementary education.¹⁷ That the diffusion of education throughout the Union was, in spite of all difficulties, so general as to be almost invariably commented on by the foreigner, speaks volumes for the substantial nature of the curriculum of all these free schools. This was strictly utilitarian, and was in most cases limited to read-

---

15 Abdy, II, 212-213, 253-254.
16 For other comments on Southern schools, see Melish, I, 263, 284, 291; Abdy, II, 254-255; Wakefield, p. 69.
17 Melish, II, 187, 220.

ing, writing, and arithmetic, the last of which was said to come "by instinct, among this guessing, reckoning, expecting and calculating people."[18] That this practical curriculum was considered the best-fitted for a republican population by some foreigners is evident. Duhring remarked in regard to it: "If possible, occasion must be given to every person to instruct himself in the general principles of true religion, in his moral and civil duties, in reading and writing, in the fundamentals of arithmetic, and of some mechanical art, or of some handicraft work. You may without risk of harm instruct the people in the general outlines of geography and history, but no farther. More is neither wanted nor desirable for the well-being of the social system."[19] A certain amount of education was said to be carried on in the home, especially in the isolated Western districts settled by Eastern emigrants, and on the plantations of the South.[20]

In many parts of the Union, exclusive of the New England states, the Americans adopted a type of elementary education which proved very useful.[21] This was the Lancastrian system of public schools, which had been instituted in America by Joseph Lancaster in 1818. Its application was observed to be very practical; it instituted a monitor and pupil-teacher scheme by which the older and more advanced students helped to teach and look after the younger ones. Certain advantages were obvious where funds were low, teachers scarce, and the desire for primary education great. Several travellers mention visits to these

[18] Hamilton, I, 217; Shirreff, p. 55.
[19] Duhring, p. 138.
[20] Melish, I, 241-242; Duhring, p. 144.
[21] For discussion of Lancastrian schools, see Fearon, p. 38; Hamilton, I, 83-84; Holmes, p. 382; Duncan, I, 235; Hall, B., I, 26; Ferrall, p. 204.

schools. They were to be seen in the greatest number in
Pennsylvania, though many of them existed in New York
State, and they were found here and there throughout the
South and West. Ferrall visited in New Orleans two
schools of this type supported by taxes on five gambling
houses. Lancastrian schools met with a great deal of
criticism on the score of sacrificing the interests of the
brighter students and retarding their progress.

The chief aim of the academies, which represented the
degree of education above that of the elementary school,
was to prepare for college. In 1815, there were 265 of these
institutions in the country, and they differed from one another as much as our preparatory schools do today. Some
of them were endowed, as those in the Southern states already discussed. In all, a tuition fee was charged. About
1818, Boston schools of this type were said to charge $100
per annum for a classical education.[22] None of them, for a
long time, admitted girls into the same school with boys.
Mrs. Trollope visited a Cincinnati girls' school in which
young ladies sixteen years old took degrees in mathematics
and moral philosophy, not knowing very much about either,
according to the author.[23]

Some dissatisfaction was expressed by visitors at the
lack of corporal punishment in American schools, though
others regarded it as an improvement.[24] Isaac Holmes remarked that a serious hindrance to American education
was the independent spirit of the children. It was noticed,
too, that in a great many details, Americans followed the
Scotch system rather than that of the English public

[22] For academies, see Rich, p. 80; Fearon, pp. 112-113.
[23] For education of girls, see Bristed, p. 371; Melish, II, 59;
Mrs. Trollope, I, 114; Martineau, II, 226 ff.
[24] Holmes, p. 382; Hamilton, I, 85 ff., also 217; D'Arusmont, pp.
310-311; Fidler, p. 40 ff.

schools, as being more suited to their character and aims.[25] Many things in the English system were repugnant to Americans, for instance, the "fagging," which might have a salutary effect on a society in which class distinctions existed, but which no independent American youth would have tolerated.[26]

In spite of the fact that the college seemed to flourish at the expense of the common school in so many of the states, there seems to have been among visitors a great deal of criticism of the higher education which they observed. In the first place, a comparatively small proportion of the population went to college.[27] Tudor says that in 1827 the entire number of students in the New England colleges amounted to 1,399; 431 of these came from Massachusetts. Then, higher education in America was charged with being superficial;[28] the curriculum embraced too many subjects to insure careful training in each. "The process of mental cultivation in America," said Murray, "is somewhat analogous to their agricultural system; in both cases they look too extensively to the quantity of produce immediately to be obtained and pay too little attention to the culture and improvement of the soil." In four years the average American college student skimmed lightly over a field which might well occupy one's attention for a lifetime. Necessarily, the standard of acquirement was low. An Englishman quotes in italics an extract from the report of the trustees of the University of Pennsylvania in regard to the course of study. "Its object is to communicate *a profound and critical knowledge* of the *classics; an extensive acquain-*

[25] Melish, I, 127; Shirreff, p. 54; Hall, B., I, 26; Hamilton, I, 222.
[26] Shirreff, pp. 55-56; D'Arusmont, p. 310; Hamilton, I, 85.
[27] Tudor, II, 523; Bristed, p. 328; Duncan, I, 171-172; Ouseley, p. 201.
[28] Latrobe, II, 65; Rich, p. 83; Murray, I, 162, II, 209.

tance with the *different branches* of *mathematical science, natural philosophy,* and *chemistry,* combined with *all the varieties of knowledge* comprehended within the sphere of *moral philosophy, logic, rhetoric, metaphysics,* and the *evidences* of *Christianity.* This course of instruction *will occupy FOUR YEARS.*" [29] The Americans were in too much of a hurry to be thoroughly educated; the young men were too anxious to get out into the world of affairs, to marry, perhaps to seek their fortunes in the West.[30] No one seemed to appreciate the intrinsic value of higher education, and the policy of the states was a parsimonious one in that they were slow to render pecuniary aid. The colleges therefore struggled in poverty and inefficiency, unable to command the services of such presidents and professors as might raise their standard. "The phrenzy for multiplying colleges all over the Union," said Bristed, "and the custom of appointing illiterate men as trustees, also retard the progress of literature by diminishing the number of students at each college, and thus lessening the means of its support, and by ensuring the appointment of absurd regulations and impractical plans of study." The number of colleges, however, was defended on the score that they achieved the aim for which they were founded — to produce not a very few learned scholars but more well-informed and liberal-minded citizens.[31] The usurpation of the professorial chairs by clergymen was sometimes deplored. This custom prevailed in colleges of all denominations, and was criticised on the score that the average American clergyman had not that wide culture which would redeem his lectures from narrow sectarianism.[32]

[29] Hamilton, I, 350-355.
[30] See Hall, B., II, 170; Mrs. Trollope, II, 177; Fidler, p. 60; Bristed, pp. 327-328; Duncan, I, 111.
[31] D'Arusmont, p. 307.   [32] Bristed, p. 329.

The attitude toward the classics, as indicated by the college curriculum, was another point at issue.[33] It was charged that they were too much neglected because they did not fit the student with practical equipment for his later busy existence. If the classics were not studied within the college walls, would they meet with any regard outside, asked the traveller. What was to give the American youth "that deep-laid foundation of knowledge which can resist the business and dissipation of life?" It was no wonder, then, that the wealthy young college graduates sought pleasure in horse-racing and billiards rather than in literature. One cannot help being amused at the dismay which this insensibility to the nobler forms of literature caused the occasional traveller. The Rev. Isaac Fidler, in 1832, tried to establish a school in New York City for the study of the Eastern languages, but met with no success. "The Americans do not yet want anything with the East Indies," said the friend whose advice he asked. "They are not colonizing other countries, but peopling their own; and have more need of being taught how to handle the axe or the spade than how to read the Hindoostanee." "A little further inquiry," said the discomfited Fidler, " . . . soon induced me to abandon the intention of opening a school for instruction in Eastern languages."[34]

One of the earliest pictures that we have from travellers of an American college is given us by Weld, to whom we owe many vivid descriptions of institutions of various kinds. In 1795, he visited William and Mary College, an institution which he says Jefferson described as bearing a very close resemblance to a brick-kiln, except that it had a

[33] For attitude toward the classics, see Duhring, p. 135; Blane, p. 470; Hall, B., II, 169-170; Murray, II, 188; Fidler, p. 79; Murray, I, 162, also II, 188, 209.

[34] Fidler, pp. 38-39.

roof. "The students were about thirty in number when I was there," he says; "from their appearance, one would imagine that the seminary ought rather to be termed a grammar school than a college; yet I understand the visiters since the present revolution, finding it full of young boys just learning the rudiments of Greek and Latin, a circumstance which consequently deterred others more advanced from going there, dropped the professorships for these two languages, and established others in their place. The professorships as they now stand are for law, medicine, natural and moral philosophy, mathematics, and modern languages. The bishop of Virginia is president of the college, and has apartments in the buildings. Half a dozen or more of the students, the eldest about twelve years old, dined at his table one day that I was there; some were without shoes and stockings, others without coats. During dinner, they constantly rose to help themselves at the side board. A couple of dishes of salted meat and some oyster soup formed the whole of the dinner. I only mention this, as it may convey some little idea of American colleges and American dignitaries." [35]

Harvard, as being the oldest and best known of the American institutions, was most often visited by sight-seeing foreigners.[36] As a result, many books of travel include a description of this college, which seems to have impressed the average visitor with no overwhelming admiration, though there are many instances of politely eulogistic description, especially by those observers who had letters of introduction to the president, or to some other officer of

[35] Weld, I, 167-168; Matthews, W., I, 171.
[36] For Harvard College in this period, see Tudor, I, 370-371; Duncan, I, 74 ff.; Finch, pp. 131-132; Bristed, p. 328; Kendall, III, 11-17; Rich, p. 84; Hamilton, I, 165-166; Vigne, II, 230-231; Boardman, p. 293; Fidler, p. 66.

the institution. Most of the visits recorded took place in the period from about 1820 to 1835. Duncan visited it in 1818 or 1819; at the time it boasted twenty professorships, from three to four hundred students, and a library of over 17,000 volumes. The latest mention of the institution in this period (in 1833) estimates the number of volumes in the library at 35,000. It was universally conceded to be the best collection of books in the country. "The whole annual expenses of an undergraduate," says Vigne in 1832, "do not amount to more than $250; for this he is boarded and instructed by the lectures of different professors on every subject from divinity to obstetrics and medical jurisprudence." [37] The study of the American constitution was always a part of the curriculum, as it was in all American colleges, and largely accounted, it was said, for the general diffusion of information in regard to the principles of government.[38]

Yale was the institution that, after Harvard, provoked the most interest.[39] Its site was described with enthusiasm as being an ideal place for such a college. Wansey, who visited it in 1794, was much disappointed at the general poverty of the institution. He says that the library was especially poor, and the books in bad condition. Tudor says in 1829, that it had 496 students, who were boarded and educated for $125 a year. In 1833, we are told by Abdy, the average expense was $175 a year, and the number of students 541. "One sitting-room with two bed chambers is, as at Harvard College, appropriated to two students, who take their meals at a common table with the rest of

[37] Vigne, II, 231.
[38] See Palmer, p. 191.
[39] For Yale College in this period, see Duncan, I, 125 ff., 147-148; Wansey, pp. 50-51; Tudor, II, 523; Abdy, III, 205-206; Kendall, I, Chap. XXVII.

the community. There are two halls, at one of which the board is about one dollar seventy-five cents per week — at the other, one dollar twenty-five cents." The college at this time was under the care of the president, who also taught, six professors, and eight tutors. The curriculum included chemistry, with mineralogy and geology, mathematics including astronomy, rhetoric, divinity, Latin, and Greek.

Other colleges that were sometimes visited were Columbia, Princeton, and the University of Pennsylvania. Boardman thus describes Columbia about 1830: "It is a large and handsome stone building surrounded by noble trees. The number of students is considerable, and they enjoy the advantages of a good library, as well as an extensive philosophical apparatus. New plans are being formed, as the present plan of study is considered by many to be too strictly classical." Finch, about 1833, visited this institution and was particularly impressed by the medical school, where he attended lectures by the celebrated Dr. Hosack. "The students attend lectures," he says, "on Botany, Chemistry, Surgery, Medicine, and Anatomy; and the most inattentive cannot fail to carry with them some fondness for those pursuits."[40] The University of Pennsylvania was also noted for its medical school. Thomas Hamilton says it was the most distinguished of American colleges out of New England. Princeton apparently was not much visited, perhaps because of its retired location. One traveller, however, says that it was as nearly perfect as an institution of that kind could be.

It must be confessed that foreign opinion of American literature throughout this period was not very high. Impatient at the limitations of the Americans in this respect,

[40] For other colleges, see Boardman, p. 68; Finch, p. 23; Kendall, III, 195-197, 270; Neilson, p. 49; Hamilton, I, 348-349; Duncan, I, 171-172; Finch, p. 281; Fidler, p. 58.

many Englishmen gave the subject little real thought, and either criticised hastily, or dismissed the matter contemptuously, like Sydney Smith with his question — "Who reads an American book?" In his attempt to account for this backwardness in literary matters, Bristed quotes Buffon's theory that something peculiar in the soil and climate of America produced a constant diminution of physical and mental strength in her inhabitants, and says soberly that he cannot believe it.[41] Broad-minded visitors saw, back of the condition, certain causes which, as long as they operated, would necessarily retard literary progress in America. "Literature in America is an amusement only," said Thomas Cooper in 1794. " . . . though not in abilities, the Americans are inferior to you in the opportunities of knowledge; their libraries are scanty, their collections are almost entirely of *modern* books; they do not contain the means of tracing the history of questions; this is a want which the literary people feel very much, and which it will take some years to remedy."[42] Bristed gives the best summary of the conditions under which the Americans labored: "A comparatively thin population, spread over an immense surface, opposes many serious obstacles to the production and circulation of literary effusions; the infancy of its national independence, and the peculiar structure of its social institutions do not allow a sufficient accumulation of *individual* and *family* wealth to exist in the community, so as to create an effectual demand for the costly or frequent publications of original works; the means of subsistence are so abundant, and so easy of attainment, and the sources of personal revenue so numerous, that nearly all the active talent in the nation is employed in prosecuting some commercial or agricultural or professional pur-

[41] Bristed, pp. 306-307.
[42] Cooper, p. 64; Howison, pp. 344-345.

suit, instead of being devoted to the quieter and less lucrative labors of literature; the scarcity of public libraries and of private collections of books, renders any great attainments in science and erudition exceedingly toilsome and difficult; the want of literary competition, rewards and honors, the entire absence of all government *patronage,* whether state or federal, together with the very generally defective means of liberal education, necessarily deter men of high talents from dedicating themselves *solely* to the occupation of letters; and consequently prevent the appearance of those finished productions, whether in verse or prose, which can *only* find an existence when the efforts of genius are aided by undisturbed leisure and extensive learning."[43]

Some optimistic observers, nevertheless, were hopeful in spite of the situation. One could not yet expect, they said, that in the higher branches of literature and arts the Americans would equal the older nations, yet they were constantly making great progress, and were beginning to evince a growing taste for the better things of life. This improvement was sometimes attributed to their system of free education, or to the unshackled press, which disseminated knowledge of what was passing in the world.[44]

On the other hand, the faults which we have already pointed out in the system of education, formed, to the minds of some travellers, an insuperable obstacle to the progress of American literature. Not until some wiser generation should take control of American affairs and do away with the "vulgar and unworthy sophistry" concerning education, would ignorance cease to be perpetuated. Particularly was this true of the clergy, who wielded a great influence, and whose education and training were, even as late as 1830, considered to be shockingly deficient.

[43] Bristed, pp. 310-311.   [44] Fowler, p. 213.

Many saw in the conditions no promise for the future. "In the present generation of America," says Hamilton, "I can detect no symptoms of improving taste or increasing elevation of intellect. On the contrary, the fact has been irresistibly forced on my conviction, that they are altogether inferior to those whose place, in the course of nature, they are soon destined to occupy. Compared with their fathers, I have no hesitation in pronouncing the younger portion of the richer classes to be less liberal, less enlightened, less observant of the proprieties of life, and certainly far less pleasing in manner and deportment."[45]

In spite of this lack of taste, and the indifference to literature that the average American displayed, it was generally agreed that many books were sold in the United States. The majority of these were reprints of foreign books, chiefly English, in their original dress, or in the cheaper American copy. It is interesting to see what English works were most in demand.[46] Novels and poetry were in the lead; they were imported immediately upon publication and quickly reprinted. Fearon says that in Philadelphia "Manfred" was received, printed, and published all in one day. Walter Scott, Lady Morgan, Moore, Miss Edgeworth, Miss Porter, Lord Byron, and Mrs. Opie were all favorites. The popularity of the Waverley novels was a subject of frequent comment. Blane says that he met several gentlemen in St. Louis (1822) who had read them all, including "The Fortunes of Nigel," which had

[45] Hamilton, I, 358-359, 366-367.

[46] For discussions of the English books read by Americans, see Neilson, p. 76; Fearon, p. 35; Mrs. Trollope, I, 125-127, II, 155. See Wansey, Appendix, pp. 264-270, for partial list of books reprinted in America, also of original works. Alexander, II, 125-126; Howison, p. 343; Candler, p. 349; Martineau, II, 310-311; Duncan, I, 108; Holmes, p. 381; Blane, p. 196; Fearon, p. 35; Bristed, p. 311.

just been published. He was told that the books were received in that remote district fourteen to sixteen weeks after their first appearance in England. "Scott is idolized," said Miss Martineau, "and so is Miss Edgeworth, but I think no one is so much read as Mr. Bulwer. I question whether it is possible to pass half a day in general society without hearing him mentioned." Hannah More was said to be more popular than Shakespeare — which fact was accounted an indication of the religious taste of the people, though her popularity was probably just as great in England at this time. Another favorite was Mrs. Hemans. Carlyle was declared to have a great influence through "Sartor Resartus," especially on the clergy, whose preaching in many cases he had been the means of regenerating. Wordsworth's admirers were few but enthusiastic, as was also the case with those of Lamb and Coleridge.

Standard works, like those of Shakespeare, Milton, Blair, and Johnson were reprinted in great numbers, as were theological books of an orthodox nature. Bristed remarked that moral essays and history were not much read, and that books on metaphysics, political economy, and philosophy slept securely on the shelves.

The knowledge of foreign literature other than English was limited to numerous light French novels, and to some scientific works in French. There was no interest in Spanish or Portuguese literature, it was noticed. One traveller mourned the fact that Rousseau, Voltaire, and Diderot, who were read by the older generations of Americans, had by 1830 become known "as naughty words rather than as great names."[47] In regard to the stream of French novels that came into the country, an American writer uttered a protest. "It might be expected that the injudicious instruction of so many of our youth in a language which is

[47] Mrs. Trollope, II, 154.

improperly regarded by many parents as a merely ornamental accomplishment, without any care being taken to make it an introduction to profitable associates or useful books, would naturally lead too many to dangerous sources of amusement. . . . O, this business of learning modern languages is full of abuses. One abuse, however, sometimes prevents a greater one. It is a comfort, in this view, to reflect that probably not one in ten of those who pretend to learn French ever reads it, and not one in fifty, perhaps, ever speaks it.''[48]

The more enlightened booksellers and publishers constantly tried to direct public taste into better channels. Many of these booksellers were men of property and education, and did much for the cause of literature in America. Philadelphia had a number of fine book shops, as well as a multitude of publishing houses, and more than one traveller mentions a visit at Eastburn's in New York, or at Carey and Lea's in Philadelphia, places that were deservedly popular.[49] The country suffered from lack of good reviews, and a consequent dearth of high standards of judgment. A great deal of trash was insistently demanded and promptly turned out by American publishers. ''The press teems,'' complained an English visitor, ''with those mushroom productions of folly which are engendered by the conjunction of ignorance with impertinence.''[50]

The quality of the product of the American press was considered quite inferior to that of books printed in England.[51] The type was poor, and the paper of a cheap

[48] See "Notes of a Traveller" (anon.), p. 57.

[49] Rich, p. 103; Hamilton, I, 369; Davis, J., p. 225; Fearon, p. 36; Lambert, II, 79; Hall, B., II, 358.

[50] Bristed, p. 311; Hall, B., II, 357.

[51] For remarks on the books printed in America, see Hall, F., p. 14; Hall, B., II, 357; Mrs. Trollope, I, 130; Lambert, II, 79; Fearon, p. 357 ff.; Hamilton, I, 371-374.

quality; the size of the book too, was reduced. One traveller says that the transformation of an English book to an American edition was sometimes very amusing. "The metamorphosis reminds one of a lord changing clothes with a beggar. The man is the same, but he certainly owes nothing to the toilet." Englishmen complained that while Americans could hold copyright in England, the privilege was withheld from the foreigner in America, and that all English books were charged thirty per cent duty at American ports. There was really no reason for this second restriction, they said, as the expense of copyright in England and the cost of transportation served to keep the market for American books.

"If the national mind of America be judged of by its legislation, it is of a very high order, . . . If the American nation be judged by its literature, it may be pronounced to have no mind at all." So spoke an Englishwoman who prided herself on regarding sympathetically the land she was visiting.[52] It is quite evident that the majority of travellers who saw the scanty evidences of an American literature agreed with her. During this period, there were but few native writers who received any marked attention from outsiders. The best known of these was Irving, of whose work there were many criticisms,[53] and whose "Salmagundi Papers" met with special approval. "This little work," remarked Lambert, "bids fair to be handed down with honor to posterity. It possesses more of the broad humor of Rabelais and Swift than the elegant morality of Addison and Steele, and is therefore less likely to become a classical work, but as a correct picture of the people of

[52] Martineau, II, 300-301.
[53] See on Irving, Duncan, II, 298 ff.; Lambert, II, 98; Fearon, p. 390; Hall, F., p. 15; Martineau, II, 306; Candler, pp. 373-374; Finch, p. 380; Bristed, pp. 359-360.

New York and other parts of the country . . . it will always be read with interest by a native of the United States." "For amusement, wit, talent, and satire, I could conceive it could have few equals," said the critical Fearon. Lieutenant Francis Hall praised Irving's "History" by Diedrich Knickerbocker, whom he considered deserving of "a niche by the side of Cid Hamet Benengli, and the biographer of my Uncle Toby." Miss Martineau was inclined to regard Irving indulgently as a writer who had enjoyed a certain amount of vogue which was already passing. Candler explained his popularity by the fact that he was such an anomaly in American literature that he aroused curiosity; then, too, his position was enhanced by favorable articles in the English *Quarterly Review*, the publisher of which also brought out Irving's "Sketch Book." "He has the merit of a flowing, mellifluous style," said Candler, "produced by the collocation of the words in so artful a manner as to conceal the labour which has been bestowed. . . . He has been represented as almost a faultless writer; yet it may be observed that his words, however beautifully arranged, are often ill-chosen; that his narratives are unskillfully told; and that his humor, happy as it sometimes is, is often as misplaced as roses in a garden by the side of poppies. If his famous tale of the Legend of Sleepy Hollow be read with attention, it will be found to contain numerous faults of the kind I have mentioned."

While native tales depicting American life were generally admired, the novels were not regarded with much consideration.[54] Judge Hall of Cincinnati and John P. Kennedy, author of "Swallow Barn," were ranked among the best known and most deserving of the story writers. Miss

[54] Howison, p. 344; Latrobe, II, 67; Fearon, p. 386; Rich, pp. 128-129; Mrs. Trollope, II, 155, 158; Davis, J., pp. 162-163; Bernard, pp. 250-252; Hall, B., II, 74; Martineau, II, 305.

Sedgwick's novels received commendation for their "moral beauty." English travellers, with one or two exceptions, seem to have been entirely oblivious of the work of Charles Brockden Brown, and to have read very little of Cooper.[55] In the most lengthy and most significant criticism of this latter novelist, he is accused of not being true to life, and of drawing poor female characters. Perhaps Mrs. Trollope had Cooper in mind when she said of American fiction-writers: "Even in treating their great national subject of romance, the Indians, they are seldom either powerful or original." Bristed remarked that there was not much scope for fiction in America, as the country was quite new, and all that had happened in it from the first settlement was known to everyone. "There is, to be sure, some traditionary romance about the Indians; but a novel describing these miserable barbarians, their squaws and their papooses, would not be interesting to the present race of American readers." [56]

Very little American poetry could be regarded as above mediocrity.[57] A few travellers mention Bryant as a promising figure, but most of the native talent in this form of literature was scattered among the members of a small group that is now almost forgotten by the average reader. Some of the native effusions that are mentioned are Barlow's "Columbiad," "which is left even at home to gather dust"; Pierrepont's "Airs of Palestine," characterized as "palpably an imitation of Campbell"; the poems of Per-

[55] On Cooper, see Finch, p. 29; Martineau, II, 306-309; Mrs. Trollope, II, 155-158.

[56] Bristed, pp. 355-356.

[57] For comments on American poetry, see Martineau, II, 307; Finch, p. 29; Mrs. Trollope, II, 156-157; Rich, p. 130; Kendall, I, Chap. XIII; Moore, T., "Epistle to Thos. Hume" (1853 ed.), p. 318 ff.; Lambert, II, 98; Fearon, p. 390; Candler, p. 370-371; Faux, p. 136 (also note).

cival, the "Fredoniad" by Dr. Emmons, and Paulding's "Backwoodsman," which was criticised as "delightfully original" but as wanting more polish before it was adapted to the drawing room. Woodworth drew from Isaac Holmes the praise that his work was "far beyond mediocrity" and that he was among those who would have prospered if he had been well-paid for his first production.

The long lists of works of various types found in travel literature, show the trend of American interests at this period. Travellers praised the books of William Wirt, whose "Life of Patrick Henry" was nevertheless criticised as being spoiled by bombastic language.[58] Works of the type of Wilson's "Ornithology" were in great demand, and were conceded to be authoritative.[59] The general historical books, for many reasons, did not meet with approval. Marshall's "Life of Washington" was "too cumbersome,"[60] Ramsay's "History of the United States" was "incomplete." Books of travel, even those describing America, were generally disappointing, as in the case of Long's "Expedition to the Rocky Mountains," and Hunter's "Captivity among the Indians." Griscom's "Year in Europe," Silliman's "Tour in England," and Somerville's "Letters from Paris" were discussed critically.[61] One field of writing in which the Americans could well take pride was that of the state and local histories, of which there were many promising specimens. These included, according to Bristed, "those of New York and New Jersey by Smith, Trumbull's History of Connecticut, Ramsay's History of South Carolina, . . . Holmes' Annals, McCall's Georgia, Darby's Louisiana, and Stoddart's Account of that State, Jefferson's Notes on Virginia, Borman's Maryland, Prud's [Proud's] Pennsylvania, William's Vermont, Belknap's

[58] Fearon, p. 387; Candler, p. 367.
[59] See Hall, F., p. 14.
[60] Candler, p. 358.
[61] Ibid., pp. 361-366.

New Hampshire, Hutchinson's Massachusetts, Sullivan's Maine, Minot's History of Shay's Rebellion and Drake's History of Cincinnati, together with divers accounts of the late war, mostly written in that crusading style which revolutionary France has rendered current throughout the world."[62]

Very few English writers could conscientiously say that the United States had as yet produced any work of great value, especially before the time of Cooper and Irving. "Liberty and competition," said *The Edinburgh Review* in 1810, "have as yet done nothing to stimulate literary genius in those republican states. Noah Webster, we are afraid, still occupies the first place in criticism, Timothy Dwight and Joel Barlow in poetry, and Mr. Justice Marshall in history; and as to the physical sciences, we shall merely observe, that a little elementary treatise of botany appeared in 1803; and that this paltry contribution to natural history is chronicled by the latest American historian among the 'remarkable occurrences since the Revolution.' In short, federal America has done nothing, either to extend, diversify, or embellish the sphere of human knowledge. Though all she has written were obliterated from the records of learning, there would, (if we except the works of Franklin) be no positive diminution either of the useful or the agreeable."[63]

The Americans, it was complained, wasted what literary talent they had on political pamphlets and newspaper articles, two forms of literature developed by the peculiar circumstances of American life. "Their party pamphlets," it was admitted, "though disgraced with much intemperance and scurrility, are written with a keenness and spirit

[62] Bristed, p. 355.
[63] *Edinburgh Review*, XV, 445 (January, 1810).

that is not often to be found in the old world."[64] Foreigners believed that the United States had no consistent policy in its intellectual habits. To this fact were attributed the rise and early decline of the numerous reviews and periodicals, few of which continued very long.[65] The general tone of this kind of literature was considered low; it was prejudiced and partial in criticism, and too often took on a political cast. Lack of originality was another charge, in that they copied long extracts from English reviews; on the other hand, the native effusions which they sometimes included were mediocre and discreditable. *The Portfolio*, founded by Joseph Dennie, was one of the few long-lived periodicals in the United States at this period. Travellers make little more than casual mention of *The Analectic Magazine, The American Review, The Boston Anthology, Knickerbocker Magazine, The Portico, The American Magazine and Review*, and *The Southern Review*. In 1810, Obadiah Rich says, there were twenty-four periodicals in the United States, of which *The Portfolio* and *The Anthology*, he says with truth, were the most important. In 1830, there were about one hundred. In 1832, *The American Monthly Review* was founded, especially for the criticism of American literature. *The North American Review*, begun in 1815, was obviously considered the best of this type of literature in the country. It was ranked with *The Edinburgh* and *The Quarterly*, both of which were reprinted in America. In 1820, the reviewer of the "Sketch Book" for *The Edinburgh* says: "We have received a copy of the 'North American Review or the Miscellaneous Journal.'

[64] Ibid., II, 448 (July, 1803); Bristed, pp. 316 ff.
[65] On periodicals and reviews, see Holmes, p. 381; Bristed, pp. 317-318, 358; Martineau, II, 308; Kendall, II, 307; Davis, J., p. 223 ff.; Rich, p. 105; Hodgson, II, 241, note; *Edinburgh Review*, XXXIV, 161 (1820); Candler, pp. 354-356; Duncan, I, 83; II, 302.

EDUCATION AND LITERATURE   227

It appears to us to be by far the best and most promising production of the press of that country that has ever come into our hands. It is written with great spirit, learning and ability, on a great variety of subjects; and abounds with profound and original discussions on the most interesting topics." Its chief defect was said to be that it was prejudiced in favor of American institutions. Its attempts at wit, too, were not appreciated, though it was admitted that it had not "fallen into the flippant petulance so observable in the early numbers of the Edinburgh Review, nor into the arrogant acerbity so often conspicuous in the Quarterly." One traveller compliments its editor on his good sense in translating quotations from foreign authors, instead of taking for granted that the knowledge of those languages was too widespread to require their translation. A great source of anxiety to the pious Duncan was the fact that it issued from the Harvard press. "Would that its theological opinions were from a purer source," he says, "happily they are but seldom obtruded."

Literary interest, for the average American, was centered in the newspapers. According to one report, there were, in 1801, 203 of these in the United States; in 1810, there were 358; and about 1830, the number had increased to 1,200.[66] Several travellers make the statement that there were, all through this period, more newspapers published in the United States than in any other country in the world. Melish (1810) gives a table showing the annual publication of about 22,500,000 copies.[67] One saw newspapers everywhere in America. There seemed to be no family too poor to have one; travellers commented on seeing carters and draymen reading them while waiting for

[66] Rich, pp. 104-105.
[67] See Melish, II, 457-458; Tudor, I, 23; Lambert, II, 78; Ouseley, p. 207; Davis, S., p. 75.

work, or while driving along in their wagons.[68] Many foreign language papers existed before the end of this period.[69] Besides, it was the duty, rather than the amusement, of every man to see just what his government was doing, therefore each took the paper that suited his particular kind of politics. His busy life forbade the spending of much time in reading; with a newspaper he could "pick up critical dictums or read snatches of English poetry in the intervals of work."[70] Knowledge acquired in this way might be superficial, but to its general diffusion was attributed that knowledge of the world, that lack of rusticity, peculiar to the laboring classes of America.[71] It was a cheap form of education too; in 1823, papers were only 1¾d. each; Lambert says they never cost more than 2½ or 3d. sterling; to send them to the subscribers cost one cent within the state and a cent and a half outside the state.[72]

The newspaper of those days was quite different from the one with which we are familiar today.[73] There was no reporting of events, except the proceedings of Congress. Nor was this regarded as a fault in some cases. Boardman quotes an example of national egotism that he found in a native paper. "We thank Heaven that our papers are barren of interest to the recorders of midnight assassinations, of accidents by flood and field, of the tale of strife and blood, and of titled profligacy. We reprint; they (the English) originate." Though Boardman says that this was not strictly true, he adds, "no namby-pamby trash of

[68] Mrs. Trollope, I, 129; Boardman, p. 76; Lambert, II, 498.
[69] D'Arusmont, p. 303.
[70] D'Arusmont, p. 303; Mrs. Trollope, I, 128-129.
[71] Lambert, II, 499.
[72] Lambert, II, 498; Rich, pp. 104-105; Ouseley, p. 205; Hamilton, II, p. 387.
[73] For contents of American newspapers, see Boardman, p. 78; Fearon, p. 384; Lambert, II, 499.

fashionable movements, routes, and dinners find their way into its columns." Important speeches in the legislature or in Congress were given in full, though they often took up the greater part of the space in the paper. Political dispute always made up a portion, as did the latest news from England; in the coast states, an important addition was the shipping news.

The unrestrained liberty of the press and the amount of personal abuse which the papers consequently exhibited, were a source of astonishment to the foreigner.[74] "The Americans are a calm, rational, civil, and well-behaved people," said one traveller, "not given to quarrel or to call each other names; and yet if you were to look at their newspapers, you would think them a parcel of Hessian soldiers. . . . Were a foreigner immediately after landing, to take up a newspaper, he might suppose that the whole political machine was about to fall to pieces, and that he had just come in time to be crushed in its ruins." No public official, no matter how high his office, was safe from attack; no epithets were too virulent to use. Englishmen complained that even personal honor was not immune; enemies, political and otherwise, used the newspaper for the exposure of private matters, the public mention of which often disgusted the foreigner; innocence of the charge was no protection from this mud-slinging. It was regretted that the dependence of newspapers on the masses of people for support, forced them to cater to the taste of their patrons.

The Englishman with a sense of humor often found the advertisements the most amusing part of the paper.[75] For

[74] Fearon, p. 384; Holmes, p. 382; Duhring, pp. 134-135; D'Arusmont, p. 298; Hamilton, II, 384-387.

[75] See Coke, I, 36; Boardman, p. 76; Neilson, p. 77; Mrs. Trollope, II, 152; Lambert, II, 204; Bernard, pp. 194-195.

the publisher, advertisement was cheap, as there was "no duty on materials, publication or contents," but the advertiser paid a high rate. Neilson says that in 1823 the usual price was sixty-two and a half cents for the first insertion and twenty-five cents for subsequent ones. Runaway slaves and apprentices were described, often in circumlocutory style. Warnings were sent out against swindlers. New publications were advertised in gushing language. Mrs. Trollope copied from a New York paper an advertisement of a partnership volume of poems of a Mr. and Mrs. Brooks. "The lovers of impassioned and classical numbers may promise themselves much gratification from the muse of Brooks, while the many-stringed harp of this lady, the Norna of the Courier Harp, which none but she can touch, has a chord for every heart." Lambert says that the newspapers published in Charleston (about 1808) were so full of advertisements that they left little space for the news of the day. He goes on to say, "Advertisements are often drawn up in ludicrous style; and rewards offered for lost or stolen property, that are not likely to facilitate their recovery. *One cent* reward is sometimes offered to those who will apprehend a negro fellow or wench that has absconded from a plantation, and I once saw a reward of thirty-nine lashes offered for the recovery of a pair of saddle-bags that had been stolen off a horse."

The interest in the drama and the theatre increased steadily throughout this period. The hostile attitude which the colonists had held toward this form of entertainment changed first to acquiescence, then to interest, in the years after the Revolution.[76] An English traveller in 1797 commented on the changed point of view in Boston, where dramatic pieces had been introduced a few years before

[76] Weld, I, 23; Kendall, I, 164-168; Wansey, p. 114; Boardman, p. 280; Rich, p. 123.

under the name of "moral lectures." Now that theatres
were licensed, Americans had run to extremes and had *two*
theatres in Boston, involving an enormous expense which
was bound to bring the venture to bankruptcy.[77] Some of
the performers in these Boston theatres received as much as
twenty pounds a week; Mrs. Whitlocke (Mrs. Siddons' sister) even commanded the enormous salary of 180 pounds
sterling for six nights. Wansey had seen this same actress
in 1794 in Philadelphia when she played in Mrs. Inchbald's "Every One Has His Faults"; so "elegant and
convenient" was the theatre and so well-behaved was the
audience that the Englishman could almost believe he was
in his native country.[78] Weld comments on this same Philadelphia theatre in 1795, and says that, though it was neatly
fitted up, it was hardly large enough for the town.[79]

After 1800 we have a constant repetition in travel literature of brief mention of theatres visited by observers.[80]
Some of these accounts are favorable to actors and audience, some quite otherwise. Certain facts stand out, however, in regard to the American theatres at that time. One
of these is the scarcity of women in the audience, which
was commented on frequently, and at widely separated
dates.[81] When Tyrone Power played in 1833 in New York
to a crowded house, there were, he says, not more than
twenty women present. He noticed the same thing in Boston. Other travellers remarked, too, that women never,
under any circumstances, sat in the pit of the theatre; also

[77] Priest, pp. 157-158.
[78] Wansey, p. 113.
[79] Weld, I, 23-24.
[80] See, for instance, Murray, II, 130; Fearon, p. 209; Boardman, p. 79; Hall, F., p. 12.
[81] For presence of women in American theatres, see Power, I, 62, 123; II, 172; Hall, F., p. 12; Fearon, p. 87; Boardman, p. 80; Howison, p. 335.

that they did not take the performance seriously enough to put on their best clothes for it. Another curious trait of behavior was noticed among the male part of the audience, many of whom kept on their hats during the performance. When Lieutenant Coke saw Forrest in "The Gladiator" in Philadelphia (1832), the house was so crowded, and so many of the men in the dress circle wore their hats, that the poor stranger caught only an occasional glimpse of the star performer during the evening.[82] Mrs. Trollope's denunciation of American manners at the theatre is classic. At Cincinnati, she saw men sitting during the performance without their coats, and with their shirt sleeves tucked up, and their heels higher than their heads. The spitting and the noises were perpetual. One could attribute this very conveniently to the unsettled state of the Middle West, if the same charge were not made against audiences in Philadelphia and New York. Shirreff says that he saw, in New York, an example of Mrs. Trollope's influence. Some men in the boxes assumed a lounging attitude, and immediately the audience called out "A Trollope, a Trollope!" until the offenders withdrew. Coke says that he saw the same thing happen at the American début of Fanny Kemble in New York.[83]

The Americans were accused generally of indifference to the claims of the drama, though the performances were usually well-attended. "Though the play was pathetic and affecting," said Howison, after a visit to a New York theatre, "I could not discover the least symptom of feeling in any of the faces around me; and this observation harmonized with the idea I had previously formed, of the total

[82] Coke, I, 37; Fearon, p. 86; Power, I, 62; Howison, p. 335; Welby, p. 320.
[83] Mrs. Trollope, I, 186, II, 88, 194; Janson, p. 225; Neilson, p. 19; Shirreff, p. 9; Coke, I, 154.

insensibility of the American people to all the finer sources of emotion."[84] Fearon tells of a very funny burlesque of "Hamlet" that he saw in Pittsburg; the audience, he says, "did not move a muscle of their *intelligent* faces."[85] English actors confessed that they missed the constant laughter and applause with which they were greeted at home, but that the audience was usually attentive and intelligent.[86]

Most of the plays seen in American theatres were of English authorship and acted by English players.[87] Travellers went in the larger cities to see Hodgkinson, or Miss Fontenelle, or some other actor whom they had admired at home. A great deal of Shakespeare seems to have been given, judging from the parts played by such persons as John Bernard and Tyrone Power. Bernard gives us the best English account of the stage from 1797 to 1811. He came to America at the earlier date, under the management of Wignell of Philadelphia, who paid him a salary of a thousand pounds a year. For fourteen years, he was an important figure on the American stage, playing comedy parts chiefly, but also acting as manager, going about to all the large cities, and not only enjoying life to the full but collecting information on every phase of American life. He tells us so much about the theatre that it is difficult to determine just which of his remarks are most valuable. In speaking of the great profit which often accrued to the managers in the early days of this period, he says: "But however advantageous to the manager's pockets, this was also a period that respected his pleasures. It gave him lit-

[84] Howison, p. 335.
[85] Fearon, p. 210; also Hall, F., p. 12.
[86] Bernard, p. 50; Power, I, 63, 88, 123 ff., 210.
[87] Fearon, p. 365; Mrs. Trollope, I, 182-183, II, 87; Boardman, p. 204; Shirreff, p. 10; Fearon, pp. 209-210.

tle other trouble than to attend to his treasury. Both his system and actors were imported from England, and the one, for some years, worked as well as the other. The modern rage for novelties had not yet set in. The drama itself was a novelty which proved quite sufficient. Thus a manager, in those days, was not perplexed for new pieces, or obliged to risk a fortune on those abysses of capital — modern ballet and spectacle. As yet, even the melodrama was unknown to the stage; the nearest approach to it being serious pantomimes, such as 'La Perouse' and 'Don Juan,' . . . Shakespeare and O'Keefe were the staple attractions, varied with Farquhar and Cumberland, Goldsmith and Sheridan, and the performances also were only three nights a week, and yet probably averaged as much as our six. Thus he had nothing to do at the opening of the season but to put up a cast of the common stock plays — 'Hamlet,' 'Othello,' the 'West Indian,' and the 'Rivals'; with the 'Padlock,' the 'Poor Soldier' and the 'Agreeable Surprise.' The actors were all studied, hardly a rehearsal was needed, and if the fever kept off, the house filled and closed without one jar to his nerves. . . .

"The actor's position was quite as good as the manager's. As yet, the supply of talent was not beyond the demand, and consequently incomes maintained a fair level. There was no salary at this time under four pounds a week, while many reached as high as twelve and fifteen, and as benefits occurred at least twice a year, these ordinarily added one-third to the amount. If an actor were unemployed, want and shame were not before him: he had merely to visit some town in the interior where no theatre existed, but 'readings' were permitted; and giving a few recitations from Shakespeare and Sterne, his pockets in a night or two were amply replenished."[88]

[88] Bernard, pp. 262-263.

Boardman says that many of the English plays were altered "to suit the political atmosphere of America."[89] It was complained, too, that many of the more vulgar jokes of Great Britain were transported to America and appeared on the native boards.[90] The stage Yankee had by 1830 become a part of the American tradition, and the inability to outwit him became one of the favorite themes of the native play.[91] Englishmen seem not to have visited many plays written by Americans. Coke saw Mr. Hackett in a very interesting one in Philadelphia, called "The Raw Kentuckian, or The Lion of the West." The scene was laid in the more uncivilized Western region, and the play delighted the audience exceedingly, though to the visitor many of the expressions used were unintelligible.[92] This same traveller saw Forrest, the "Roscius of America," in Dr. Bird's "The Gladiator." The most famous American actor all through this period was Thomas Cooper, the first great tragedian.[93] John Bernard tells us a great deal about him, of his charm as an actor and as a man. Vigne saw him in Philadelphia in 1831, and admired his voice particularly. "I remember that I thought him dignified but rather stiff, without however being the least awkward in his acting." The scarcity of American actresses was commented on; Tyrone Power, particularly, believed that there was a great deal of latent dramatic talent in America, and expressed his wonder that American women did not turn their good looks, easy carriage, and imitative ability to that account.[94]

[89] Boardman, p. 80.
[90] Fearon, p. 365.
[91] Boardman, p. 81.
[92] Coke, I, 35-37; Mrs. Trollope, II, 194-195.
[93] For Cooper, the tragedian, see Bernard, p. 164; Vigne, I, 45; Janson, p. 254.
[94] Power, I, 211.

236   THE ENGLISH TRAVELLER IN AMERICA

Many museums and libraries were visited by the stranger, especially in the larger cities.[95] One traveller accounts for the diffusion of science through the country by the founding of museums in every town of over 10,000 inhabitants. The institution most frequently visited was Peale's Museum at Philadelphia. It was noted for its collection of minerals and fossil remains, among which the traveller never failed to observe the bones of the mammoth found in New York State in 1801.[96] This same city had in 1824, it was said, sixteen public libraries, containing a total of over 65,000 volumes; of these institutions the Franklin Library was the oldest and most progressive.[97] Melish, in 1810, quotes the history of it from the "Continuation of the Life of Franklin." At the time when the English merchant visited it, the library owned 14,000 books. It was run by a stock company of 500 subscribers, each of whom paid $40 entry fee and $2 annual dues. The former, Melish thought, was too high for the mass of people, while the annual tax might be easily increased without laying too heavy a burden upon the people. In Baltimore, where the library was considered very excellent, and where the same subscription system was in use, the dues were $4. Strangers commented on the fact that in any American library, strangers could use books freely and could take them out overnight by paying a small fee.

New York had, of course, many libraries with facilities

[95] For some museums visited, see Howison, pp. 335-336; Boardman, p. 192, 195-196; Lambert, II, 80; Kendall, III, 24-25; Candler, p. 447; Finch, p. 26.

[96] For Peale's Museum and the mammoth, see Fearon, pp. 153-6; Janson, p. 193; Neilson, pp. 146-150; Finch, pp. 86-87; Duncan, I, 195; Faux, p. 67; Flint, p. 55 (note 21).

[97] For the Franklin Library, see Finch, p. 86; Hall, B., II, 366; Duncan, I, 200; Davis, J., p. 42; Boardman, p. 176; Janson, pp. 187-191; Melish, I, 162-164, 184.

for circulating books. The New York Library had been founded before the Revolution; in 1806, it contained 10,000 volumes; in 1832, it had doubled that number.[98] Howison complains of the custom here of making everyone who took out books pay for a week's loan, no matter how rapidly he read the book. The Englishman carefully explains that the reason for this is the great slowness with which Americans read, and which would make it extremely expensive for them to borrow books by the night. Fowler mentions another important library in New York—the Society Library. This, he says, had been established in 1740; during the Revolution, its 3000 volumes were destroyed or carried away by British troops. It was re-established in 1789, and by 1830 had 20,000 volumes.[99] The contents of the Library of Congress in Washington were also, it was said, destroyed by the British, in the War of 1812, but in 1832, this flourishing institution had 20,000 books.[100] Melish mentions an interesting one which he visited in Lexington, Kentucky. It had in connection with it a *youth's* library, which seems to have been an innovation, a prototype of our "Children's Room" of today.[101]

Probably the finest library throughout this period was the Athenaeum at Boston. Early in the century, it contained 18,000 books; about 1830, this number was said to have increased to 30,000. It was noted especially for its fine collections of casts, coins, and medals.[102]

It has already been said that the frequent mention of

[98] For the New York Library, see Howison, p. 344; Boardman, p. 72; Lambert, II, 79-80.
[99] Fowler, pp. 225-226.
[100] Mackenzie, p. 39.
[101] Melish, II, 187.
[102] For the Athæneum in Boston, see Duncan, I, 84; Alexander, II, 314; Fearon, p. 105; Boardman, p. 277; Power, I, 121; Hamilton, I, 241; Kendall, II, 2*i*

lectures indicated their popularity with Americans. "It has become the fashion in New York," an observer tells us, "to attend lectures on moral philosophy, chemistry, mineralogy, botany, mechanics, etc., and the ladies in particular have made considerable progress in those studies. . . . The desire for instruction and information indeed is not confined to the youthful part of the community; many married ladies and their families may be seen at the philosophical and chemical lectures, and the spirit of inquiry is becoming more general among the gentlemen."[103] The investigations of the American Philosophical Society were known all over the world, we are told, and its library in Philadelphia was supposed to be a particularly fine one. In New York was another organization of the same type, known as the Lyceum of Natural History.[104]

No discussion of means for promoting culture in this period would be complete without some mention of "Wistar parties."[105] These were the meetings of an organization in Philadelphia which was founded by an eminent physician for whom the club was named. It met weekly, for the encouragement of science and literature, and had a great influence on the thought of the country. To it came noted men from foreign countries, and several English travellers tell of the profitable evening spent at one of these meetings, which brought together men of different interests, and promoted free interchange of opinion.

The results of America's progress in the fine arts met with small consideration from the stranger. The collections were very indifferent, and the quality of American

[103] Lambert, II, 95-96; Boardman, p. 279; Hamilton, I, 241.
[104] See Hall. B., II, 328, 366.
[105] For "Wistar parties," see Alexander, II, 271; Finch, p. 88; Harris, W. T., p. 76; Boardman, p. 212; Hall, B., II, 339; Hamilton, I, 334-335.

work poor.[106] The best known names in the arts were evidently those of Trumbull and Washington Allston.[107] Trumbull was commissioned to paint a series of national pictures for the Hall of Congress, for each of which he was to receive $4000. Howison saw his "Surrender of Cornwallis" and found it very inferior and "unfortunate in choice of subject." "Col. Trumbull is the most ladylike painter in the world; his colors appear to be laid on with the utmost timidity; he shows as much aversion to strong shadows as the Chinese do, and his faces have an expression of red-cheeked stupidity about them which denotes a corresponding want of soul in the artist."

There was some attempt at ornamental architecture in the cities, in the churches, and other public buildings. The Capitol at Washington sometimes received praise.[108] Bristed remarked that "the city hall of New York, a marble edifice, probably surpasses in magnificence and beauty every European building out of Italy."[109] But on the whole, the opinion of American art was a mean one, as Englishmen did not hesitate to affirm. Some of the critics tried to indicate the reasons for this, and to hold out promise for the future. "With regard to the *fine arts*," said Bristed, "our *sculpture* extends but little beyond chisseling grave-stones for a church yard, and our *painting*, for want of individual wealth, is chiefly confined to miniatures, portraits, and landscapes. . . . But American genius is equal to that of Europe for the fine arts, as it is evident from the United States having produced West, Trum-

---

[106] Mrs. Trollope, II, 84; Bristed, p. 364; Howison, p. 337; Coke, I, 133; Hall, F., p. 171; Candler, p. 446; Fearon, p. 85.

[107] Mrs. Trollope, II, 84; Boardman, p. 277; Howison, p. 337; Bristed, pp. 363-364; Vigne, II, 234-235.

[108] See, for instance, Candler, pp. 448-450.

[109] Bristed, p. 364.

bull, Stuart, Copeley, Allston and Leslie. The Academies of the fine arts at New York and Philadelphia contain some fine paintings, and a few good pieces of sculpture, imported from Europe."[110] One branch of the arts in which the Americans were conceded to excel was engraving, especially of the practical sort. The bank notes, for instance, turned out by American engravers were the finest of their kind.[111] The quality of American art was indeed, some travellers said, as good as one could expect, considering the small amount of patronage artists received, and the peculiar circumstances of American life, which put small value on aesthetic pleasures. "The trade of a carpenter," said one indignant observer, "opens up an infinitely better prospect [than painting], and this is so well-known that nothing but a genuine passion for the art could beguile anyone to pursue it."[112]

It seems to have been the common belief among travellers that the Americans prided themselves on speaking the English language more correctly than did the English themselves.[113] Nothing was more galling to the latter than to be complimented on the purity of their language, by people of the United States. Coke says that he was frequently told by casual acquaintances in the States, "Well, I should have imagined you to be an American, you have not got the *English brogue,* and aspirate the letter *h* when speaking."[114] In spite of the fact that there was no standard pronunciation of the English language in America,

[110] Bristed, pp. 363-364.
[111] See Holmes, p. 379; Duncan, I, 203.
[112] See Mrs. Trollope, II, 174; Hall, F., pp. 175-176; Holmes, p. 378.
[113] On this belief, see Blane, pp. 504-505; Duncan, II, 304; Coke, I, 154-155; Abdy, I, 186; Kendall, II, 172; Chap. XLIX.
[114] On uniformity of language, see Bristed, p. 335; Candler, p. 327; Vigne, II, 70; Stuart, I, 326.

it was noticed that there was more general uniformity throughout the land, than in most European countries. In no place, except perhaps among the Pennsylvania Dutch, was an unintelligible jargon spoken. The constant movement of the population, too, helped to unify vocabulary and pronunciation. "To travel by the mail for two or three hundred miles," says Vigne, "and to sit beside a coachman who spoke as good English as the one with whom I first started, had, certainly, at least, I thought so, the effect of shortening the distance."

Americans were said to be more careless in regard to grammar and syntax than were Englishmen. This was especially true of the educated classes; the lower types of people spoke more correctly than did the same class of people in England. The deficiency in grammar arose perhaps, as one traveller suggested, from the lack of necessity for endeavor to free one's self from provincialisms, and from the fact that attention was seldom called to the niceties of language. The use of careless phrases, or slang, was much deplored; Candler thus expresses himself: "Some amongst them seem too fond of adopting those cant expressions, which from time to time, become current with persons who affect the airs and behavior of coachmen, stable-boys and the like; which expressions were condemned by Swift, as the most ruinous of all corruptions in language." [115]

The greatest curiosities to the foreigner were the changes in the pronunciation and in the use of words. Captain Basil Hall records an amusing altercation with a New York school mistress. During a visit to the school, he criticised her pronunciation of certain words. "I could not resist saying," he remarks, "that in England, the word

[115] For carelessness in language, see Hamilton, I, 227; Abdy, I, 186; Duncan, II, 306; Candler, p. 331; Vigne, II, 75.

combat was pronounced as if the *o* in the first syllable were written *u,* cumbat; and that instead of saying *sh*ivalry, the *ch* with us was sounded hard as in the word, chin; and that I believed the dictionary alluded to [Walker's] would bear me out in this." When the teacher protested, he carried on the argument until she took refuge in "You in Scotland may do as you like, but we Americans have a perfect right to pronounce our words as we please."[116] Four or five years later, Boardman, on a visit to Boston, heard a young Harvard orator pronounce "chivalry" and "chicanery" in the manner approved by Captain Hall. "He pronounced them both in a style that would have fully satisfied the gallant officer, and made ample amends for the pertinacity of the New York 'school madam' who did not conceive that 'they who go down to the sea in ships' are the best models in scholastic matters."[117]

Candler says he recalls only two or three instances of difference from English pronunciation. "The second syllable of *engine* is pronounced long, . . . the word *learned,* which, when used adjectively, we pronounce in two syllables, they pronounce in one. We make *clerk* rhyme to *bark,* while they make it rhyme to *jerk.* There are most likely some others which either escaped my notice or have slipped from my memory."[118] Other travellers were not willing to dismiss the subject so lightly. "The American error," says Vigne, "is detected in the formal and decided accentuation of particular syllables in several common words, and in the laughable misuse of many others; and not in any mispronunciation of the language generally. The word *engine,* for instance, is pro-

[116] See Hall, B., I, 28-29.
[117] Boardman, pp. 293-294.
[118] Candler, pp. 328-329.

nounced *engīne;* favorite, *favorīte;* European, *Eurōpean,* etc."[119] The word *does* was remarked to be split into two syllables and pronounced *do-es, where* became converted to *whare,* and *there* to *thare.* Words like *oratory* and *dilatory* were pronounced with the penult syllable long and accented, *missionary* became *missionairy, angel, ângel,* and *danger, dânger.*[120]

It was the wrong use of words, generally, that amused or provoked the stranger, according to his disposition.[121] This failing called forth many comments, and not a few imaginary dialogues. Duncan analyzed the peculiarity as consisting "partly in an uncanonical use of good English words, partly in illipses to which we are not accustomed, partly in an occasional word surviving from the language of the first settlers, and in a few that appear to be of republican coinage." Vigne tells us what some of these are: "There are about half a dozen words in constant use, to which the English ear is unaccustomed in the sense they are meant to convey; such as to fix, to locate, to guess, to expect, to calkilate, etc. The verb 'to fix' has perhaps as many significations as any word in the Chinese language. If anything is to be done, made, mixed, mended, bespoken, hired, ordered, arranged, procured, finished, lent, or given, it would very probably be designated by the verb 'to fix.' The tailor or boot-maker who is receiving your instructions, the bar-keeper who is concocting for you a glass of mint julep, promise alike to fix you, that is, to hit your taste exactly. A lady's hair is sometimes said to be fixed, instead of dressed; and were I to give my coat or my boots

[119] Vigne, II, 70.
[120] Hamilton, I, 227-228; Abdy, II, 315-316.
[121] For wrong use of words, see Davis, J., p. 221; Melish, I, 128; Vigne, II, 73-74; Duncan, II, 305; Lambert, II, 505-507; Woods, J., "The English Prairie," pp. 345-346.

to a servant to be brushed, and to tell him merely to fix them for me, he would perfectly understand what he had to do. There is a marked peculiarity in the word—'clever.' In America, a man or woman may be very clever without possessing one grain of talent. The epithet is applied almost exclusively to a person of an amiable and obliging disposition. . . . According to their meaning, Bonaparte was terribly stupid, and Lord North was a very clever fellow indeed.'' Hamilton says that when he had had drilled into him this use of "clever," he fondly believed that all trouble with the word was at an end. "It was not long, however, before I heard of a gentleman having moved into a *clever* house, of another succeeding to a *clever* sum of money—of a third embarking in a *clever* ship, and making a *clever* voyage, with a *clever* cargo, and of the sense attached to the word in these various combinations, I could gain nothing like satisfactory explanation.'' [122]

Another stumbling block was "fine," which was distorted from its usual meaning. To say that a certain lady was a "very fine woman" was to compliment her exclusively on her intellectual abilities. "Smart" for "clever"; "elegant" in the sense signifying good quality; "balance" for "remainder"; "fall" for "autumn"; "roosters" for "cocks"; "lengthy" for "long," are only a few of the perversions most frequently noticed and commented on.[123] What the outcome of these changes would be was distressing to think of. "Unless the present progress of taste be arrested," we are told, "by an increase of taste and judgment in the more educated classes, there can be no doubt that, in another century, the dialect of the Americans will become utterly unintelligible to an Englishman, and that the nation will be cut off from the advantages

[122] Hamilton, I, 228.
[123] Hamilton, I, 229; Palmer, pp. 129-131; Candler, pp. 329-331.

arising from their participation in British literature. If they contemplate such an event with complacency, let them go on and prosper; they have only to *progress* in their present course, and their grandchildren bid fair to speak a jargon as novel and peculiar as the most patriotic American linguist can desire."[124]

[124] Hamilton, I, 230.

CHAPTER IX

RELIGION

THE United States, in refusing to establish an official church, followed a policy which set it apart from the other nations, and which produced effects that are incalculable in their value and extent. The lack of an established church might perhaps be supposed to lead to a state of irreligion, or at the very least, to a carelessness in regard to religious matters, and a reluctance to support enterprises of that nature. There was danger that the spiritual things of life would be left more or less to chance, or would be made dependent on the popular whims of the day. Then too, the policy of allowing everyone to choose his own church tended, it was said, to lead to injudicious and thoughtless choosing, and to encourage a multitude of sects.[1] That most of these fears were unfounded was made evident by the actual observation of strangers who were interested in the working-out of the country's religious policy. The Americans were seen to be a race neither of atheists nor of fanatics. The churches were filled with people voluntarily attending and supporting their chosen denomination by contribution; generally a state of harmony prevailed among the congregations. However one might doubt the practice of religion in the United States, the public profession of it was nowhere else more conspicuous.[2] Of course there were many travellers who,

[1] Hall, B., II, 118-120; Murray, II, 205-206; Mrs. Trollope, I, 149-150; Hamilton, II, 397-399; Ashe, p. 28.
[2] Boardman, p. 44; D'Arusmont, p. 319; Stuart, I, 332.

even in the face of these conditions, saw only hypocrisy in so much religious activity, and remarked that churches were not religion, and that however pleasing it might be to see such a promising state of affairs, one would be more confident of the sincerity of the Americans if more honesty were seen in the every-day dealings between man and man.[3]

Public opinion in the United States was observed to be distinctly on the side of the church-goer. This may be seen early in the history of the nation in the various acts of legislation on this matter in the different states. In several parts of the country, limitations were put on the citizen who refused to affiliate himself with one of the many sects. By 1822, Blane says, all the States had dropped their restrictions, but he reckoned without Massachusetts, which until 1834 enjoined upon its citizens the necessity of contributing to some form of religious organization, though the choice was unrestricted.[4]

It was not, however, because of legislation on the matter that public opinion was so firmly fixed on the side of the church. There is no doubt that the Americans as a whole seemed to be a distinctly religious people.[5] This might be accounted for, as was suggested, by the close connection that they made between virtue and the church, and by their belief that a high standard of morality could not exist without that institution. Part of this interest may have originated in New England, the inhabitants of which, in their emigrations, disseminated a joint interest in churches and schools along the ever-receding Western frontier. At any rate, in spite of the wave of infidelity which

[3] Hodgson, II, 211, 213; Welby, p. 307; Fearon, p. 113.
[4] Blane, p. 482; Melish, I, 245-246, 292-293; Fearon, p. 114; Tudor, I, 421; Martineau, II, 349; Vigne, II, 231-232.
[5] D'Arusmont, p. 319; Hamilton, II, 395-396; Bristed, p. 414; Mrs. Trollope, I, 150.

entered America with the interest in French affairs after the Revolution, it is evident that the person who went so far as openly to avow himself an atheist or a deist was exceedingly rare.[6] This is testified to by the attitude toward the few who thus exposed themselves to public criticism. Sutcliffe, the English Quaker, was one of those who actually saw a professed atheist. His account of the meeting must be given in his own words: "At the last mentioned inn [in central New York] I met with what I had often heard of, but seldom, if ever, seen, a professed atheist, who openly avowed his opinions. To all appearance he was sober; yet his arguments were extremely weak; indeed, the poor man seemed to be laboring under great mental darkness. Although this was the season of the year in which thunder and lightning are not common, yet it was very remarkable that during the time the atheist was delivering his opinions, the thunder rolled over our heads in an awful manner, accompanied with vivid flashes of lightning. . . . This, however, he seemed not to regard." Tudor met, on his passage to America, two daring atheists with whom he foolishly tried to argue. One of them avowed himself a worshipper of Neptune, a confession which had the result of reducing the Englishman to a horrified silence. Frances Wright, in her lectures through the country, was regarded by the majority of the population as a disseminator of radical doctrines which were wicked but fascinating. Englishmen as well as Americans regarded her in this light. Ferrall in 1832 uttered a warning against her, and her opinions, quoting *The New York Enquirer* to the effect that her followers were already boasting of the results of her lectures. " 'Two years ago,' say they,—'*twenty persons* could scarcely be found in New

[6] On atheists, see Candler, p. 163; Sutcliffe, pp. 146-147; Tudor, I, 4-5.

York who would openly avow infidelity. Now we have
twenty thousand.' "[7] Bristed maintained that in the
South and West there existed societies modelled after the
atheistic organizations of France and Germany. The states
were therefore in danger of being over-run, in a few years,
with "unbaptized infidels, the most atrocious and remorseless banditti that infest and desolate human society."[8]

The passing of the observance of Sunday was a source
of anxiety to some English visitors, just as it must have
been to many Americans. It was in the West and the
South that this was particularly noticeable. Weld, in 1794,
comments on the fact that there was little observance of
Sunday in Virginia, and that the churches were going to
decay.[9] Janson says that the same thing was true of the
Carolinas, where Sunday was spent in "riot and drunkenness."[10] In the winter of 1814-15, the legislature of
Louisiana rejected a bill for the improvement of conditions,
among them the desecration of the Sabbath; the bill was
characterized as "persecuting intolerance."[11] Sunday observance was undoubtedly neglected in the more remote
sections of the country where ministers were scarce, where
there were few churches, and very little religious activity
of any kind.[12] In New England, only scattered traces remained of the severe laws that had distinguished those
states in the days before the Revolution, but Puritan ancestry was discernible in the manners and in the attitude
toward religion. Even by 1835 not much time had elapsed
since the days when a man was forbidden to travel on

[7] Ferrall, pp. 332-333.
[8] Bristed, p. 394; also Martineau, II, 324 ff.
[9] Weld, I, 177.
[10] Janson, p. 103.
[11] Bristed, p. 395; Alexander, II, 17.
[12] Hodgson, II, 222-223; Ferrall, p. 81.

Sunday.[13] Many travellers noticed the custom which prevailed in some of the cities, of throwing chains across the streets during the hours of the church service to prevent vehicles from passing. In the cities all along the Eastern coast, the stranger noticed the attention generally paid to the external observance of the Sabbath, though it was remarked that as one passed out of New England the severity was less evident.[14] Most people regarded this attitude toward Sabbath-keeping in a favorable light. Miss Martineau, however, objected strongly to a custom which must necessarily bring religion down to a ceremonial, and ultimately work evil.[15]

About 1815 to 1818, there seems to have been a great increase in religious activity in the United States. Among the various phases of this was the introduction of the Sunday School.[16] It is true that various embryonic gatherings of this type had been held for several years before 1816. The earliest form originated in Philadelphia in 1791. It was called the "First Day or Sunday School Society" formed on non-sectarian principles by several prominent citizens, including Bishop White of the Episcopal Church, Benjamin Rush, and Mathew Carey. The teachers received compensation, the expenses being defrayed by subscription. By 1800, more than 2,000 pupils had been admitted. It was in 1816 that the present voluntary teaching system was inaugurated. Interest in Sunday schools was aroused, and the institution became an influence for good throughout the

[13] Janson, pp. 101-102; Duncan, I, 117-119; D'Arusmont, p. 319, 321-322; Kendall, I, Chaps. XXIX, XXX.

[14] Mrs. Trollope, II, 95; Duncan, II, 375; Tudor, II, 408; Hodgson, II, 212; Coke, I, 163.

[15] Martineau, II, 341.

[16] For the American Sunday School, see Stuart, I, 207; Cooper, p. 221; Bristed, p. 415; Coke, I, 217; Shirreff, p. 309; Duncan, I, 121, 211, 246; II, 27, 380; Hodgson, II, 212-213.

land. One traveller remarked about 1818 that it had already greatly diminished the ignorance, poverty, and vice of the largest cities. Not the least reason for its influence, it was said, was the fact that it united secular and religious instruction. The principal object of attention seems to have been English reading, with the Bible of course as a text book. John Duncan, whose primary interest was religion, gives us the best descriptions of these schools shortly after they were founded. He visited them whereever he had an opportunity, and never failed to comment on them. Evidently the instruction was of a very simple kind; each student prepared a portion of Scripture of whatever length he wished, a lack of uniformity which, to the mind of the Englishman, greatly diminished the usefuless of the institution.

Another influence for good was the American Bible Society, which was founded as a national institution in 1816.[17] Before that time, there had been many local branches, the work of which had been chiefly restricted to the conversion of the Indians. The national society was said to have by 1818 over one hundred and fifty auxiliary branches, which an enthusiastic Englishman characterized as "organizations which, perhaps, constitute the most important and most comprehensively useful institution that has ever blessed the human race, since the day-star of the *Reformation* first dawned upon a benighted world." The greater part of the Bibles distributed went to the South and West, especially to the Mississippi Valley. Missionaries who went out to that region discovered a shocking state of affairs—a huge tract of land with a scattered population of thousands without a minister or a church. The only form of religious instruction was brought by the circuit riders,

[17] For the American Bible Society, see Hodgson, II, 212-213; Blane, p. 497; Bristed, p. 416 (quotation); Duncan, II, 378.

chiefly Methodists, who appeared at intervals of a month or more, and who scattered stray crumbs of religion which were consumed long before the time of their next visit. To this isolated and often indifferent population, the Society sent thousands of copies of the Bible.

The duties that fell to the average American preacher, and the circumstances which attended his ministration, were characteristic of the national life. Most visitors to his church did not consider his lot a particularly enviable one.[18] In the first place, he held his charge only with the approval of his congregation. When a group of people of the same religious belief wished to found a church, they got together, raised money for the purpose by subscription, and proceeded to "call" the pastor whom they wished. His salary was assured from the rental of the pews, from marriage and baptismal fees, and from voluntary contribution. If he failed to please his congregation, the pastoral relation was severed without much ceremony. Strangers saw many defects in this system; it not only rendered conditions extremely precarious for the clergyman, but it must necessarily affect his moral independence, and the sincerity of the doctrines he expounded.

Another disadvantage was the relatively small income that he received.[19] This was particularly true of the parishes in the country districts. Ouseley, who made a study of the ecclesiastical finances of the United States, maintains that the pay of a travelling Methodist minister was as low a $60 a year in money, if he was unmarried;

[18] On this point, see Bristed, p. 408; Cobbett, p. 244 ff.; Alexander, II, 17; Duhring, p. 44; Murray, II, 206; Martineau, II, 352-353.

[19] On income of clergy, see Coke, I, 216; Abdy, I, 248-249; Ouseley, pp. 120, 127, 129; Fidler, p. 30; Vigne, II, 232; Lambert, II, 269; Martineau, II, 351; Bristed, pp. 413-414; Kendall, I, 222.

about twice that if he was married. These ministers were "boarded around" of course, by numerous parishioners. Lieutenant Coke says in 1832 that the clergyman's salary in small towns was generally $1,000 a year; in cities from $1500 to $2500. Ouseley quotes these figures also, but says the estimate is much too large; he is inclined to agree rather with Fenimore Cooper, who set the average salary, for ministers in New York State at least, at less than $400. It is true that many of the clergy in the smaller parishes were unable to devote their time exclusively to religion, but eked out their salary by teaching or by small farming; in that case they became mere preachers rather than pastors, officiating in the church on Sundays, but attending to few of the multifarious duties which usually fall to the pastor's lot. Too often the minister's salary was supplemented by "donations"—gifts which degraded his office and which often did not afford practical relief to the situation. In the city churches the salaries, it was said, were much more respectable, just as they are today. From the accounts of observers it would seem that they ranged from $1000 to $3000. Lambert tells of an enormous salary paid to a Presbyterian minister in Savannah, Georgia: $3000 in voluntary contributions, besides $7000 from pew rents. He attributes the large sum to the extravagance and enthusiasm in religion that prevailed in America. Miss Martineau said that there was in America only one way by which a clergyman could become wealthy; that was by marriage with a wealthy woman, an occurrence which was fairly common. "Not a few planters in the south began life as poor clergymen, and obtained by marriage the means of becoming planters. Not a few pastors in the north grow more sleek than they ever were saintly, and go through two safe and quiet preachments on Sunday as the price of their week-day ease."[20] Observers noticed that no provision was made for the minister's old age; from what remained of his salary after supporting and educating his usually large family, he was supposed to have saved enough for this exigency; at any rate, the responsibility was his. Another limitation put upon him by lack of finances was deficiency in education.[21] In the larger cities, this condition was not noticed; most of the clergy in the wealthier parishes were men of learning and culture, but in the country a great state of theological ignorance often prevailed among ministers.

Englishmen believed that to most Americans, especially to those in the Northern states, the minister was a man set apart.[22] He was tacitly expected not to take sides on any public question, said the observer, ignorant of the real influence which many American clergymen exerted. As he was the spiritual guide, he must be irreproachable in conduct, "as wise as serpents and as harmless as doves." One traveller quotes a remark of an American: "You know the clergy are looked upon by all grown men as a sort of people between men and women." Travellers remarked that the pastor was not on the same worldly footing with other men. Never was he seen at the theatre or at the dance; to appear at either would have subjected him to contempt and professional disgrace. When cards were introduced at a party, he was expected to leave the house. He was not only debarred from the pleasures of an ordinary citizen, it was said, but from the responsibilities as well. He was exempt from military duty, and by the

[20] Martineau, II, 351.

[21] Hamilton, II, 397-398; Rich, p. 84; Ashe, p. 66; Fidler, p. 35.

[22] For position of the clergy in American life, see Fearon, p. 47; Neilson, pp. 229-230; Martineau, II, 342, 353-363; Ouseley, pp. 124-125; Fidler, pp. 24-25.

constitution of several states, he could hold no civil or military office.

In spite of these drawbacks, the influence of the clergy was conceded to be great [23]—too great, some Englishmen thought, among them Mrs. Trollope, who compares their power to that of the Spanish Catholic priests. "Where equality of rank is affectedly acknowledged by the rich and clamorously claimed by the poor, distinction and preeminence are allowed to the clergy only. . . . I think also that it is from the clergy only that the women of America receive that sort of attention which is so dearly valued by every female heart throughout the world. . . . I never saw, or read of any country where religion had so strong a hold upon the women, or a slighter hold upon the men." Making allowance for the fact that Mrs. Trollope's pen was dipped in gall, there is still an element of truth in what she declared. Other travellers testify to the strong influence of the clergy on the women of the congregation, for which they try to find a reason. It is true that while the men nominally managed the affairs of the church, women devoted themselves zealously to the practical working-out of the schemes for its benefit.

Practically every form of the Christian church, besides the Jewish, existed in the United States. The harmony which prevailed among them, and the apparent calmness with which the American usually took his religion, were a source of astonishment to those who witnessed them.[24] The fact was the more wonderful because of the European reputation which Americans had for dislike of opposition of any kind, and for the ability to become worked up to a state of great excitement over politics, or money matters,

[23] Mrs. Trollope, I, 103-104; Martineau, II, 363; Melish, II, 61-63.
[24] Hamilton, II, 395-396; De Roos, p. 59; Hodgson, II, 229-230 (also note); Fearon, pp. 47-48.

or other vital interests. Many travellers believed that the attitude toward religion was due to apathy and lack of enthusiasm. Fearon even intimated that the Americans regarded personal interest in choosing a denomination, and that they attended a certain church, not because of any religious conviction, but because it was profitable to do so.[25]

Among the numerous sects, especially in the Middle Atlantic States, the Episcopalians generally stood foremost in social influence and in wealth, a great deal of the latter advantage having accrued to them from the income of lands granted before the Revolution.[26] This church seems to have made on English visitors a most favorable impression, undoubtedly because it closely resembled the Church of England. Travellers point out that pure Episcopacy was modified in America to suit the needs of a republican population. Certain parts of the service were eliminated, and others necessarily changed. Most Englishmen noted with approbation the omission of the Athanasian creed. Bishops and clergy were elected by popular vote, and the conventions admitted lay delegates as well as clergy, which was considered a radical change.

This church drew to itself a large proportion of the wealthy and fashionable. De Roos tells of being taken in New York to an Episcopal church especially to be shown the "principal inhabitants," though the friends who accompanied him belonged to another denomination. Hamilton had somewhat the same experience in Boston where he attended an Episcopal service, the congregation of which, he says, was generally composed of the better orders. That

[25] Fearon, p. 46.
[26] For remarks on the Episcopal church, see Boardman, p. 45; Ouseley, p. 121; Fearon, p. 47; Bristed, p. 412; Blane, pp. 488-489; De Roos, pp. 59-60; Hamilton, I, 159; Candler, Chap. XIII (entire); Flower, pp. 92-93; Woods, p. 193.

this condition of affairs in the church did not always meet with approval is evident from the remark of a traveller that the reason for the greater proportion of Episcopalians than Presbyterians among the fashionable was that the Presbyterians cared less for dress. Another attraction was the organs, of which the Episcopal churches generally had the monopoly. It was noticed that deists attended the churches of this denomination much more freely than they did the services of any other sect, a fact which might be a source of either reproach or pride to the Episcopalians, according to the personal point of view.

Probably the best-known Episcopal churches in America in this period were Trinity and St. Paul's, both in New York City. Practically everyone who visited Trinity commented on its monuments to Captain Lawrence of the "Chesapeake" and to Alexander Hamilton, also on the cemetery with its record of 160,000 to 200,000 burials. It also had the distinction of possessing the only chime of bells in the city.[27] St. Paul's was one of the first churches in the country. It also had two notable monuments: one erected to Thomas Emmet, brother of the famous Irish orator, and the other to Cook, the actor, erected by Kean of the Drury Lane Theatre.[28] Boston, too, had its Trinity and its St. Paul's, which the stranger sometimes visited. These more closely resembled the English style of churches, it was said, than did any others.[29]

There was no doubt in the minds of many travellers that the Episcopal church was destined to become the national form of religion in America. It had an admirable church

[27] For Trinity Church, see Tudor, I, 26; Coke, I, 136; Fowler, p. 226; Lambert, II, 57.

[28] For St. Paul's, see Neilson, p. 13; Lambert, II, 57; Coke, I, 135-136; Tudor, I, 25-26.

[29] Boardman, pp. 284, 286; Coke, I, 188.

government and discipline, and its ministers were among the most enlightened of all people of their profession. It had, however, a rival in Unitarianism. The English attitude toward this latter sect is quite different from that held toward the Episcopal church; on Unitarianism there was division, some denouncing its tenets as rank Socinianism, others welcoming the independence of religious thought for which this denomination stood.[30] The spreading of its influence was a source of great anxiety to the orthodox, and the opposition shown to it by Americans afforded one of the few instances, some said the only instance, of war waged by American theologians after the Revolution.

The stronghold of Unitarianism was New England, particularly Boston. "Fully half the population, and more than half the wealth and intelligence of Boston, are found in this communion," says Hamilton, who then attempts to explain the fitness of such a form of religion to that section of the country. The New Englander is more a creature of reason than of impulse—with sharp faculties and obtuse feelings; Unitarianism makes fewer demands on the faith or the imagination than any other Christian sect. "The prosperity of Unitarianism in the New England States, seems a circumstance which a philosophical observer of national character might, with no great difficulty, have predicted. Jonathan chose his religion as one does a hat, because it fitted him. We believe, however, that his head has not yet attained its full size, and confidently anticipate that its speedy enlargement will ere long induce him to adopt a better and more orthodox covering." Hodg-

[30] For remarks on Unitarianism, see Hall, B., II, 116, 119-120; Blane, p. 491; D'Arusmont, p. 320; Hamilton, I, 163-165; Hodgson, II, 237 ff.; Boardman, p. 57 ff., 201-202, 241; Palmer, p. 277; Hall, F., Appendix, p. 276; Duncan, I, 81-82.

son, too, attempted to explain the conditions among the population of Boston which were calculated to promote the extension of Unitarianism. He found them in the inability of these descendants of Puritans to suspect error in any creed with which they themselves were connected, in their consciousness of literary superiority, in their association of liberality and Unitarianism, and in their state of general ease and comfort, which had the effect of diminishing the necessity for religious consolation and inquiry. In regard to Harvard College, it was indeed a source of regret that that influential institution had fallen so entirely under the influence of this religious sect. Its liberal doctrines, we are told, prevented many parents from sending their sons there, though it was surprising, after all, to see how little this religious consideration affected the average American parent.

While most of the interest centered in New England, Unitarianism fought its way through the Middle Atlantic States as well. When Boardman visited Philadelphia in 1830, the number of Unitarians was rapidly increasing in spite of fierce attacks, he says. How far the influence of the sect penetrated is indicated by the fact that a traveller in 1821 said that Transylvania University in Lexington, Kentucky, was avowedly Unitarian in religion.

Many visitors to Boston went to hear the celebrated Dr. Channing, and even those who could not subscribe to his doctrine admired him as a great preacher. "He struck me," said a usually critical traveller," as being in many respects a very remarkable preacher, particularly in the quietness or repose of his manner. How far this proceeded from the simplicity of his thoughts, or from the unaffected plainness of his language, I cannot exactly say, but the power which it gave him of introducing, when it suited his purpose, occasional passages of great force and richness of expression, was one of which he availed himself with much skill. . . . The tone of his voice was familiar, though by no means vulgar; on the contrary, it might almost be called musical, and was certainly pleasing to the ear; but whether this arose from the sounds themselves, or from the eloquent arrangement of the words, I never thought of enquiring, as I was carried along irresistibly by the smooth current of his eloquence. . . . He gradually embarked on the great ocean of religious controversy, but with such consummate skill, that we scarcely knew we were at sea till we discovered that no land was in sight.''[31]

The philanthropic Abdy tells of a visit he paid to the celebrated clergyman, during which an argument arose in regard to the distinction between the black and the white races. The Englishman held to his view that the only distinction was one of color, and could not at all understand the position maintained by this eminent man whom reputation had credited with a liberal mind! The discussion came to nothing, and Abdy was extremely discomfited to hear afterward that the famous abolitionist had characterized him as an ''enthusiast.''

Another sect which figured largely in the religious life of New England was that of the Congregationalists, Presbyterians, or Independents, as they were variously called.[32] They were said to practice a form of worship which reconciled Presbyterians and Episcopalians to meet in one church, a kind of ''relaxed Presbyterian service.'' All matters in the church, Bristed says, were arranged by universal suffrage of the congregation. Usually the attitude toward them was favorable, as they seemed to be free from violent

[31] Hall, B., II, 112 ff.; Vigne, II, 233; Boardman, pp. 58-60, 286; Hamilton, I, 159; Abdy, III, 217 ff.

[32] For remarks on the Congregationalists, see Duncan, I, 313 ff.; Lambert, II, 66, 311, 335; Bristed, p. 313; Candler, p. 167.

RELIGION 261

heretical doctrines, while maintaining liberal views. Lambert comments on the fact that in 1806-8, the majority of Boston's 30,000 population were Congregationalists, who occupied nine places of worship. At the same time, New York, out of thirty-three churches, had only one belonging to this sect. In 1824, there was none at all in New York; newcomers who were Congregationalist usually attended one of the fourteen orthodox Presbyterian churches which the city boasted at that time, as the two sects were similar. Presbyterianism flourished generally throughout the Middle and Southern states.[33] Travellers speak of attending services of this denomination in places as widely separated as New York and New Orleans. Harriet Martineau says that in the North, Presbyterians were numbered among the most energetic abolitionists, and in the South, among the most unfeeling defenders of slavery. They were also charged with being particularly bitter against the Catholics.

This last-named denomination was much in the minority during this period.[34] They were confined chiefly to Maryland, and to the larger cities on the coast, New Orleans particularly. Baltimore was called the "headquarters of Catholicism" and had the distinction of possessing the most beautiful cathedral in the country. It was built in the form of a Greek cross, and contained the largest organ in America.[35] The Catholics apparently made few attempts to gain proselytes from the other denominations, but depended largely upon the great numbers of European emigrants, chiefly Irish, to swell their numbers. In 1824, it

[33] Palmer, p. 276; Lambert, II, 269; Alexander, II, 18, 253; Martineau, II, 318-322; Candler, pp. 172-173.

[34] For Catholics, see Holmes, pp. 387, 390; Blane, p. 489 ff.; Fearon, p. 167; Bristed, p. 413; Neilson, p. 227; Murray, I, 207; Candler, p. 190 ff.; Martineau, II, 322 ff.; Duncan, I, 241.

[35] Mrs. Trollope, I, 292; Stuart, I, 250; Boardman, p. 258 ff.; Alexander, II, 258; Duncan, I, 220.

was said that they did not comprise one-tenth of the population; ten years later, Murray calls attention to their rapid increase, especially in the Western states. In regard to the attitude of other sects toward them, there was a difference of opinion; for instance, Candler says they were nowhere viewed with jealousy, but Miss Martineau speaks of the bitter persecution of them throughout the country.

The rise of Universalism was viewed with horror by Americans and by Englishmen.[36] English travellers admitted that they did not understand the tenets of the sect, though several attempted to explain them. The general confusion of mind in regard to them is indicated by such remarks as the following by Murray: "Besides the sects above mentioned, there are a numerous body of Universalists, subdivided into Mennonites, Tunkers, and Shakers." They were particularly objectionable to the conservative types of Calvinists, on whose tenets they professed to base their faith. "The sect labors under the imputation of disguised infidelity," said Abdy, "though its origin may be traced to the Calvinistic doctrine of atonement—pushed to its extremest consequences." Its doctrines were regarded as the most dangerous to the peace and happiness of society of the newer and more radical sects, though it was admitted to be an accommodating form of religion.

The Baptists throughout this period were increasing rapidly in the Western districts.[37] Dalton says that in 1793 there were in the United States 1032 Baptist churches with 73,471 members; in 1817, the number of churches had reached 2727, and the membership, 183,245. The Baptists

[36] On Universalism, see Neilson, p. 227; Abdy, I, 236-240; Murray, II, 207; Holmes, pp. 390-391; Lambert, II, 309-310; Candler, pp. 167-168; Palmer, p. 277; Fearon, p. 45.

[37] For Baptists, see Lambert, II, 373; Bristed, p. 413; Dalton, pp. 240-241; Melish, I, 37; Murray, II, 207; Candler, pp. 211 ff.

were said to be notable for the pure democracy of their church government and for the quietness and austerity of their religious rites. Visitors to their camp-meetings witnessed no such excesses as distinguished the gatherings of their neighbors, the Methodists, with whom they shared a reputation for rapid increase.

The growing influence of this latter sect was generally acknowledged;[38] they were found throughout the country, though they tended to increase most rapidly in the West and South. In the Southern districts, Methodism tended to supplant the older Episcopal forms of worship. Its simple appeal to all classes of society was seen to be reinforced by the great amount of practical good which the Methodists accomplished. They were the first to bestow attention upon the religious and moral instruction of the slaves, and were said to be prominent in every movement to do away with vice and wickedness of all kinds. The part that they played in arousing interest in religion was conceded to be great, while the propriety of some of their rites was very much questioned. Many observers refused to take them seriously. "The preachers of that sect," said Hamilton, "are generally well adapted, by character and training, for the duties they are appointed to discharge. They perfectly understand the habits, feelings and prejudices of those whom they address. They mingle in the social circles of the people, and thus acquire knowledge of the secrets of families, which is found eminently available in increasing their influence. Through their means, religion becomes mingled with the pursuits, and even the innocent amusements of life. Young ladies chant hymns instead of Irish melodies; and the profane chorus gives place to rhythmical

[38] For Methodists, see Candler, p. 211 ff.; Duncan, II, 369; Palmer, p. 276; Lambert, II, 107, 175; Hamilton, II, 394 (quotation).

doxologies. Grog parties commence with prayer and terminate with benediction. Devout smokers say grace over a cigar, and chewers of the Nicotian weed insert a fresh quid with an expression of pious gratitude.''

Judging from the accounts of Methodist meetings visited by travellers, it was this sect that brought upon Americans the charge of fanaticism.[39] The experience of most observers seems to have been the same. Stentorian lungs were said to be the primary requisite for a minister of this sect; he harangued his audience, hurling upon sinners imprecation and entreaties to repent until half his congregation were weeping and groaning, perhaps as much from terror at his loud voice and violent gesticulations as from a conviction of sin. The appeal which this kind of preaching made on the less-educated classes was tremendous, and accounts largely for the enormous increase of Methodism.[40]

Revivals were met with in almost all the denominations. They were distinguished by a sudden excitement and enthusiasm for things religious, and might arise from a variety of causes.[41] Sometimes a public calamity brought about one of these manifestations, it was said; more often they were inspired by some powerful preacher or evangelist. The people assembled in great numbers, the meetings continuing for several days. Fervid preaching, praying, and confession of religious experience took place. Often astonishing instances of infant piety were revealed.

Travellers were much interested in the camp-meeting, which in its most distinctive and interesting form at least,

---

[39] For descriptions of Methodist meetings, see Holmes, p. 388; Boardman, p. 61; Mackenzie, pp. 203-204; Lambert, II, 179-180; 279; Fearon, p. 162 ff.; Wood, J., p. 193; Melish, I, 36-37.

[40] Candler, p. 214.

[41] For revivals, see Tudor, I, 419; Mrs. Trollope, I, 104 ff; Candler, pp. 168-170.

was limited to Methodism.⁴² It repeated all the features of the usual Methodist religious demonstration, multiplied many times, as the gathering was always a large one and numbered sometimes thousands of people. These assembled in a great open space, often a clearing in a forest, where they proceeded to pitch their tents for a week's stay. Fervent preaching and prayer went on continuously in several different places on the grounds, except during the late hours of the night, and the most extravagant demonstrations of religious enthusiasm were encouraged. Efforts were made to check anything approaching immorality, but that charge was brought frequently against these gatherings. While camp-meetings were open to criticism on many points, there is no doubt that they acted as a valuable aid to the quickening of religious life in the thinly settled regions, where any regular ministration of religion was impossible.

The religious system of the United States was seen to include many other sects, in addition to these that have been discussed. The Dutch Reformed Church, for instance, was an important part of the religious life of New York and New Jersey.⁴³ In 1831, it was said that there were 148 congregations of this sect in New York State alone, and 602 in the whole country. The Friends, or Quakers, were numerous in the Middle Atlantic States, where it was noticed that they occupied a curious and rather detached position, being much engaged in works of benevolence, but taking small part in the life about them, and thus limiting

---

⁴² For the most interesting comments on camp-meetings, see Blane, pp. 491-496; Holmes, p. 388; Lambert, II, 271 ff.; Neilson, p. 195; Palmer, pp. 154-155; Mrs. Trollope, I, 232 ff.; Flint, p. 257 ff.; Stuart, I, 262 ff.; Ferrall, p. 71 ff.; Kendall, I, 232.

⁴³ For mention of Dutch Reformed Church, see Tudor, I, 28; Abdy, I, 240-241.

their influence.⁴⁴ There was a tradition that they refused to co-operate with other sects in their benevolent schemes because of the custom of opening charitable meetings with prayer, a procedure which was contrary to Quaker religious principles. Moravians and Swedish Lutherans also abounded throughout the Middle Atlantic States, especially near Philadelphia.⁴⁵ In most of the large cities of the nation there was at least one Jewish synagogue.⁴⁶ The Jews, on the whole, were believed to be rather well-treated in America. "I am surprised," said Blane, "that all who profess the Hebrew faith do not emigrate to the United States, as they would there not only be free from civil incapacities (particularly as regards landed property), but would even find themselves eligible to the highest offices in the Republic." As early as 1806 there were many wealthy and respectable Jewish families in New York, where they seemed to suffer no invidious distinctions, according to one traveller, Lambert, though Candler includes them later (1824) with Unitarians and Universalists in the three classes of persecuted sects.

This period witnessed the beginning or development of two or three religious communistic experiments. One of these, Mormonism, did not become known till about 1830, when it had only six ministers.⁴⁷ By 1834, the sect was said to number almost 6,000 converts, with 800 ministers. Not much was said about this mysterious religion by for-

⁴⁴ For the Quakers, see Weld, I, 25-26; Duncan, I, 207; Mrs. Trollope, II, 92-94; Lambert, II, 106; Bristed, p. 413; Candler, pp. 199-210; Mackenzie, pp. 234-235; Abdy, III, 187-188; Holmes, p. 390.

⁴⁵ Weld, I, 26; Abdy, I, 240-241.

⁴⁶ On the Jews, see Abdy, I, 241; Blane, p. 488; Lambert, II, 106-107, 159; Candler, p. 171.

⁴⁷ On Mormons, see Abdy, III, 54-58, also I, 324-325; Hamilton, II, 309 ff.; Murray, II, 207 (quotation); Alexander, II, 129-130.

eigners, who evidently did not understand what its doctrines were, though one traveller designates the adherents as "fanatics, whose extravagant tenets and disgraceful immorality of practice render them undeserving of the name of sectarians." Travellers mentioned having seen them here and there throughout the country, usually en route to the West.

Far more interesting to the stranger was that peculiar "excrescence" on the religious life of the United States, as an American author calls it, known as the Shakers, or the Shaking Quakers. Very few travellers who visited one of these communities could abstain from writing a full account of it, so that we have numberless repetitions of the same facts.[48] The sect was founded by Ann Lee, the daughter of a Manchester blacksmith, who came to America in 1774 with a few followers and settled near Albany, New York. It was believed by them that the millennium had arrived and that Christ had appeared the second time in the person of the founder of the religion. Gradually communities sprang up in New York State, Massachusetts, Connecticut, Maine, and even in Ohio and Kentucky. Strangers were impressed with the neat and prosperous appearance of the Shaker farms, the order and regularity of their lives, and the manifest contentment with their lot. Men and women lived separately, with little communication except during their social meetings. The two principal tenets of their faith were celibacy and communistic sharing of all earthly possessions. Because of their industry

[48] For the best accounts of the Shakers, see Holmes, p. 392 ff.; Candler, p. 217 ff.; Abdy, I, 254 ff.; Vigne, II, 259 ff. (quotation); Hamilton, II, 290 ff.; Mrs. Trollope, I, 194 ff.; Hall, B., I, 111-112; Martineau, I, 310 ff; Coke, I, 195 ff.; Ferrall, p. 58 ff.; Wakefield, pp. 201-203; Melish, II, 303 (note); Hodgson, I, 399-400; Stuart, I, 185 ff.; Tudor, I, 152-175.

and thrift, and the excellent quality of their productions, the Shakers became very prosperous, and were known to give large sums of money for benevolent purposes.

Most people who visited them believed in their sincerity but censured their doctrines. Their indifference to the claims of natural affection repelled many observers. Their queer costumes, their disregard of everything but the most rudimentary education, their theocratic system of government, and their extraordinary method of worship, aroused little sympathy. In regard to the last, Basil Hall said that though he had witnessed some strange forms of worship in former travels, he had never beheld anything, even in Hindoostan, to match these Shakers. The following description by Vigne is perhaps as distinctive as any of the accounts: "About fifty men and women were arranged *en masse,* with their faces toward each other, and with an intervening space of about ten feet. The service commenced by an elder coming forward between them and delivering a few words of exhortation. Several others followed his example at intervals during the service. . . . Hymns were then sung by them in their places, each of them shaking the whole time. They then performed a regular dance, holding hands, advancing and retiring, to a most uproarious tune, sung by a few of them formed in a small circle, who gave the words and the time to the others as they afterwards paraded in pairs around the room, singing very loudly the whole time—hopping heavily, first on one foot, then on the other,—flapping their hands the whole time before them, with their elbows stuck into their sides, and looking for all the world like so many penguins in procession. It was not till the end of the service that they all fairly fell on their knees, and sang a hymn, as if they were asking pardon for their vagaries."

Another curious experiment of the communistic type was

worked out at Harmony, Indiana, under the direction of a German enthusiast, George Rapp. Few travellers went West without visiting this community.[49] The Rappites were much like the Shakers in many respects. Their beliefs included celibacy and communistic sharing of property. Their attitude toward life was, on the whole, considered more normal than that of the Shakers; the most curious feature of the experiment was the influence exerted by its founder. Visitors were interested to see that this strange personality dominated the entire existence of the hundreds of people who became members of the community; no language but German was permitted to be spoken, members were allowed to hold no communication with strangers, and all money which came into this prosperous, industrious community was paid over unhesitatingly to the head. In this way Rapp was said to have accumulated large sums of money, the ultimate disposal of which has always been more or less mysterious. Trouble arose inevitably in regard to financial matters, and a succession of law-suits started the downward career of the sect.

These communistic ventures were perhaps of little vital importance, ''superficial appendages without organic significance.'' As a whole, it was seen that the American people did not take kindly to strange and unusual forms of religion, nor were they carried about by ''every wind of fashionable doctrine.'' A spirit of practicality and conservatism pervaded their church life, and kept them alike from the heights and depths of religious experience.

[49] For Rapp's settlement, see Stuart, II, 251-252; Murray, I, 143-144; Blane, p. 244 ff.; Martineau, I, 315 ff.; Harris, pp. 134-135; Faux, pp. 249-251; Hulme, ''Journal,'' pp. 53-61; Birkbeck, ''Notes on a Journey,'' pp. 135-136.

CHAPTER X

FAMOUS CONTROVERSIES

THE period of fifty years with which we have to do, witnessed several spirited conflicts with the pen, engagements in which the United States became involved chiefly as the defender of her institutions and her ideals. The feeling between this country and England, which had its origin in the Revolution and its development in the growing importance of the new republic, seemed to come to a climax just about the middle of this period; by 1835, though the mutual lack of understanding persisted, the relations had become less hostile, and the two nations assumed a less prejudiced and more just attitude toward each other.

In the period before the beginning of the War of 1812, the United States was particularly unfortunate in the type of travellers who came here, and who afterward found it either their duty or their pleasure to open the eyes of their fellow countrymen in regard to American institutions. In such a comparatively new state of civilization there was, of course, much that was unusual and crude and far removed from the ordinary experiences of the average Englishman. Considering that there were practical obstacles even in the way of comfortable living, one could expect very little of the finer side of life to be revealed. Americans complained that travellers saw nothing but the inconveniences of travel. "Neither the soil," said one native writer, "its productions, its advantages or disadvantages, nor any of those subjects which occupy the attention of liberal, enlightened and scientific travellers, excite their curiosity or merit investigation."[1] Very few visitors tarried long enough to look below the surface of this disorganized, unassimilated state of society and to find the elements of strength and greatness which were bound at some time to come to the surface. The larger proportion of the accounts written in this period were not in friendly vein; many of the observers, like Parkinson and Ashe for instance, were men of limited education or of inferior character, with no capacity for taking the large and fair view of American life. Besides the works turned out by these travellers, Englishmen at home had as their guide only the newspapers, in which criticism of America was rife. These the United States could afford to ignore and did ignore; it was only when the animosity was carried into higher quarters that it became necessary for a self-respecting nation to defend herself against it. It was not until the English reviews, under the direction of some of the chief literary men of the time, turned their batteries against America, that the real conflict began.

The English *Quarterly Review* was founded in 1809, and in the November number of that year there appeared a discussion of Abiel Holmes' "American Annals." This was made the excuse for a severe attack upon American institutions and manners. The reviewer based his remarks chiefly upon the accounts of Ashe, Janson, and Weld. Of these, Weld is probably the most to be credited;[2] his works offer much valuable material, but we should hardly agree with the reviewer when he says that Weld's book has no gross exaggerations, with the exception of the story of the mosquito so enormous that it bit General Washington through his leather boot.[3] Janson was one of those travel-

[1] Paulding, J. K., "The United States and England" (1815), p. 50.
[2] See reference to Weld in *The North American Review*, I, 65.
[3] *Quarterly Review*, II, 334 (note).

lers who came to America for personal gain. He intended to practice law, it was said; having invested his money unwisely in American stocks, he lost the greater part of it. This made him very bitter against the land of his adoption. *The North American Review* says that he "was dissatisfied, and grumbled at everything, got into debt, and was obliged to make his escape from his creditors."[4] His account, like so many others, is colored by personal feeling, which leads him into ridiculous statements. When his book, "The Stranger in America," appeared in 1806, it was ornamented with sketches which the author attributed to his own skill. Paulding, later, in 1815, proved that they were copied from a set of engravings published some years before by Birch, an American.[5] Ashe also had his failings, it seems. Not only were his statements patently untruthful in some respects, but he was mysteriously concerned with the removal of some archaeological remains from the Western region that he visited.

It was on the accounts of such unreliable visitors as these that the early reviews were based, therefore one is not surprised, though one may be regretful, at the astonishing statements believed by Englishmen. The review under discussion gives a scathing account of American manners and depicts the people as living in the semi-savage state. It abounds in such sweeping statements as the following: "There is scarcely any medium in America between overgodliness and a brutal irreligion," and "Slavery exists in the Southern states and consequently hardens the hearts and corrupts the morals of the people; the Northern states have hardly outgrown their fanaticism." It patronizingly admits a hope for the future, however; "This is an unfavorable picture, yet surely not an unfair one, nor has it

[4] *North American Review*, I, 68.
[5] See Paulding, "The United States and England," pp. 21-22.

been drawn by an unfriendly hand. Let but the American government abstain from war, and direct its main attention to the education of the people and the encouragement of arts and knowledge, and in a very few generations, their country may vie with Europe."[6]

The injustice of *The Quarterly's* attitude was emphasized by the fact that *The Edinburgh Review* also, at one time or another, had occasion to mention these same travellers and estimated them at their true worth. In 1806, this periodical discussed Janson's "Stranger in America" very critically, showing that his statements were exaggerated and his conclusions unjust, and that the hand was "more employed than the head" in the making of his book.[7] The issue for January, 1810, reviewed Ashe's book as a work of "extraordinary pretensions." "His account of the Atlantic States, indeed," says the reviewers, "forms the most comprehensive piece of national abuse we ever recollect to have perused."[8] Another early traveller in the class of Ashe and Janson, who was frequently quoted by the English, was Parkinson, who, it was said, was a gardener. He came to this country to speculate in land and was bitterly disappointed in his investment. His disillusioned, prejudiced account was often used as an authority on American life. *The Edinburgh* takes up the question of this book (October, 1805) and shows how impossible it is that his statements can be true, as for instance, his assertion that there is no good land in America. What the reviewer concludes in regard to his work might be said of any of the books of this type and of this period: "In the whole of his numerous details and anecdotes, we can discover nothing asserted of that country which might not have been pre-

[6] *Quarterly Review*, II, 337.
[7] *Edinburgh Review*, X, 103 ff.
[8] Ibid., XV, 442 ff.

dicted from a little consideration of its peculiar circumstances, and no inconvenience imputed which is not susceptible of an effectual remedy, either at the present moment, or in the rapid progress of its improvement." [9]

The real beginning of hostilities was, however, to come a little later. In 1810, there appeared in New York a little book with the lengthy title of "Inchiquin, the Jesuit's Letters, during a Late Residence in the United States of America; being a fragment of a private correspondence accidentally discovered in Europe; containing a favourable view of the manners, literature, and state of society of the United States, and refutation of many of the aspersions cast upon this country by former residents and tourists; By some unknown foreigner." These letters were supposed to have been written by an Irish Jesuit who had taken up his residence in the United States. With an amused appreciation of the shortcomings of America, the author, who was later identified as C. Jared Ingersoll, a Pennsylvanian, united a lively indignation at the treatment which his country had suffered at the hands of English observers. He takes up the much disputed question of the characters of Adams and Jefferson, and shows wherein each was strong and weak. "When a little time shall have softened the asperity of faction," he says, "it is probable that the imbecility imputed to the one, and the hypocrisy charged to the other, will be in a great measure forgotten, and the patriotism of both be generally acknowledged." [10] He reviews the two books which were probably at that time the best-known in America, Barlow's "Columbiad" and Marshall's "Life of Washington," showing fairly the good qualities and the limitations of each. He puts literature and the fine arts in their proper place in American life,

[9] *Edinburgh Review*, VII, 33.
[10] "Inchiquin, the Jesuit's Letters," p. 77.

and judges the national manners and character in the light of the youth of the country and other circumstances under which they exist.[11] An important contribution that he makes is an analysis of the commercial spirit in America, showing its origin and its real and salutary influence on the character of the people.[12] In conclusion, he states the object of these ostensible letters: "Into what errors I may have been betrayed by a partiality which I am proud to acknowledge, I cannot determine: though a strict regard to the unexaggerated truth has guided my pen. Probably they are not the fewer from a feeling which all along accompanied me that I was repelling prejudices, the demolition of which was to be the first step toward my object. An affectation of contempt for America is one of the only prejudices in which all the nations of Europe seem to concur. . . . The soil has been represented as parsimonious and abortive; the climate as froward and pernicious; the creatures as stunted and debased below their species; the manners, principles, and government as suited to this universal depravity. These absurdities appeared engraved with the stamp of knowledge and authority, their circulation was general and accredited, and it is amazing how current they continue to this day, notwithstanding the proofs that have successively adduced themselves of their falsification and baseness."[13]

Though this little book was moderate in statement and apparently sincere in aim, it became the starting point of a bitter discussion. In the number of January, 1814, notice was first taken of it by *The Quarterly*, which made the review the excuse for another unwarranted and scathing denunciation of America. This article is wrongly at-

[11] "Inchiquin, the Jesuit's Letters, p. 129.
[12] Ibid., p. 139 ff.
[13] Ibid., pp. 164-165.

tributed to the poet laureate, Southey[14]; one wonders how anybody could have seriously made those sweeping generalizations, such as "In America, the 'man of the people' is one who frequents the grogshops, smokes his segar, and harangues the populace with violent and inflammatory abuse of the hostile faction;" "Most of the members (of Congress) may be said to be the representatives of peach brandy and rye whiskey;" "There are no impartial decisions in the courts;" "There is no respectable country gentleman known in America," etc. The writer declares that the religious life of America is uniformly gloomy, that slaves are treated like mere cattle, and that Americans are a race of intemperate, knavish, immoral people. Even the English language is not safe in their hands; Americans are attempting to get rid of it, not only by barbarizing it, but by doing away with it entirely and by making a new one of their own.[15]

This open abuse from such a source could not pass unchallenged. It called forth in America three works in vindication; these were published almost simultaneously. *The North American Review,* in its first number (1815) rushed to the rescue. It exposed the character of *The Quarterly's* authorities, Priest, Wansey, Burnaby, Parkinson, Moore, Cobbett, etc., all of whom were more or less unreliable. The reviewer employed a weapon which came to be very much used in these wordy battles, that is, facts in regard to the enemy's affairs, by way of odious comparison. In short, the article endeavored to show either that many of the outrageous statements regarding the United States were not to be credited at all, or that, if

[14] See Dwight, T., "Remarks on the Review of Inchiquin's Letters," 1815, Preface, p. vi; also Southey's letter of denial republished from *The London Courier* in *The North American Review,* I, 442-443.
[15] *Quarterly Review,* X, 501-528.

certain disadvantages existed, such faults were not peculiar to America alone.

In a note at the end of the article, the reviewer states that another vindication has just come to his attention. This was a small book called "Remarks on the Review of Inchiquin's Letters Published in the *Quarterly Review;* Addressed to the Right Honorable George Canning, Esq. by An Inhabitant of New England" (Boston, 1815). That this was to offer a more spirited defence was evident from the preface. Its author, Timothy Dwight, president of Yale College, criticises both *The Quarterly* and *The Edinburgh,* the latter of which, he says, "sometimes exhibits superior talents but, as a whole, . . . is a nuisance to the world."[16] It is impossible, in this discussion, to do more than touch upon the points that Dwight refutes. He takes up in detail the statements of *The Quarterly,* and denies most of them. If denial is impossible, he shows that an equally bad state of affairs prevails in England. He incidentally throws light upon contemporary opinion of the policies of Jefferson and Madison, and of the conduct of the War of 1812.[17] He maintains the decency of American elections, the impartial justice of the bench, and the dignity of religious toleration.[18] On the score of religion, he attacks the English clergy for non-residence and neglect of duty.[19] Throughout his discussion he emphasizes a general criticism of all English remarks on the United States, — that is, that the adverse statements were based on isolated instances of bad manners, cruelty, injustice, intolerance, etc., without taking into account much that was said to the contrary, sometimes by the same traveller. He takes up the question of the slave trade in the United States, not extenuating the horrors of it, but showing that

[16] Dwight, Preface, p. vii.
[17] Ibid., p. 15 ff.
[18] Ibid., pp. 37 ff., 44 ff., 50 ff.
[19] Ibid., p. 63 ff.

England's record in that respect is much more to be criticised.[20] On no point has the reviewer been more scathing than in regard to the genius and learning of America—"a subject which I believe no British Journalist who has meddled at all with America, and scarcely a single British traveller who has visited its shores, has passed by."[21] How ridiculous some of these strictures of *The Quarterly* are, is shown by the statement that with Barlow's "Columbiad," which is criticised severely, may be classed "a poem by a Mr. Fingal, no descendant, we believe, of the Caledonian bard of that name." The reference is of course to Trumbull's "Mac Fingal," as Dwight shows.[22] One of the most interesting parts of the discussion takes up the question of the English language and the changes which the Americans have made in it; the author appends a long list of English words which are daily mispronounced in London.[23]

Dwight's reply to *The Quarterly* article was reinforced by James K. Paulding's "The United States and England," published in Philadelphia in 1815. The author says in his "Advertisement" that the only attempt that he has seen "to answer the uncandid and swaggering attack made upon the reputation of the people of the United States ... is contained in a series of letters published in an Eastern paper. This *defence* consists pretty much in an admission of most of the charges, provided an exception is made in favour of New England. For ourselves, we know of no such discriminating patriotism as this; and however it may be the fashion in that part of the Union to offer up their brethren as sacrifices to their own interests, we do not admire it enough to make it the object of our imitation." The reviewer, Paulding says, "is no less a person than the poet laureate of all England. This office was instituted

[20] Dwight, p. 23 ff.
[21] Ibid., pp. 106-107.
[22] Ibid., pp. 107-108.
[23] Ibid., p. 140 ff.

on the abolition of that of King's fool, which had become a sinecure on account of their majesties' playing it generally themselves." [24] However, the purpose of the writer is not to enter into a contest of vulgar abuse. "Our object is simply to show . . . that if instances of senatorial indecorum, vulgar immorality and habitual intoxication are to be the standards of the public manners and morals, they may be found even in England; and that if one case is to condemn a nation, the claims of his [the reviewer's] country to either religion, refinement, or morality, will be rather difficult to establish." [25] It is on this principle that the book is written; on the question of the corruption of the United States courts, the conditions of the prisons, the number of illegitimate religious sects, the bad state of manners and morals, retaliation upon England is made by the use of carefully chosen facts.

Hardly had the echoes of this controversy died away when a second one was precipitated by the publication of another American book. This was Robert Walsh's "An Appeal from the Judgments of Great Britain Respecting the United States of America" (1818). This book, Allibone says, was "the earliest considerable remonstrance against the derogatory estimates of America, then the fashion of English travellers." The author in his preface avows his purpose to be "not merely to assert the merits of this calumniated country; I wish to repel actively, and if possible to arrest, the war which is waged without stint or intermission, upon our national reputation. This, it now appears to me, cannot be done without combating on the offensive; without making inroads into the quarters of the restless enemy." He has long indulged the hope, he says, that the false impressions of the higher class of English

[24] "The United States and England," p. 13.
[25] Ibid., p. 17.

critics would disappear in view of the real conditions which palpably existed in America, but *The Edinburgh* and *The Quarterly* have lately put beyond question the insufficiency of any amount of evidence to work the reformation. In his retaliation upon England he intends to use the highest authority, "the records of Parliament and the oracles of the British Empire." He takes up the question of the most recent book on America, which Earl Grey has quoted as an authority at a public dinner, and which has just been reviewed in *The Quarterly*, Fearon's "Sketches of America." Inasmuch as this author has been discontented with the condition of affairs in England, the reviewer censures him; when he attacks American institutions he is praised.[26] In regard to the few favorable remarks that he makes about America, as for instance, that in New York every industrious man can get employment, *The Quarterly* is careful to state that the traveller has been hasty in his judgments, or that in this matter he is not competent to speak. "One valuable quality, indeed, Mr. Fearon possesses," the reviewer tells us, "and it is this which, in spite of numerous defects, renders his book one of the most interesting and amusing that ever came before us. He is a lover of truth, and so far as he discerns it, is ready to set it forth. We cannot recollect an instance, during the whole of our progress through his voluminous work, in which a suspicion of his veracity as to what he saw and heard, crossed our minds."[27] Walsh convicts this author not only of "flippancy and rancour" but of absolute falsehood as well.[28] Having disposed of him in his preface, he goes through the early history of America, telling of the

[26] *Quarterly Review*, XXI, 125-126

[27] Ibid., XXI, 166.

[28] See Walsh on Fearon's remarks concerning redemptioners, for instance. Preface, p. xxviii ff.

difficulties surmounted, and of the numerous acts of injustice suffered by the colonists at the hands of the British. He emphasizes the aid which the Americans gave the English in the French and Indian Wars, and the commercial value to England that America has always represented. Then follows a bitter denunciation of both *The Edinburgh* and *The Quarterly;* "They have indeed carried opposite ensigns, and made their attacks in modes somewhat dissimilar. The hostilities of the English critics have been more direct and coarse, and accompanied with fewer professions of moderation and good will; those of the Scottish have been waged almost always with protestations of friendship, and at times with the affectation of a formal defence of the object." [29] He traces the remarks on America in *The Edinburgh* from the fourth number, which reviewed John Davis's "Travels in America, 1798-1802," to the time at which he is writing. He complains that, though the infamous accounts of such men as Ashe were undoubtedly held up to reprobation, the reviews were made the excuse for sly ridicule and derision of the Americans.

The Quarterly was still more of an enemy, from its intimate connection with the English government. The political object, therefore, said Walsh, was the chief consideration in its criticism.[30] Through such criticisms, however, as those on Inchiquin's "Letters," "The Travels of Lewis and Clark," and Colden's "Life of Fulton," it had taken the opportunity to revile America. Walsh devoted a whole section to the strictures on the slave trade as it existed in the United States; "the side on which we appear most vulnerable and against which the reviewers have directed their fiercest attacks . . . If there is any nation upon which prudence and shame enjoined silence in regard to the negro bondage of these States, England is that nation,

[29] Walsh, p. 214.   [30] Ibid, p. 249.

but it happens precisely as in all the other questions open to the most direct recrimination, that it is from her the loudest outcries and the sharpest upbraidings have come.'' He shows the impractability of the freeing of the slaves in the United States, and exposes the fallacy of some of the statements regarding cruelty toward the free and the enslaved blacks.[31]

The Edinburgh Review, immediately upon the publication of Walsh's book, took up the discussion in its own defence.[32] It considered the work ''a vehement and unjust attack on the principles of this journal.'' It attempted to explain what had been meant by the criticisms of certain authors, Barlow and Chief Justice Marshall, for instance, and it disclaimed all attempt to excite animosity. The attitude of the review was, that the Americans were supersensitive and were cherishing imaginary wrongs. ''The sum of it is, that in point of fact we have spoken far more good of America than ill, that in nine instances out of ten, when we have mentioned her, it has been for praise, — and that in almost all that is essential or of serious importance, we have spoken *nothing but good,* while our censures have been wholly confined to matters of inferior note, and generally accompanied with an apology for their existence and a prediction of their speedy disappearance.'' Even now, though as a book, Walsh's work was not particularly admirable, the reviewer agreed with him on many points, and wished well to his labors. As one reads today through the files of *The Edinburgh,* one is impressed with the justice of the review's attitude.

The North American Review of course took up the defence of Walsh, and gave a detailed review of his book, section by section.[33] It is sufficient to say that this article

[31] Walsh, p. 306 ff.   [32] *Edinburgh Review*, XXXIII, 395 ff.
[33] *North American Review*, X, 334 ff.

considered Walsh justified in his remarks. "The United States," it said, "has been attacked by grave authorities, but derived from ignoble and contemptible sources." Walsh's book was said by the English reviews to have been instrumental, with *The North American Review* in impressing "upon America that she has become in this country the object of systematic hatred and contumely."[34] This was refuted by *The North American;* "It was only when tourists, to whom grammar was a mystery and a decent coat a despaired-of treasure, who fled from the English bailiffs to America, and back again from the American constables to England, — it was only when this worthy class of travellers was espoused, quoted, and believed, . . . that we thought the quarrel worth taking up."[35]

That hostilities went on more or less through the next few years, may be seen from the publication of several American books on the subject, and from the reviews of English travels printed by English periodicals. The best known of the former type of work were two books by James K. Paulding, "A Sketch of Old England by a New England Man" (1822) and "John Bull in America, or the New Munchausen" (1824), and James Fenimore Cooper's "Notions of America, Picked up by a Travelling Bachelor." These were more or less serious attempts to reveal the injustice of the average English traveller to the United States. When we turn to the reviews of travels in *The Quarterly* for the decade after 1820, we find the hostile attitude still consistently revealed. In 1822, this periodical published discussions of four books on America.[36] Two of these accounts were favorable to the United States — William Tell Harris's "Remarks Made during a Tour through

[34] See article in *The New London Monthly,* February, 1821.
[35] *North American Review,* XIII, 26.
[36] *Quarterly Review,* XXVII, 71 ff.

the United States of America," and Frances Wright D'Arusmont's, "View of Society in America." Concerning these two books, nothing complimentary could be said; Harris was characterized as being "strongly disposed to find all things as they should be"; Madame D'Arusmont was attacked bitterly. Her book was called "an impudent attempt . . . to foist into public notice, under a spurious title, namely that of an *Englishwoman,* a most ridiculous and extravagant panegyric on the government and the people of the United States." The reviewer added that he had at first believed the book to be by Walsh, "who, finding that his former work had made no converts on this side of the Atlantic . . . had attempted to revive it under a more taking title." A third book reviewed, Flower's "Letters from the Illinois," was passed over rapidly as "adding little to our knowledge," while Welby's "Visit to North America, 1819-20" was highly approved. This book sets forth America generally in an unfavorable light. The author, *The Quarterly* said, "is tolerably free from prejudice, though he, too, occasionally talks nonsense about the taxation and oppression of England."

In no case is this prejudice of *The Quarterly* so well revealed as in the review of Faux's "Memorable Days in America."[37] It was true that the author was vulgar and coarse, that he constantly betrayed the hospitality of those who entertained him, but, it was said, he was honest and told the truth to the best of his knowledge and belief. "From such a man, one practical page is worth all the radical trash of the Halls,[38] the Wrights, and the Tell Harris's in enabling us to form a just estimate of an emigrant's prospects in a 'land of boasted liberty!' "

It was the same traveller whom *Blackwood's* dismissed

[37] *Quarterly Review,* XXIX, 338 ff.
[38] Hall, Lieut. Francis.

summarily as "a simpleton of the first water," and to whose account credence was denied by that periodical.[39] *The North American Review* ignored the work until the article in *The Quarterly* brought up the matter and made it seem necessary to attempt some defence.[40] Faux was shown to have come to America, not for his ostensible purpose of investigating the conditions and prospects of English emigrants, but to look after some real estate connected with his family. The editor of Paulding's "John Bull in America" says that the review of this book was thrown out of the American republication of *The Quarterly*, so notoriously untrue were its statements.[41]

It is true that on both sides efforts were constantly being made by certain writers to produce a better feeling. The best-known attempt was that of Irving in his "English Writers on America" included in "The Sketch Book" (1819). While deploring the credence lent in England to the unjust and incomplete accounts of the United States, he says: "I shall not, however, dwell on this irksome and hackneyed topic, nor should I have adverted to it, but for the undue interest apparently taken in it by my countrymen, and certain injurious effects which I apprehended it might produce upon the national feeling. We attach too much consequence to these attacks. They cannot do us any essential injury. The tissue of misrepresentations attempted to be woven around us are like cobwebs woven around the limbs of an infant giant. Our country continually outgrows them; one falsehood after another falls off of itself. We have but to live on, and every day we live a whole volume of refutation." Many English observers,

[39] See *Blackwood's Magazine*, XIV, 562 ff.
[40] *North American Review*, XIX, 92 ff.
[41] See Paulding, "John Bull in America," p. 174. Preface of Editor to First Edition.

several of them among the most reputable of travellers, admitted the shortcomings of their countrymen in observation and in tact. Hodgson remarked that English travellers often saw only one side of American life, and that there were often important omissions in their works. The tone of discussion in England concerning America, was sometimes, he admitted, neither just nor liberal.[42] De Roos, in speaking of the Americans, says: "Though vilified in our Journals and ridiculed upon our Stage, they will be found upon nearer inspection to be brave, intelligent, kindhearted, and unprejudiced. Though impressed with an ardent, perhaps an exaggerated admiration of their own country, they speak of others without envy, malignity, or detraction."[43] In regard to the feeling of enmity which America was supposed to cherish toward England, many visitors declared that they could perceive none of it. Blane and Francis Hall both believed that America was doing her part to provoke a good feeling — the name of Englishman, Blane said, was a passport to kindness and attention.[44] Melish, too, maintained that, so far as he could see, there was no animosity in the United States against the British *people,* but against the *government,* at the hands of which America had suffered a long list of wrongs.[45]

But these books were an exception to the rule. Mr. Tuckerman thus sums up the condition that prevailed through most of this period: "There was, indeed, from the close of the War of 1812, for a series of years, an inundation of English books of travel, wherein the United States, their people, and their prospects, were discussed with a monotonous recapitulation of objections, a superficial knowledge, and a predetermined depreciation, which render the task of analyzing their contents and estimating their

[42] Hodgson, II, 267.
[43] De Roos, pp. 67-68.
[44] Blane, p. 500; Hall, F., p. 37.
[45] Melish, I, 44.

comparative merit in the highest degree wearisome. Redeemed, in some instances, by piquant anecdote, interesting adventure, or some grace of style or originality of view, they are, for the most part, shallow, egotistical, and more or less repetitions of each other."[46]

The last two of these accounts we have still to consider; the works of Captain Basil Hall and of Mrs. Trollope. To Americans of that time these two books were the best known of all the English travel literature, and they exerted the most influence. Captain Hall came to America in 1827; part of his stay was spent in Canada; during the remainder of the period he travelled extensively through the United States, from New England south to Georgia and up the Mississippi. He had been a traveller all his life, having entered the Royal Navy in his fourteenth year; he therefore considered himself competent to judge American institutions and to speak dogmatically of what he saw. "In former days," he says, "I confess I was not very well disposed to the Americans; a feeling shared with all my companions on board, and probably also with most of my superiors. But as the duties of a varied service in after years threw me far from the source at which these national antipathies had been imbibed, they appeared gradually to dissipate themselves, in proportion as my acquaintance with other countries was extended, and I had learned to think better of mankind in general. My next anxiety naturally was to persuade others that there really were no just grounds for the mutual hostility so manifestly existing between America and England.

"Probably therefore, there seldom was a traveller who visited a foreign land in a more kindly spirit. I was really

[46] Henry Tuckerman, "America and Her Commentators," pp. 219-220.

desirous of seeing everything relating to the people, country, and institutions, in the most favorable light."[47]

Though the captain came to this country in such a professedly kindly mood, his book had the effect of arousing a storm of angry feelings in the Americans. Travellers who passed through the country after his visit complained that hospitality was withheld from them because of the feeling this work had aroused. "The mistress and boarders of the house where we first resided," says one traveller, "informed us that the publication of Captain Hall's Travels had shut the entrance against any future reception of English gentlemen into American society. 'No Englishman will hereafter,' said they, 'be caressed in the States,' I did not find this to be absolutely true, yet I have no doubt it is accurate to a great extent."[48] It seemed the prevailing idea among Americans that Hall had been sent by the Tory government of England "to depreciate republican institutions, and to repress the growing spirit of freedom at home."[49] Two notable American protests followed the publication of the work. One was an account of the book in *The North American Review;* the other an anonymous refutation published in 1830, and later proved to be by Richard Biddle.[50] In the review, the character of the captain was chiefly emphasized. This he himself had revealed by his ungracious acceptance of favors, and his carping criticism of American hospitality. He travelled with a wife and child, besides servants, and he admitted that the party sometimes gave their hosts a great deal of trouble, and that his temper under difficulties compared most unfavorably with that of

[47] Hall, B., I, 3-4.
[48] Fidler, p. 84; also Tudor, II, 55.
[49] Boardman, p. 255; Mrs. Trollope, II, 219.
[50] *North American Review*, XXIX, 522 ff.; "Captain Hall in America, by an American" [Richard Biddle] 1830.

the Americans at those times.[51] He seemed to be unable to remain silent whenever he saw anything to criticise, and it is evident that he was a thorn in the flesh to everyone with whom he came in contact. The review concluded: "We repeat, we have been actuated by no ill-will towards the traveller, but we appeal to the impartial reader that we have shown him to be in possession of prejudices under which he could not, and to have committed errors which prove he did not, see the country as it is. His work will do considerable mischief, not in America, but in England. It will furnish food to the appetite for detraction, which reigns there toward this country. It will put a word in the mouths of those who vilify because they hate, and hate because they fear us." [52]

The anonymous "Captain Hall in America" did not dismiss the case as purely one of bad temper, though that trait was dwelt on as well. There were much more serious faults to be attacked. The Englishman had criticised the American government and the judiciary, comparing them unfavorably with the English institutions, of which, Biddle showed, he knew nothing.[53] The same was to be said of his discussion of primogeniture. His statements in regard to the several state governments were incorrect, or at best, half-truths. His disingenuous air in his remarks on slavery was exactly of the sort that would produce a wrong impression of that institution in England.[54] "As to the state of *Manners* in the United States, the tourist has confined himself to certain dark and seemingly very ominous hints, to which it is, of course, quite impossible to offer any reply." [55]

[51] See, for instance, Hall, B., I, 15, II, 184-185.
[52] *North American Review*, XXIX, 574. See on this book, *Quarterly Review*, XLI, 417-447; *Blackwood's Magazine*, XXXIV, 288.
[53] Biddle, p. 19 ff. [54] Ibid., p. 54. [55] Ibid., p. 61.

Coke says, speaking of Captain Hall and Mrs. Trollope, that never were two authors so abused as these two; that every newspaper teemed with violent remarks and personalities, which were substituted for refutation. He also quotes from Paulding's novel, "Westward Ho," an American conversation in which Captain Hall is held up to ridicule.[56] Mrs. Trollope devoted an entire chapter to the defence of Hall in illustration of the extreme sensitiveness of the Americans. "Of this, perhaps," she says, "the most remarkable example I can give, is the effect produced on nearly every class of readers by the appearance of Captain Basil Hall's 'Travels in America.' In fact, it was a sort of moral earthquake, and the vibration it occasioned through the nerves of the Republic, from one corner of the Union to the other, was by no means over when I left the country in July, 1831, a couple of years after the shock . . . the internal conviction on my mind is strong, that if Captain Hall had not placed a firm restraint on himself, he must have given expression to far deeper indignation than any he has uttered against many points in the American character, with which he shows, from other circumstances, that he was well acquainted. His rule appears to have been to state just so much of the truth as would leave on the minds of his readers a correct impression, at the cost of pain to the sensitive folks he was writing about."[57]

But even Captain Hall's book sank into comparative insignificance beside the work from which this quotation was taken; namely, Mrs. Trollope's "Domestic Manners of the Americans," which was published in 1831 and ran through several editions immediately. Obadiah Rich remarked in his "Bibliotheca Americana Nova," in 1832, that it was not much to the credit of the taste of the British

[56] Coke, I, 149.
[57] Mrs. Trollope, II, 216, 223-224.

public that the malicious effusions of a disappointed old woman should pass through three editions in about three months.[58] Mrs. Trollope had come to America with her husband in 1829, and had set up a small fancy-goods store or bazaar in Cincinnati in a building which she had had erected, and which Murray later described as the most "absurd, ugly and ridiculous building in the town."[59] The venture did not prove a success, and after a stay of three years, Mrs. Trollope returned to England very much at odds with America. Her book, the result of her observations, is full of personal feeling. An English traveller, staying in New York at the time of its appearance, tells of the demand for it. "The Tariff and Bank Bill were alike forgotten, and the tug of war was hard, whether the 'Domestic Manners' or the cholera, which burst upon them simultaneously, should be the more engrossing topic of conversation. At every corner of the street, at the door of every petty retailer of information for the people, a large placard met the eye, with, 'For sale here, with plates, Domestic Manners of the Americans, by Mrs. Trollope.' At every table d'hote, on board of every steamboat, in every stage coach, and in all societies, the first question was, 'Have you read Mrs. Trollope?' And one-half of the people would be seen with a red or blue half-bound volume in their hand, which you might vouch for being the odious work, and the more it was abused, the more rapidly did the printers issue new editions."[60] We are told that a great many Americans believed that Captain Hall and Mrs. Trol-

[58] Rich, "Bibliotheca Americana Nova," II, 240. In regard to this book, see *Blackwood's Magazine*, XXXI, 829-847; *Edinburgh Review*, LV, 487; also Asa Greene's "Travels in America" by Geo. Fibbleton, Esq. (a satire).
[59] Murray, I, 147-148. See also Hamilton, II, 171.
[60] Coke, I, 148-149 (also note).

lope were one and the same person, or that Hall had written the book from Mrs. Trollope's notes.

As may be imagined, the publication of the work was the signal for the beginning of a literary battle. *The Edinburgh Review* ridiculed the book generally;[61] *Blackwood's* qualified its praise of the truth of delineation shown by the author by saying that it was "very palpably varnished and exaggerated for the purpose of impression."[62] *The Quarterly*, however, published a glowing eulogy: "This is exactly the title page we have long wished to see, and we rejoice to say that, now the subject has taken up, it is handled by an English lady of sense and acuteness, who possesses very considerable power of expression and enjoyed unusually favorable opportunities for observation." Apparently, it was a book much needed, when "so much trash and falsehood pass current concerning the West." Many excerpts from the work are included in the review, all of which are characterized as "clever," "lively and amusing,"[63] etc. As a matter of fact, Mrs. Trollope visited only a small portion of the country, she did not mingle with the higher social ranks of people, and she judged simply from what she saw. It is interesting to note the attitude of subsequent English travellers toward this work. Most of them believed it would do some good; in fact, actual results were already to be seen, as in the experience before narrated, of Coke and Shirreff in the theatres.[64] All, however, did not believe that the book had gone about the work of reformation in the best way. Shirreff remarked: "The clever, and to some people, amusing work of Mrs. Trollope will have different effects from what its admirers in Britain contem-

[61] *Edinburgh Review*, LV, 479 ff.
[62] *Blackwood's Magazine*, XXXI, 829 ff.
[63] *Quarterly Review*, XXVII, 39 ff.
[64] See Coke, I, 153-154; Shirreff, p. 9.

plate. The many sketches of low and incidental character which the book contains, and given as belonging to the people generally, wounded the feelings of the inhabitants of the United States. . . . From much I saw and heard, the keen satire of this authoress is likely to produce in a few years, the usual improvement of a century; on the other hand, her caricatures of manners and institutions fostered the prejudices of many of the inhabitants of Britain, and engendered dislike to political changes taking place in that country . . . the popularity of Mrs. Trollope's book may be regarded as evidence of want of discernment, if not of vitiated religious and moral feeling in a portion of the reading population of Britain.'' James Stuart attacked Mrs. Trollope bitterly, and showed, in several particulars, how different had been his experience, and how little the Englishwoman had understood and appreciated America.[65] Tudor devoted an entire chapter to refuting some of her statements regarding the manners, religion, and standards of morality in the United States.[66] Ouseley says in regard to her representation of religion, that it would be as fair to judge the church system of England "by the proceedings of a meeting of Jumpers or Ranters in some remote village, or by the hallucinations of the followers of Johanna Southcote" as to generalize the religious state of America by her account.[67] Her son, Anthony Trollope, admits that no observer was less qualified to judge of the prospects, or even of the happiness of a young people. "If a thing was lovely in her eyes, it ought to be lovely to all eyes, — and if ugly, it must be bad. . . . The Americans were to her rough, uncouth, and vulgar, and she told them so."[68]

[65] Stuart, II, 281 ff, 305.
[66] Tudor, II, 390 ff.
[67] Ouseley, p. 12 (note).
[68] See Trollope, A., "Autobiography," Chap. II.

The North American Review published a long discussion of this work, and refuted many of its statements.[69] The remarks about American grammar, American prudery, and fanaticism in religion were shown to be false, and based on insufficient evidence. Mrs. Trollope was one of the many travellers who brought against the Americans the charge of extreme sensitiveness to criticism. This the *North American* reviewer thought it well to answer. The periodical, he said, had made a study of this trait for fifteen years. "We aver upon our consciences, that we do not remember an occasion on which a good-natured joke from any quarter, on any part of America has been taken amiss."

Before we are tempted, like Mr. Tuckerman, to find the analysis of these quarrels too wearisome, we must consider another controversy, more limited in its scope, but as bitter in spirit, namely the one that concerned the so-called English Prairie in the south-eastern part of the state of Illinois. The experiment which was there worked out became the center of the discussion on emigration to America after the peace of 1815. The settlement was founded by Morris Birkbeck and George Flower, both of whom were Englishmen of considerable wealth and influence, who became dissatisfied with conditions at home, and conceived the scheme of transplanting large numbers of their countrymen into the new land. The controversy grew out of the popularity of the settlement in spite of the efforts of detractors to kill it. In 1817 and 1818, Birkbeck published two books on the venture, "Notes on a Journey in America" and "Letters from Illinois." In the preface to the former, the author spoke of the hopeful future: "There are advantages before us greater than I had in contemplation, and apparently attainable with less difficulty and sacrifice. I have, therefore, nothing to regret in the step I have taken,

[69] See *North American Review*, XXXVI, p. 1 ff.

and in my present knowledge, I should find stronger motives for it." He set forth candidly the plans that he and Flower had made, to purchase from the government one or more entire townships, part prairie and part woodland, which would be offered to Englishmen on the most favorable terms possible. "To obviate the sufferings to which emigrants . . . are exposed on their arrival, it is a material part of our plan to have in readiness for every poor family, a cabin, an inclosed garden, a cow, and a hog, with an appropriation of land for summer and winter food for cows, proportioned to their number."[70] The members of the community were to be bound by no ties except mutual interest, and to be subject to no law, except the law of the land. In his second book, Birkbeck took up the discussion of the details of the settlement, its limitations and its advantages, answered numerous questions that had come to him, and gave much gratuitous information in regard to the manners and character of the inhabitants.

It was inevitable that Birkbeck should be bitterly opposed by certain classes of people in England. *The Quarterly,* in reviewing his "Notes on a Journey in America," made the following scathing remark: "Whatever 'New America' may have gained by the name of Birkbeck having ceased to be found in the list of the citizens of Old England, the latter has no reason to regret the loss. Many more of the same stamp may well be spared to wage war with the bears and red Indians of the 'back woods' of America."[71]

The chief American opponent of the new settlement was William Cobbett, the noted Radical, "self-exiled from England to avoid prosecution for libel and consequent fines."[72] Cobbett seems to have wished to confine all experiments in

[70] Birkbeck, "Notes on a Journey," p. 160 ff.
[71] *Quarterly Review,* XIX, 78.
[72] See Thwaites, "Early Western Travels," X, 11.

emigration to the land along the Atlantic coast. In part of his book, "A Year's Residence in America" (1818), he made an attack on the English Prairie, basing his facts ostensibly on the "Journal" of Thomas Hulme, one of his followers. The latter, it is well to say, was a conscientious observer, and intended to write nothing against the Western settlement, but Cobbett distorted his statements to give a derogatory account, and affixed a letter of Birkbeck which urged the advantages of the East over the West, as a place of settlement. These remarks were answered in turn by Birkbeck and by Richard Flower (father of George Flower), who wrote "Letters from Lexington and the Illinois, Containing a Brief Account of the English Settlement in the Latter Territory, and a Refutation of the Misrepresentations of Mr. Corbett" (1819). This honest, straightforward account set forth the difficulties of the new venture, extenuating nothing, but showing the promise of the future. One of Cobbett's chief strictures had been on the point of the inferior healthfulness of the West, a matter to which Flower gave a great deal of care and discussion.

It is impossible to go into all the controversial literature which grew out of this experiment. Faux took a part in the quarrel with his characteristic vigor and disregard for truth. He showed what a disappointment the colony had proved, how difficult the land was to cultivate, how the people suffered from lack of water, and how progress was retarded by lack of a market for produce. He maintained that Birkbeck was already declining the responsibility of advising people to emigrate, and that Flower was saying, "Tell your countrymen to stay at home by all means, if they can keep their comforts."[73] Fearon, too, affixed to his "Sketches of America" an examination of Birkbeck's works on the English Prairie, and tried to prove that on

[73] Faux, p. 191 ff, 252 ff.

many points the author was evading the truth. "I have been thus free with Mr. Birkbeck's 'Letters,' " said he, in conclusion, "because I have seen the effects which they have produced upon your minds, and I believe that effect to be an improper one. This has arisen, I apprehend, more from the *mode* in which the information is conveyed than from the information itself, for it appears to me that throughout the work, there are those *admissions* which no colouring ought to prevent the mind of the reader from viewing as most serious considerations connected with an Illinois settlement." [74]

The question was settled only by the actual fact of the growth of the settlement, and its prosperity. Echoes of the trouble were heard from time to time, but the colony flourished in spite of them. The service that these English settlers rendered to the country is well summed up by Thwaites: "When a new constitution for the state was agitated, one that should admit slavery to its borders, it was the sturdy opposition of the English leaders that turned the scale in favor of freedom. . . . Largely to English devotion to free institutions, it was due that the attempt to foist 'the peculiar institution' upon the new West failed, and the state which was to shelter and train Abraham Lincoln was made a free land." [75]

Even today, as we read through the history of these old quarrels, we find the numerous criticisms of the new republic irritating. The frequent repetition, the astonishment at facts that should have been taken for granted, the lack of a broad outlook on life, and of a real understanding of the institutions observed,—all of these failings on the part of the average English traveller arouse our ire and make us

[74] Fearon, p. 391 ff.
[75] Thwaites, "Early Western Travels," X, 14-15; see also for the English Prairie, Welby, p. 248 ff; Woods, J., p. 179 ff.

wonder that there was not more recrimination when the criticisms were published. Misunderstandings and verbal encounters are not pleasant at best. It is with a strong sense of relief that we read a statement like the following, in *The Quarterly* of September, 1835: "Let us hear no more then,—at least, let us hear nothing in harsh, contemptuous, or arrogant language about the petty circumstances which may happen to strike an English eye—as offensively characteristic of the people of America in their interior domestic intercourse among themselves."[76] When our chief antagonist calls a truce, it is a promising omen for the future.

[76] *Quarterly Review*, LIV, p. 408.

CHAPTER XI

CHARACTER

THE American character was considered by most visitors to be something distinct, and belonging peculiarly to the country. One who reads through the English travels in the United States is impressed with the fact that so much emphasis was laid on the effects of separation from the Old World, and the difficulties of life in the New. *The Quarterly,* in a review of Paulding's "Lay of the Scottish Fiddle" set forth America's limitations in no very kindly terms: "In a nation," said the reviewer, "derived from so many fathers, it has justly been a matter of wonder that there should hitherto have existed so tame a uniformity and that the composition of such various elements should produce the merest monotony of character the world has yet seen. It is not our business to trace why the thoughtfully dissolute, and turbulent of all nations, should, in commingling, so neutralize one another that the result should be a people without wit or fancy. We will only observe that when the vulgar and illiterate lose the force of their animal spirits, they become mere clods, and that the founders of American society brought to the composition of their nation few seeds of good taste, and no rudiments of liberal science."[1]

On the other hand, the diversity of character met with on a long journey through America could not be ignored. It was to be expected in a land of such latitude and longi-

[1] *Quarterly Review,* X, 463 ff.

tude, and made generalizations in regard to one part of the country inapplicable to the rest. Latrobe, at the very end of this period, maintained that the people of America could not be said to have a national character; in fact, they could never unite sufficiently to acquire one. "It is even to be doubted whether they will ever amalgamate sufficiently, under the great difference of temperament, style of life, and habits consequent upon such diverse climates alone, to admit of one picture, however broadly sketched, being in every particular characteristic of the whole. . . . Turn to whichever part of the Union you may, manners perfectly distinct from each other, traceable to the stock from which the individual sprang, in person, dwellings, prejudices, prepossessions and modes of expression, are distinguishable."[2] One might as well try to include all the countries of Europe in one general description, it was said, as to attempt to characterize the United States.[3] Hence there grew up a tradition, stimulated by the opinions that prevailed among the Americans themselves, that North, South, and West, particularly, had developed a distinct character. Blane expresses what many Americans and Englishmen firmly believed in regard to the differences between the North and the South: "Thus the White inhabitants of the Southern and slave-holding States are high-spirited, fiery, and impetuous, with difficulty restraining their passions, and possessing all those characteristics (many of them very odious) that mark the slave-holder. In those States, no one deigns to work, and the gentry, or wealthy planters, occupy their time in sporting, and particularly in horse-racing and cock-fighting. They also indulge in the pleasures of the table much more than their Northern fellow-citizens . . . the inhabitants of the free States are not only much less im-

[2] Latrobe, I, 59-60.
[3] Welby, p. 170; Flint, pp. 171-172; Hodgson, II, 248.

CHARACTER

petuous, and much more cautious than the Southerners, but are also superior to them in morality, and perhaps even in politeness and urbanity of manners."[4] It was this belief in the disparities of American character that helped to give the Ohio River the reputation for being "the greatest thoroughfare of bandits in the Union," that pictured the inhabitants of the West generally, as a lawless, fighting, "gouging" population, and the people of New England as shrewd, cautious, and not too honest.[5]

As it is impossible to analyze any phase of American life without bringing out the nature of the people as well, it is to be hoped that much of the character of the nation has already been revealed in this discussion. It remains to stress certain dominant traits which Englishmen most frequently noticed, or believed that they saw. Concerning one of these, we may be allowed some repetition, particularly as it had a close connection with another important characteristic. This was the acute sensitiveness to opinion that the average American revealed.[6] It was said that fear of opinion kept people from taking office or from assuming other public responsibilities; travellers remarked that Southerners particularly plunged heavily into extravagance to escape the imputation of poverty, and that all over the Union, men preferred to risk death in a duel to bringing upon themselves the suspicion of cowardice. Englishmen found that it was fatal to utter even the most harmless critical remark about any part of the country; that the quarrel of one division of the nation was the quarrel of all. "To see a gentleman of Boston or Baltimore resenting

---

[4] Blane, pp. 501-502.

[5] See, on local differences, Hall, F., p. 266 ff; Martineau, II, 158; Flint, p. 167; Candler, p. 451; Woods, p. 317; Alexander, II, 58-59.

[6] On sensitiveness, see Martineau, II, 156; Hodgson, II, 39; Latrobe, I, 61.

by word and deed the sketch published to the world of the society of a district of the West, borders on the ludicrous," said a traveller, "the more so as, if untravelled, they are frequently as ignorant of the real state of things there, as a stay-at-home Englishman might be supposed to be. . . . This weakness almost amounts to a national disease."[7] Tudor tells of having wounded the feelings of a young American woman by commenting critically on the carriage of some raw recruits at drill. "I was reproached," says the dismayed Englishman, "with the injustice I had done to her countrymen; and it required the lapse of some hours before her wonted complacency and kindness of temper returned."[8] Even writers kindly disposed to the United States in other respects, sided with Captain Hall and Mrs. Trollope in their criticism of this trait, of which their books were full. It is amusing to us to notice that Captain Hall attributes to this sensitiveness the fact that he was not able to write freely concerning the American people.

This general fault was closely connected with another, or was perhaps the result of it — namely, the national vanity. Charitable travellers attributed this to the successful struggle for independence and to the republican institutions.[9] Strangers, it was complained, were not only obliged to tolerate conditions, but to praise them as well. Americans were not content to hear their country spoken of respectfully; it must be admitted as almost beyond any improvement. The accusation of vanity is too nearly universal to be dismissed as resulting from prejudice. Candler, whose "Summary View of America" was praised on both sides of the Atlantic for its justice and fair-mindedness, makes this one of the few points for adverse criticism. He tells of one

[7] Latrobe, I, 61.
[8] Tudor, II, 423 ff.; Hall, B., I, 14; Mrs. Trollope, II, 218.
[9] Candler, p. 106.

or two encounters he has had with the national trait: "Having had a long conversation with a naval officer on different subjects, he asked my opinion of the country. I spoke strongly in its favor, and assured him, that next to my own, it stood first in my regard, at the same time pointing out several things that I disapproved. I had not the remotest idea that I should, in consequence, be condemned for a want of candour, for controversy we had none, and were both in good humour and apparent harmony; and yet a few days after, I was told by another person that this officer had reported that I was going as a spy through the land, and intended, on my return home, to vilify it like other English travellers. As I was in a stage coach, the conversation turned on the improvements going on, and the Erie Canal was adverted to. One of the passengers described it as the wonder of the world, as the glory of the age. I remarked that it certainly was a great and useful work, and manifested conspicuously the spirit and enterprise of the people, but that I could not think such strong language as he used, was altogether applicable to it. Some hours after, another passenger asked me what State I was a native of. I told him that I was an Englishman. 'I thought so,' said the first, 'from your remarks on the canal: you did not speak of it like an American.' . . . A gentleman who also spoke of the canal, told me, that taking the circumstances of the people into consideration, it was equal to the Pyramids of Egypt, or the wall of China.'' [10] Tudor came into collision with this trait in his very first conversation with a native American. Everything that the Englishman mentioned in regard to his own country, the American attributed to his, to a hundred-fold degree of superiority; even the English colonies did not escape, for though the American had to admit that his country had none, he de-

[10] Candler, pp. 120-123, 476.

clared that it would very soon possess them more extensively than did England.[11] One cannot help feeling that Englishmen were charitable when they said mildly that American patriotism was "warm but not properly moderated with reflection," on being asked if there was any building in Europe equal to the Capitol at Washington, and whether London or Paris possessed any houses as good as those in New York or Philadelphia. "The *national vanity* of the United States," said Bristed, "surpasses that of any other country, not even excepting France. It blazes out everywhere and on all occasions, — in their conversation, newspapers, pamphlets, speeches and books. They assume it as a self-evident fact, that the Americans surpass all other nations in virtue, wisdom, valour, liberty, government and every other excellence. All Europeans they profess to despise as ignorant paupers and dastardly slaves. Even during President Washington's administration, Congress debated three days upon the important position that 'America was the most enlightened nation on earth' and finally decided the affirmative by a small majority." [12]

One of the most vulnerable points of attack was the question of the conduct of the wars with Great Britain. The Americans found it hard to believe that the English did not take the same absorbing interest in those wars as they themselves did, and more than one Englishman was accused of being bigoted when he said so. One traveller even went to the length of advising Englishmen to read up well on the wars before coming to America, in order to avoid an embarrassing exposure of ignorance. American books on the subject betrayed this type of vanity. Englishmen objected to having themselves represented as cowards, while the

[11] Tudor, I, 85; also Fidler, p. 80; Murray, II, 219 ff.
[12] Bristed, pp. 460-461; see also Moore, T., "Epistle to Hon. W. R. Spencer" in "Poems Relating to America."

Americans figured throughout as heroes of the occasion; they protested that skirmishes were promoted to the rank of battles, and were compared to the conflicts of Marathon and Trafalgar.[13]

It is encouraging to read that some of the observers limited the aggressive display of vanity to the less-educated classes, absolving the more enlightened. James Flint says that the trait met with more reprobation from the educated American than from the average Englishman.[14] Several travellers, too, believed that the ardent patriotism of the United States was quite natural, and was something to be admired. "I am very far from viewing it as a heinous offense," Latrobe tells us, "or as deserving the animadversions which have been so generally bestowed upon it. In truth, I know not any nation that has ever been distinguished in history, where this has *not* been a national characteristic; and certainly it has never been carried to a greater height than in Britain. . . . If I were an American, I confess I should be proud of my country, proud of its commercial enterprise, — proud of its gigantic resources, — of its magnificent rivers, and forests, and scenery — still more proud should I be of its widely diffused education and independence, and the imperishable memory of its heroic father and founder!"[15] Hodgson, too, believed that the Americans had an excuse for their vanity, and that they must be more than mortal not to boast, so great was the promise for the future.[16]

The spread of this defect was traced to the inflated language of the native newspapers, and to the influence of American orators. Abdy quotes from a speech of Martin

---

[13] Candler, pp. 478-479; Blane, p. 503.
[14] Flint, pp. 167-168; Hodgson, II, 31.
[15] Latrobe, I, 219-220.
[16] Hodgson, II, 32; also Melish, I, 44.

Van Buren at the New York Convention to illustrate this. Mr. Van Buren declared that it was "the boast and the pride and the security of the American nation, that she had in her bosom a body of men who for sobriety, integrity, industry and patriotism, were unequalled by the cultivators of the earth in any part of the known world; nay more, to compare them with men of similar pursuits in other countries, was to degrade them."[17] Bristed says that President Monroe, in his tour through the Union, told the people of Kennebunk, Maine, that the United States was certainly the most enlightened nation in the world.[18]

Another result of this feeling of national superiority was the self-confidence and independence which were noticed in all classes and ages of people. This passed the bounds of moderation and became a fault. It has already been seen that the independent manners of the laboring classes met with little sympathy from the English traveller. The worship of equality was seen to produce contempt for any assumption of superiority, whether of wealth, family connection, or intelligence. Even differences in political opinions, it was observed, never seemed to operate as a cause of separation.[19] Weld complained that on account of this equality of all classes, civility could not be purchased from the Americans on any terms; that there seemed to them to be no other way of convincing the stranger that he was in the land of liberty but by being surly and ill-mannered in his presence.[20] Cobbett argued just the opposite: "No man likes to be treated with disrespect; and when he finds that he can obtain respect only by treating others with respect,

[17] See Abdy, II, 277-278; Fearon, p. 374; Hodgson, II, 31.
[18] Bristed, p. 461.
[19] Bristed, p. 460; Mrs. Trollope, II, 159; Cobbett, 205; Flint, p. 292; Tudor, I, 82.
[20] See Weld, I, 30.

he will use that only means. When he finds that neither haughtiness nor wealth will bring him a civil word, he becomes civil himself, and I repeat it again and again, this is a country of *universal civility.*" [21] In spite of this glowing tribute, travellers continued to take offense at the frequency of the expressions "This is a free country" and "One man is as good as another."

This assiduity in maintaining the equality of all men seemed the more amusing to the Englishman in view of the undeniable fondness for titles of all kinds.[22] The Honorable Charles Augustus Murray tells of being called "Charlie" by his American host on the very evening of his arrival, though, as he says, "the curious observer of character . . . may find . . . the small tavern where he lodges kept by a general, the broken wheel of his waggon mended by a colonel, and the day-labourers and mechanics speaking of one another as 'this gentleman' and 'that gentleman.' " The multiplicity of titles is of course to be largely accounted for by the institution of the state militia; a title thus acquired was never dropped, though the term of service may have been very brief. Vigne tells an anecdote, of a time-worn type, in regard to this. He narrates the story of the captain of an American steamboat who asked at dinner, "General, a little fish?" and was answered in the affirmative by twenty-five of the thirty men present. If an American became a magistrate or justice of the peace, he acquired the title of "Squire," which he kept for the rest of his life, "even when dismissed for misconduct," says the astonished James Flint. Another title that amused Englishmen

[21] Cobbett, p. 205. See also Fearon, p. 375; Dalton, pp. 18-19; Flint, pp. 168-169.
[22] For fondness for titles, see Murray, I, 92; Weld, I, 236-237; Flint, pp. 169-170; Vigne, I, 170-171; Hamilton, I, 237; Neilson, pp. 230-233.

was that of "Captain," as applied to the persons in charge of keel boats. "Except where such names as those just alluded to, are applied," Flint says, "Mr. is the epithet of every man; the wife is of course Mrs., the daughter and maid servant are indiscriminately saluted Miss or Madam. All are ladies. . . . I do not wish to be understood as approving of giving an appellation to one man and withholding it from another, but would only observe that, where all are Mr., Mrs., and Miss, these terms do not imply a distinctive mark, and that the simple Christian names would be more discriminately useful in the affairs of life, if not almost as respectable."

In some respects, this air of independence and self-confidence was rather admirable than otherwise. "Nothing has hitherto struck us more forcibly," said Dalton, "than a certain apparent independence which every American carries about with him. It does not seem to be derived so much from mere assurance, as from the idea, that every citizen is upon terms of equality with his fellows and equally eligible to any office of trust or emolument."[23] This feeling extended even to the backwoodsmen, of whom a traveller says: "They are a most determined set of republicans, well versed in politics, and thoroughly independent. A man who has only half a shirt, and without shoes and stockings, is as independent as the first man in the States, and interests himself in the choice of men to serve his country as much as the highest man in it, and often from as pure motives, — the general good, without any private views of his own."[24] Even Faux became eloquent at the contemplation of American independence: "The American walks abroad in the majesty of freedom; if he be innocent, he shrinks not from the gaze of upstart and insignificant wealth; nor sinks beneath the oppression of his fellowman. Conscious

[23] Dalton, p. 52.   [24] Woods, p. 317.

of his rights and of the security he enjoys, by the liberal institutions of his country, independence beams in his eye, and humanity glows in his heart. Has he done wrong? He knows the limit of his punishment and the character of his judges. Is he innocent? He knows that no power on earth can crush him. What a condition is this compared with that of the subjects of almost all the European nations!"[25]

At this period, the Americans already had the reputation for being a money-loving and a money-getting people.[26] So universal was this belief that it is with surprise that we see any denial of it. Cobbett was one of the very few who ventured a defence. "That anxious eagerness to get on;" he says, "which is seldom unaccompanied with some degree of envy of more successful neighbors, and which has its foundation, first in a dread of future want, and next in a desire to obtain distinction by means of wealth; this anxious eagerness so unamiable in itself, and so unpleasant an inmate of the breast, so great a sourer of the temper, is a stranger to America where accidents and losses which would drive an Englishman half mad produce but very little agitation." It is true that the enterprise of the Americans could not be charitably attributed to a dread of future want, nor did it seem to most Englishmen that they were consciously actuated by a "desire to obtain distinction by means of wealth,"— their attitude toward gain was quite different from either of these. Perhaps it grew out of the abundance of resources, and the certainty of a competence with a relatively small amount of labor. Flint said it was the security of property and the high profits on capital that tended to promote this disposition. Fowler attributed the eagerness to accumulate to the fact that in the

[25] Faux, pp. 27-28; also Fowler, p. 212.
[26] For love of money, see Cobbett, p. 205; Fowler, p. 212; Flint, p. 170.

absence of titles and all acknowledged distinctions in rank, wealth constituted the primary basis of contrast between individuals. At any rate, this trait became to foreigners an integral part of the American nature. "There are two features in the American character," remarked Abdy, "that few strangers fail to observe. . . . The Americans are too anxious to make money, and they spoil their children."[27] Birkbeck said that the chief consideration of the Americans in founding towns seemed to be gain, and that this fact led to much bad calculation, as they often omitted the important consideration of salubrity in their choice of a situation.[28] Mrs. Trollope said that an Englishman, of long residence in America, told her that he had never overheard Americans conversing without the word "dollar" being pronounced between them. "Such unity of purpose," adds Mrs. Trollope, characteristically, "such sympathy of feeling, can, I believe, be found nowhere else except, perhaps, in an ants' nest."[29]

This desire for getting on was not confined to the accumulating of money. Visitors remarked that there was a certain economy which pervaded many American institutions — economy of time, for instance. It was a saving of time to import books rather than to write them; a fact to which Englishmen ascribed much of the poverty of native literature.[30] A certain parsimony was characteristic of the Americans in ventures the result of which could not be immediately seen; one recognizes traces of it in their policies for promoting education, and their neglect of roads in anticipation of the coming railroad. This economy was strangely at variance with a practice of which Americans

[27] Abdy, I, 70-71.
[28] Birkbeck, "Notes on a Journey," p. 69.
[29] Mrs. Trollope, II, 136-137.
[30] See Hall, F., p. 177.

were accused by many travellers — that of waste of resources, food for instance. Observers tell of the great quantities of food served at each meal, and of the daily waste of what remained. One's plate at the table was literally loaded with viands, not half of which were consumed. There were very few poor to receive the bounty of others, and those few would have indignantly spurned charity.[31] Another kind of wastefulness prevailed in certain places, usually the more isolated country districts. There shiftlessness made itself evident; farming implements were not taken care of; borrowed property was sometimes not returned at all, sometimes sent back to the owner in an unsatisfactory condition. Complaints were made that manufactured articles, in many parts of the country, were never finished as well as they might have been, but were only put in such shape as might sell them readily.[32]

There were more serious consequences of this love of gain. Speaking of the American trading classes, Hamilton observed: "One cannot but be struck with a certain resolute and obtrusive cupidity of gain, and a laxity of principle as to the means of acquiring it, which I should be sorry to believe formed any part of the character of my countrymen. I have heard conduct praised in conversation at a public table, which, in England, would be attended, if not with a voyage to Botany Bay, at least with total loss of character. It is impossible to pass an hour in the bar of the hotel without being struck with the tone of callous selfishness which pervades the conversation, and the absence of all pretension to pure and lofty principle. The only restraint upon these men is the law, and he is evidently considered the most skilful in his vocation, who contrives to over-reach his neighbor without incurring its

[31] Hodgson, II, 37; Welby, p. 276.
[32] Hall, B., II, 25-26.

penalties."[33] In no particular, it was considered, was this disregard of probity more conspicuous than in cases of insolvency. Failure in trade was generally the means of building up a new fortune. It was said that this laxness was due to the difference in the laws in the various states, and to the consequently confused ideas of right and wrong. At any rate, the schemes to which the Americans resorted were considered a disgrace to the country. Foreigners, many of whom had a personal interest in the matter, bewailed the fact that creditors were paid arbitrarily, interest dictating to the insolvent whether they should receive anything or not. Breaches of trust in responsible positions were considered to be everyday occurrences. Many Englishmen were afraid to have commercial dealings with American traders, so generally unreliable were these supposed to be. "I must complain much of American roguery," said an English resident of Kentucky to Faux. "Hardly anybody cares about poor honesty and punctuality. If a man can, or is disposed to pay, he pays; if not so disposed, or not able, he smiles and tells you to your face, he shall not pay."[34] The New England Yankee of course, bore the brunt of the accusation, particularly because he was looked upon by his fellow-countrymen as the embodiment of "smartness" and trickery in business.[35] Travellers narrate stories that have been told them of wooden nutmegs, or of watches sold at auction without works, or of common sheep with Merino wool sewed upon them. Melish

[33] Hamilton, I, 124-125.

[34] Fearon, pp. 379-380; Parkinson, II, 504; Hodgson, II, 254 ff; Faux, p. 189; Fidler, p. 81; Bristed, p. 456; Janson, pp. 244-245; Moore, T., "Epistle to Lord Viscount Forbes from the City of Washington;" Weld, I, 403-404.

[35] Hamilton, I, 225, 249, 261-265; Alexander, II, 58-59; Neilson, pp. 233-234; Hall, F., pp. 266-269; Mrs. Trollope, II, 137-138; Faux, pp. 117-118.

limits trickery in business to the seaport towns, where the commercial spirit was so strong that principle was often sacrificed at the shrine of commerce,[36] but in general, very few exceptions were made to the rule of business dishonesty. It was even believed that Americans prided themselves on getting into debt and then showing how adroitly they could get out of paying. Nor was it customary, it was said, for these people to point out defects in goods, or errors in accounts, when these were in their favor.[37] The fondness for lotteries was another indication of dishonesty which professedly horrified Englishmen. It was declared that even churches were built by means of them. "Lotteries pervade the middle, southern and western States," said Bristed, "and spread a horribly increasing mass of idleness, fraud, theft, falsehood, and profligacy throughout all the classes of our labouring population. . . . Our state legislatures never assemble without augmenting the number of lotteries."[38] This lack of a fine sense of honesty was the more astonishing in view of the probity in other matters, and the comparative absence of crime in the country.[39] Pilfering and house-breaking especially were commented on as being conspicuously absent. English visitors were surprised to find that doors and windows were left open night and day, and that possessions of all kinds were left lying about, often over night, with no apprehension entertained by their owners. Americans also gave their visitors credit for being honest; money was lent freely to Englishmen in distress. Francis Hall tells of an experience in Elmira, New York, where a storekeeper offered him money to go to Philadelphia without any other se-

[36] Melish, I, 44.
[37] Faux, pp. 96-97.
[38] Bristed, pp. 435-436; Hodgson, II, 258.
[39] Hodgson, II, 253; Stuart, I, 150; Abdy, II, 305; Candler, p. 454.

curity than his word. Hall says his surprise was the greater because he had been told that Americans never failed to cheat and insult Englishmen.[40] This scrupulous personal honesty was attributed to the slight temptation to theft in a country where there was ample facility for obtaining a livelihood.[41]

In spite of the prevalence of certain vices, the great amount of drinking that went on, the gambling and the duelling, the quality of American morality was generally conceded to be high.[42] This has been seen to be especially true of the chastity of American women. Mrs. Trollope maintained that the standard of general morality in the United States was much lower than in Europe, but travellers frankly disagreed with her. It is to be remembered, besides, that Mrs. Trollope did not visit New England, where the standard was universally thought by foreigners to be the highest in the country. Hamilton, a true Scotchman, admitted that not even in his own land was morality at so high a premium as in this section.

Notwithstanding the many comments on the independence of manner and the defective education of the American children in this respect, there was observed to be a certain conservatism in American ideas, a kind of holding back from that which was new and strange. Men tended to follow, for instance, the religious and political opinions of their fathers. "In the United States," said Hamilton, "one is struck with the fact that there exist certain doctrines and opinions which have descended like heirlooms from generation to generation, and seem to form the subject of a sort of national entail, most felicitously contrived

[40] Hall, F., p. 156.
[41] Candler, p. 454.
[42] Hodgson, II, 251-252, 260-261; Candler, p. 480; Mrs. Trollope, II, 138; Hamilton, I, 163.

to check the national tendency to intellectual advancement in the inheritors. The sons succeed to these opinions of their father, precisely as they do to his silver salvers, or gold-headed cane; and thus do certain dogmas, political and religious, gradually acquire a sort of prescriptive authority and continue to be handed down, unsubjected to the test of philosophical examination. . . . Enquire their reasons for the inbred faith of which they are the dark, though vehement apostles, and you get nothing but a few shallow truisms, which absolutely afford no footing, for the conclusions they are brought forward to establish.''[43] A feature of this conservatism in opinion was the high value that was attached to the authority of certain individuals. Men like Washington and Jefferson, for instance, were constantly being quoted, sometimes in connection with matters in which they probably were poor authority. Candler objected to hearing Jefferson's opinions on literature explained repeatedly. He says that an American told him that Jefferson was considered the most learned man in the world.[44]

In their attitude toward one another, the Americans were considered most praiseworthy; their charity and helpfulness to those in distress was generally acknowledged.[45] It is true that Mrs. Trollope remarked that there was less almsgiving in America than in any other Christian country on the face of the globe, but she did not explain what other travellers pointed out, that there was also less occasion for alms, and fewer objects of charity. Among the members of a community, misfortune always called forth the

[43] Hamilton, I, 128.
[44] Candler, p. 108.
[45] Hodgson, II, 38; Birkbeck, "Notes on a Journey," pp. 114-115; Mrs. Trollope, 167; Tudor, II, 411-412; Cooper, p. 57; Martineau, II, 194; Fowler, p. 214; Hall, F., Appendix, p. 266; Neilson, p. 194.

kindest and most practical expressions of sympathy. This feeling grew up as a matter of course in a new country where a certain amount of dependence upon one's neighbors was inevitable. Miss Martineau noticed that though there was nothing that men prized so much in America as time, there was nothing that the people were more willing to give to the service of others. Whole families of children were often taken over by some relative of the deceased father or mother, and brought up as a matter of course. So common was this that one traveller remarks that it ceased to meet with praise, it was merely a performance of duty. Appreciative visitors regretted that this helpful side of American character did not seem to be so patently exhibited as were the faults. The sympathy of the Americans was not so evident, it was said, because their social system did not compel them to suffer; it is only oppression that engenders pity.

The stranger generally not only saw the greatest kindliness prevailing among neighbors, but felt it extended to himself. Even Basil Hall's book is full of instances of this lavish hospitality, which, however, many strangers observed to be relative. "From Massachusetts to Maryland," said Thomas Cooper, "inns are plenty, and strangers frequent them when they travel; from the south boundary of Pennsylvania to South Carolina, taverns are scarce and dear, and hospitality is on the most liberal scale." [46] Francis Hall made a very amusing comment on the tradition of hospitality in certain parts of the Union. He believed that the old time virtue was fast disappearing—at least the sort of hospitality of which Jefferson had told him—which waylaid strangers on the roads and compelled them to come in. "While I was in the North," Hall says, "I was constantly told of the hospitality of the

[46] Cooper, p. 52.

South; at Philadelphia I found it ice-bound; at Baltimore there was indeed a thaw, but at Washington, the frost, probably from the congenial influence of politicks, was harder than ever; the thermometer rose but little at Richmond, and when I arrived at Charleston, I was entertained, not with its hospitality, but with an eulogium upon that of Boston. I did not retrace my steps to put the matter to proof."[47] Other travellers, less analytical of the kindness which sheltered and fed them, paid glowing tribute to the Americans in this respect. Candler devotes two entire chapters to instances of unsolicited hospitality and politeness, extended to him in different parts of the country; one sees incidentally that the credit should not be attributed entirely to his hosts.[48] Murray tells with gratitude of the kindly treatment he met with while seriously ill with cholera in Cincinnati. He says that an American acquaintance came to see him two or three times a day, bringing him comforts from his own home, in which he invited Murray to take up his invalid abode.[49] The lack of ostentation in entertaining guests was a subject of comment. Very little change was made in the meal; guests were well supplied with food, but were not urged to eat and drink more than they wished[50]. Miss Martineau declared that American hospitality was so remarkable, and the stranger usually so grateful, that there was danger of its blinding him to the real state of affairs in other particulars.[51] On the other hand, Abdy maintained that it had

[47] Hall, F., pp. 245-246.
[48] Candler, Chaps. X and XI, p. 125 ff; also Hodgson, II, 38; Weld, I, 143-145; Hamilton, I, 120; Neilson, pp. 270-271; Fowler, p. 214; Power, II, 347.
[49] Murray, I, 150-151.
[50] Stuart, I, 299.
[51] Martineau, I, 229.

a wonderful effect in sharpening the discriminating faculties of the mind![52]

The patience and good humor of the Americans were almost proverbial. How could the stagecoach passenger complain of the frequent breaking of the springs on the rough road, when the driver, on whom alone rested the responsibility of repairs, set to work patiently and good-humoredly to "fix" the broken part? Travellers tell of long journeys beguiled by the cheerfulness of native fellow-passengers, and of the philosophical calm displayed by these Americans in emergencies.[53] No one, however, would have thought of calling the American gay; many strangers noticed the habitual gravity of his expression. Hamilton was surprised at the apparent lack of happiness in New England, where "the materials of happiness were so widely and plentifully diffused." The countenances of the people were furrowed with care; no one seemed to have a light heart; soul and body were "withered up by the anxieties of life."[54] Francis Hall says that the usual gravity of manners and deportment were attributable to the fact that the Americans were habitually occupied with matters of deep interest.[55] Though not without wit, the inhabitants of the United States seemed lacking too in a certain kind of humor, the humor of the more boisterous kind. John Davis remarked that this quality was not indigenous to Americans. "The pleasantries of a droll would not relax the risible muscles of a party of Americans, however disposed to be merry; the wag would feel no encouragement from the surrounding countenances to exert his laughter-moving powers, but like the tyrant in the tragedy, he would

[52] Abdy, II, 306.
[53] See, for instance, Martineau, I, 240; D'Arusmont, pp. 126-127.
[54] Hamilton, I, 256.
[55] Hall, F., Appendix, p. 266.

be compelled to swallow the poison that was prepared for another." [56] This lack of a joyous spirit was noticed in both young and old alike. Blane commented on the fact that he never saw even American school-boys playing at any game whatsoever. "Cricket, football, and quoits, etc., appear to be utterly unknown, and I believe if an American were to see grown-up men playing at Cricket, he would express as much astonishment as the Italians did, when some Englishmen played at this finest of all games in the Cascina at Florence." [57] Welby offered as a reason for this lack of national amusement, the great number of elements in American life, agreeing only in devotion to religious and political liberty, and the resulting lack of a national character, "the effect," he says "is an evident want of energy, of heart and soul in everything animating to other nations. I am just returned from witnessing the celebration of the anniversay of their Liberty . . . such a festival might well be expected to call forth every spark of enthusiasm, but even then, not an eye, either of spectators or actors, glistened with joy or animation, the latter seemed walking to a funeral; the others contemplating the melancholy ceremony! Nothing could dispel the illusion but the gay clothes of the female spectators, to which their countenances in general bore a strong contrast." [58]

A trait which seemed to be apparent to Scotch visitors particularly was the lack of local attachment.[59] Americans seemed to be always moving about. Bristed remarked that they were "undoubtedly the most locomotive and migrating people in the world." A love of change was indeed obviously manifested in American life; it even ex-

[56] Davis, John, p. 104.
[57] Blane, pp. 502-503; also Weston, pp. 198-204.
[58] Welby, p. 170.
[59] See Murray, I, 111; Hamilton, I, 223; Bristed, p. 427.

tended to the frequent changing of the officers of administration, as has already been said.

The government was regarded as the greatest unifying force in the formation of American character. "The common qualities which may be said to be generated by this influence," said Francis Hall, "are intelligence or a quick perception of utility, both general and individual; hence their attachment to freedom and to every species of improvement, both publick and private; energy and perseverance in carrying their plans into effect . . . gravity of manner and deportment, because they are habitually occupied upon matters of deep interest; taciturnity, which is the offspring of thought."[60] Hamilton confessed that the political relations of the Americans were hard to understand though their other characteristics were marked and their peculiarities lay on the surface. "The patriot of one company was the scoundrel of the next," says the perplexed Scotchman.[61] Everywhere there was evidence of fervent party spirit, and yet the harmony of the country in regard to the great principles of government was too manifest to be ignored.[62]

The number of Englishmen who made any real attempt at analysis of American character is relatively small. Incidental and local comments of course are more numerous, but one feels the lack of a complete and philosophical discussion. Perhaps the Englishman did not understand the American well enough to analyze him; it is more likely that he regarded the native traits as secondary in interest to the institutions of which they were largely the result.

[60] Hall, F., pp. 265-266.
[61] Hamilton, I, 282, 292.
[62] Weld, I, 413; Hamilton, I, 209-210; Moore, T., Preface to "Poems Relating to America" in "Poetical Works" (1853 edition), Vol. II, 203.

CHAPTER XII

THE FUTURE OF THE UNION

BECAUSE the United States represented such a unique experiment in statecraft, her ultimate destiny seemed to have an unusual importance for the other nations of the world. If she could demonstrate that a government established on her principles, and composed of various elements, could withstand the wear and tear of internal and external dissension, and come forth triumphant from her trial, she could do much to remove from the consciousness of the world the close connection that existed between revolution and bloodshed; between republics and lawlessness. "If a government founded upon a republican model does not succeed there," said Latrobe, "surely the question of its suitableness to the state of mankind as they are, should be considered as determined forever."[1] This period witnessed only the beginning of the country's existence as a nation; consequently it was the time when conjectures as to the probable destiny of the United States were particularly numerous. Certain policies of the government were still in their infancy, and had not yet demonstrated their practicability. One was therefore at liberty to make surmises in regard to them, and, in so doing, to indulge to the full the desire to explain one's own theories of government.

It has been said before that the greatest and most inevit-

[1] Latrobe, II, 57. See also Faux, p. 28.

able distintegrating force was considered to be the institution of slavery. This was to be dreaded in both its moral and economic effects.[2] Those who emphasized the moral side of the question dwelt upon the injustice of the institution. What nation could expect to flourish and to become permanent when it was basely ignoring the first principles of justice and the rights of the slaves as human beings? The Americans were professing to be lovers of liberty, and at the same time were making capital of an enslaved race. This lack of consistency in theory and practice could not expect to go unpunished. "If the laws of God and the arrangements of man are incompatible, man's arrangements must give way." The past history of other nations afforded melancholy instances to show that, economically, slavery was destined to be the ruin of the nation, in its pernicious effects on industry and agriculture. The greatest evil, however, which could arise from this institution, as the foreigner saw it, was the separation of North and South. This was the only one of the definite prophecies of evil which has as yet been justified by subsequent history. Such disputes as those over the tariff, and over the admission of new states as slave or free, were destined in time, it was said, to be the opening wedge of the division. "Before Washington's bones are dissolved in the tomb, the sword of civil discord will be drawn in the land to which he bequeathed the fatal gift of democratic freedom." "The worldly inteersts of the minority," said Miss Martineau, ". . . are bound up with the anomaly. . . . The minority may go on for a length of time in apparent harmony with the expressed will of the many—the law. But the time comes when the anomaly clashes with the law." Practi-

[2] For effect of slavery, see Flower, pp. 97-98; Candler, pp. 397-399; Martineau, I, 132; Duncan, II, 331-334; Hamilton, II, p. 227; *Blackwood's Magazine*, XXXIII, 225.

cally no English visitor who expressed himself at all on the subject, needed to be convinced that the United States could not long exist unless she extirpated the curse of slavery.

Granted that she did so, her future was still insecure and problematical because of certain defects in the policy of the government, all of them details in themselves, but important in their bearing. Some of these had to do with the manner of electing officials. The most trivial of these defects was the custom of voting by ballot.[3] Most Englishmen believed that voting should be done viva voce, and that the paper ballots used by the Americans were liable to corruption. "The less secrecy and mystery there is in political matters, the better," said one of these critics, "everything in a land of freedom should be open to public inspection." "This system," said another, "excludes the open, wholesome influences of talent and property at the elections, and encourages a perpetual course of intrigue and fraud, by enabling the cunning demagogue to impose upon the credulity of the weak and ignorant. Indeed, the frauds practised by the substitution of one set of ballots for another, in every electioneering campaign throughout the country, are in themselves innumerable and shameless; and the success of elections generally depends upon the adroitness of intrigue exhibited by the more active political partisans."

Another defect was the frequency of the elections, an imperfection extending through the whole system of American government.[4] The drawbacks of this repeated change of office were obvious to the travellers. It was criticised as

[3] See Candler, pp. 388-389; Bristed, p. 120; Brothers, p. 132 ff; Matthews, I, 74.
[4] On this point, see Duhring, p. 9; Bristed, pp. 116 ff; Hamilton, II, 62-63; Hall, B., II, 266 (quotes DeWitt Clinton); Kendall, I, 157.

making the representatives of the people too local in their policy, and too dependent upon the will of their constituents; a candidate who wished to accomplish anything of importance in his office was obliged to stand for re-election. So short was the term of office in some cases, it was pointed out, that it was difficult to investigate and annul spurious elections before it was time to consider another candidate. Frequent elections, too, kept the people generally in a turmoil during the greater part of the year; time that should have been spent in useful and productive occupations was wasted in unprofitable politics. Such a method of procedure was inevitably destined to make the country poorer and the people less industrious. The evil had also a wider application; a Congress which was changed so frequently was of necessity without a settled policy in regard to the conduct of national affairs and the development of the country's resources. "One man will not plant, that another may reap the harvest of his labors; he will not patiently lay the foundation of a structure, the plan of which is continually liable to be changed by his successor, on whom, if completed, the whole honours must ultimately devolve. In short, it is an inherent and monstrous evil, that American statesmen must legislate for the *present*, not for the *future*. . . . Immediate and temporary expediency is, and must be, the moving and efficient impulse of American legislation."

State representation in the electing of the president was also considered to be much in need of re-adjustment. The influence of each of the states was in exact ratio to the number of its population. As the increase of population in some states was greater than in others, the former tended to secure to themselves the electing power. Thomas Hamilton foresaw the time when the three states—New York, Pennsylvania, and Ohio, would together possess the numerical majority of the population and could therefore elect the president. If the other states tried to amend the constitution on this point, their attempt would be futile, because these three states would also have a majority in the House of Representatives.[5]

The most serious evil connected with the elections and regarded with apprehension by these borrowers of trouble, was, however, the tendency toward universal suffrage,[6] which became practically a fact in the first part of the nineteenth century. Even if the nation did away with all religious restrictions, said the critics, would it not have been well to keep the property qualification, especially, as one traveller pointed out, since the lack of property in a country like America, full of opportunities, stamped one as idle and thriftless? Besides, "property has a tendency to bind a man more strongly to the interest of his country; and, if so, he is the more likely to be careful and considerate to do nothing that has a tendency to involve the country in difficulties; for by doing so he would put in jeopardy his individual property that he or his forefathers have taken so much pains to obtain." Much was said in regard to the connection between universal suffrage and bribery.[7] Some foreigners asserted that bribery existed in the United States; others tried to show that it was improbable. Most of the former believed that the practical difficulties which were said to stand in the way of corrupting such large numbers of people, offered no obstacle to the practice. The natural result of a universal suffrage was

[5] See, for system of representation, Hamilton, II, 49, I, 311; Vigne, I, 204-206; Hall, B., II, 254 ff.

[6] For universal suffrage, see Duhring, p. 10; Duncan, II, 335; Hamilton, I, 313-314; Brothers, p. 244; Bristed, pp. 120-121; Vigne, I, 191 ff.

[7] Ouseley, p. 32; Duhring, p. 10; Candler, pp. 383, 394; Vigne, I, 192-193; Duncan, II, 335.

that much-dreaded state of affairs—a mob rule which kept office-holders subservient to its interests, and tended to exclude from the administration of the government "men of talents, character, and property." The evil effects of this extension of the suffrage could not yet be seen; perhaps, as Duncan hopefully suggested, some antidote might yet be discovered, but it was quite certain in the minds of many people that the interests of the United States were destined to suffer, at some time in the future, because of the adoption of this policy.

Another serious question was the relation of the executive to the legislative department of the government.[8] It was believed that the states had acted unwisely in excluding executive officers from all places in the representative bodies, thus "discarding a powerful and efficient guarantee for the honest and upright administration of their affairs. The knowledge that every political measure will be subjected to a rigid and unsparing scrutiny, and must be defended to the satisfaction of honorable men in open discussion, is assuredly the most effective safeguard which has yet been devised to secure the integrity of public men." Other observers complain of an exactly opposite tendency to merge the two departments of state. Basil Hall said that the constant aim of the populace was "to draw within their circle as much of the executive power as possible, and to blend this with their legitimate authority; two things which universal experience elsewhere shows ought always to be kept separate."

In their attitude toward their executives, from the president down to the smallest official, the Americans were characterized by what Englishmen called distrust and sus-

[8] Candler, p. 395 ff; Duhring, p. 9; Hamilton, II, 66-67; Hall, B., II, 311.

picion.⁹ The tendency of the government was believed to be toward circumscribing more and more the influence of the executive, and putting more power into the hands of the people. Some foreigners looked upon this as the chief error of the American constitution, and thought it absurd that the president, for instance, could conclude no treaty without the consent of the Senate. In general, the president's power was considered to be altogether too limited and controlled for a vigorous government. In emergencies there was liable to be much procrastination in getting policies adopted. "Liable to impeachment and dismissal from office for the commission of treason and other high crimes and misdemeanors, he [the president] may do much good, but he can do no essential harm. The powers he derives from the constitution are in fact mere duties."

The anxiety which was felt in regard to the relations between legislature and executives was extended to those that existed between the several states and the Federal government.¹⁰ These had been, since the founding of the nation, the subject of many disputes. Englishmen seem to have taken the side of the states almost entirely. Hodgson said that it was a common idea in England that the stability of the Union was much endangered by the trouble between the central government and the states, and that the former was inclined always to usurp the prerogatives of the latter. It was the belief, however, that the Federal government could not misuse its rights for any length of time without being checked by the states; what was chiefly to be feared was the alienation of the two.

⁹ For attitude toward officials, see De Roos, p. 29; Hamilton, I, 363; Duhring, p. 9; Welby, pp. 334-335; Hall, B., II, 262-263, 311; Hodgson, II, 178-179.

¹⁰ Duhring, p. 5, 11-14; Bristed, p. 218; Hodgson, II, 190-196; Mrs. Trollope, II, 20-21.

Less important than these defects in the constitution, just discussed, seemed a group of considerations none of which commanded a general credence, but which are interesting as showing the kind of condition which might operate against the Union, and detract from its prosperity and efficiency. These ranged from the exclusion of the clergy from official positions [11] to the lack of the law of primogeniture.[12] The levelling propensity betrayed in the custom of the equal sharing of property in the family, was to the mind of the observer not an unmixed blessing. It prevented the growth of a wealthy class which might be extremely useful to the community, and which might fittingly make a part of the state legislatures. On the other hand many Englishmen feared for America an increase in her poor.[13] Hamilton in discussing Miss Wright's "Workies," says that they present an aspect menacing to the government. Let luxury and poverty increase, and the cities become congested, and the so-called lower classes would be something with which to reckon. It was true that the poor were now so comparatively few in number as to be a "mere hydra in embryo," but the real time of trial for America was in the future. "Hitherto," says De Roos, "the Americans have enjoyed the advantage of occupying a country where the evils of an overflowing population have not been felt; where every man is either a farmer or a merchant; where there are no idlers; and more than all, where there are no poor; for vile indeed must be the American who cannot, in some capacity, earn an ample maintenance. When, however, the means of carrying off a superfluous population begin to fail, which, at some period must

---

[11] Bristed, pp. 122-123.

[12] Hall, B., II, 309.

[13] Hamilton, I, 295-297. See refutation of Hamilton in Shirreff, p. 291 ff; Vigne, I, 247-249.

THE FUTURE OF THE UNION 329

be the case, . . . we may expect to see the disadvantages of a popular government."[14] One of the greatest drawbacks to the future prosperity of the country was, in Miss Martineau's opinion, the general apathy in regard to the duties of citizenship.[15] "In England," she said, "the idea of an American citizen is of one who is always talking politics, canvassing, bustling about to make proselytes abroad, buried in newspapers at home, and hurrying to vote on election day." The true situation was quite different from this. Many of the more respectable men were extremely apathetic and indifferent in regard to voting, not appearing to realize the harm they were doing to the public good. Fear of criticism kept many from assuming the responsibility of office, a circumstance by which the corrupt element profited.

These were only relatively unimportant defects of government policy, the action of which, or the combination of which, might interfere with the progress of the nation. The imagination of the average traveller, however, was not satisfied with these trivial bugbears. Much more serious to him was the disparity of interests that prevailed in the different parts of the country.[16] No two sections were alike, and each defended itself against the rest with the fiercest jealousy. Could it be expected that unity of government should be compatible with great diversities of interest in the governed? One traveller cited the instance of Florida and Maine. "In Florida and Louisiana they grow sugar; in Maine there is scarcely enough sun to ripen a crop of

[14] De Roos, p. 28.
[15] Martineau, I, 115 ff; also Duncan, II, 328.
[16] For disparity of interests, see Hamilton, I, 306-308; Matthews, I, 75-76; Candler, p. 397; Tudor II, 508-509; D'Arusmont, p. 287; Bristed, pp. 234-235; Flint, pp. 210-211; Martineau, I, 135-143.

maize. The people of these states are no less different than the productions of their soil. They are animated by no sentiment of brotherhood and affinity. Nature has divided them by a distance of two thousand miles; the interests of one are neither understood nor cared for in the other. In short, they are connected by nothing but a clumsy and awkward piece of machinery most felicitously contrived to deprive both of the blessing of self-government.'' There was not only the difference between North and South; it might be expected that at some time in the future the East and the West would come into conflict. The practical difficulty of representation for so large a field was urged. If this obstacle were surmounted, the result would still engender strife. The great extent of territory west of the Mississippi afforded space for numerous future states, which, with a growing population and a proportionally increasing representation, would soon be able to outvote the East in Congress. Eastern interests would inevitably suffer in that event. ''The tendency of all this,'' said Bristed, speaking of the growing preponderance of Western influence, ''beyond a peradventure, is either to break up the Federal Union, and entail a perpetuity of anarchy and civil broils throughout the whole continent, or to crush the Atlantic States beneath the enormous hoofs of the western mammoth.'' James Flint, who was thoroughly familiar with the Western district, did not believe that that section of the country would ever separate from the East. ''The western settlements,'' he says, ''have the strongest incitements to remain in close conjunction with their eastern neighbors. A separation from them in times of war would cut off all communication by land with the eastern coast; an inconvenience that would greatly aggravate any attempt to blockade the mouth of the Mississippi. A separa-

·tion would retard the ingress of population, it would injure internal trade, it would occasion additional expense in supporting a separate government, and it would deprive them of the protection of the United States navy. It will scarcely be alleged that the Eastern States have an interest in dissolving the compact with the Western; as by that step, they would not only forego a rapid accumulation of strength, but would incur the danger of converting fellow-citizens into the most powerful enemies. They would lose that important branch of revenue which arises from the sale of public lands, and they would no longer participate in the fur trade.''

This sectional jealousy was necessarily inconsistent with sound and wholesome legislation.[17] Each representative, it was urged, in protecting the interests of his own part of the country, would estimate measures, not by their tendency to benefit the whole union, but by their bearing on particular interests. The disparities were the more serious because they arose largely from climate and soil and were therefore beyond legislative interference. A circumstance which might lead to serious inconvenience, was the difference in the laws of the various states. This resulted from the great number of separate state governments, and was regarded by the foreigner as a disintegrating circumstance, for, as one Englishman said, nothing tends more to unite a people into general harmony and to make them feel a common interest, than the being subject to the same laws in all parts of the country.[18] Unfortunately, in the United States the tendency was in the opposite direction.

Facing all these obstacles to growth and longevity, the United States might well be expected to fail to achieve a

[17] Hamilton, I, 196, 376-377; Vigne, I, 260.
[18] Candler, p. 387.

glorious destiny.[19] She was still, as it were, in her infancy; her real time of trial had not yet come but it was none the less inevitably coming. Even the most pessimistic critics did not set a very early date for her dissolution. Vigne is the only observer who predicts that it will probably be less than a half century before the United States "will fall to pieces by its own weight." But the seeds of dissolution, it was said, had had their origin with the government, and might be expected to come to fruition at some future time.

It is by no means true that all English travellers looked upon the United States as a nation doomed to destruction. To many, the signs of the times were too hopeful to justify gloomy predictions.[20] Some steered a middle course, and prophesied that the government would slowly assume a new form, eliminating one by one the faults that impeded the country's progress, and, as one traveller expressed it, "fixing its rule upon the broad and firm foundations of property and talent." It was to be hoped and expected that America's practice of government would approach more nearly to her theory, which was conceded to be almost ideal.

The necessity of the preservation of the Union for the ultimate welfare of the several states was emphasized.[21] Let this confederation once be dissolved, and all the advantages peculiar to the United States would be lost. The parts could not be separated without disturbing the happiness of

[19] See Smyth, J. F. D., "A Tour in the United States of America" (1784), Vol. II, Chap. LXXV entire. Smyth was in America during the Revolution, and accordingly suffered at the hands of the Americans. His chapter is an interesting prophecy in view of the fact that the separation of England and the United States was scarcely consummated at the time it was written. Vigne, II, 273.

[20] See Bristed, p. 218; Fearon, p. 363; *Blackwood's Magazine*, XXXII, 93.

[21] Duhring, pp. 19-20; Bristed, p. 211, 213-214 (quotation).

the whole. It behooved the Americans to remember the evils surmounted in the past by the aid of such men as Washington and the other founders of the republic, and by that memory cling to and protect the Federal union, "that *federal union* which, if once dissolved, ensures the breaking up of the foundations of civil order, peace, and safety, over all the range of this extensive territory; ensures a perpetuity of . . . anarchy, civil war, carnage, and desolation. . . Better, far better, would it be for the United States to endure an entire century of *foreign* war, or to labour fifty years under the burden of *domestic maladministration,* than by severing the federal Union into a multitude of petty principalities, to entail upon all the extent of the northern continent of America the prevalence of *foreign* factions, French, Russian and British, perpetually interfering with, and confounding, all their *home* movements and measures; and above all, to ensure a perpetuity of *feudal* anarchy and brigandage; of castellated feuds; of partisan warfare; of hereditary hostility, of arbitrary incarceration; of inquisitorial torment; of military execution; of private assassination; of public pillage; of universal oppression and all the calamities incident to afflicted humanity, when *force* and *fraud* are the arbiters of right and wrong."

If these states could be kept united, a glorious future lay before them, as they had within themselves all the materials for greatness.[22] Observers cited, as elements of strength, the civil and religious equality, the adaptability of the separate state governments to the different parts of the country, the natural advantages, the similarity in manners and in language. As James Flint said, it was an organiztion "well adapted to insure internal tranquility and protection

[22] Hodgson, II, 190; Flint, p. 213; Candler, pp. 397-401; Duhring, p. 11; Bristed, pp. 245-246; Matthews, I, 78.

against invasion." It could reasonably be expected that the country would add to its territory, and that it would in time extend "from the Atlantic to the Pacific; from Mexico to the shores of the arctic ocean." It was quite probable that the United States would seek to gain possession of Canada, in order to have the free navigation of the St. Lawrence and to prevent future hostilities from the British provinces. It was even suggested that Canada should be given to the United States for a consideration, in order to prevent future trouble. As for the West Indies, it was generally believed that they would in time become part of the new republic, though Candler said in 1824: "As to Mexico, California, and the West Indies being added to the Union, a circumstance which some of the Americans are pleased to anticipate, the probabilities are so remote, that it is not worth while to examine them."

In short, many visitors believed that far from being peculiarly susceptible to the danger of dissolution, the United States represented as nearly ideal a form of government, and as stable a one as could be imagined.[23] She could reasonably be supposed to last as long as any other human institution, particularly since, by her legislation, the interests of the people were regarded; that kind of government, it was maintained, has always lasted longest. Her inhabitants had fought together for liberty, and the independence and self-confidence of the American character, which had resulted from this fact, were sufficient guarantees of the stability of the government. "I see no reason," an Englishman remarked, "why, in the ordinary course of things, this grand Confederation might not continue for ages. . . . It is destined, I trust, to exhibit to the world at large a grand and successful experiment in legislation." "As a friend of

[23] Hodgson, II, 196 (quotation); Duhring, p. 6 ff., 127 (quotation); D'Arusmont, p. 265, 297; Hall, F., p. 332; Ouseley, p. 7.

liberty and of free institutions," said another, "I implore from the Almighty the salvation of the American Union! May this noble, verdant, and flourishing tree of liberty, planted by a free hand on a savage but fertile strand, which has already struck its roots deeply in the American soil and produced the richest and most abundant fruits, still gain in strength and in majestic stateliness! May its bark be preserved from any injury; its wood from the meanest worm! May its roots never moulder; its sap never dry!"

CHAPTER XIII

CONCLUSION

WHEN the reader of this mass of travel literature tries to reduce the facts to some kind of system, he notices frequent gaps. The sins of omission are sometimes curious ones, and difficult if not impossible to account for.

We notice immediately that observers usually describe the same parts of the country. This is easily understood if one remembers that few travellers went aside from the beaten paths because of the very practical difficulties in the way of transportation. For instance, those Englishmen who visited New England usually travelled over the roads between Albany and Boston, or between Boston and New York. There was very little going aside from two or three main-travelled routes. A few observers, as has been said, visited the White Mountains, and others saw as much of Vermont as was visible from the eastern shore of Lake Champlain, as they passed southward from Canada. Kendall was an exception to the rule in that he visited the isolated districts of Maine. Generally speaking, that section of the country was untouched, and the almost solitary Englishman, Melish, for instance, who wrote about the untravelled regions of New England, drew his picture, not from what he had actually seen, but from information gleaned from other sources.

The same is true of the rest of the country. Travel books abound in descriptions of New York, Philadelphia, Baltimore, Washington, Charleston, New Orleans, and Cincinnati. The best-known routes have already been traced in a previous chapter. The territory on either side of these roads remained an unknown land to the average traveller. Exceptions to the rule were men like Francis Baily and John Bradbury, who penetrated into comparatively unsettled parts and who give us our few pictures of those regions. So great was the tendency to follow the known road that even Fowler, who made a study of New York State, went from New York to Niagara and back in 1830 by practically the same route.

Another kind of omission has to do with the details of American life. On some of these, information is sadly lacking. We are told, for instance, very little of the appearance of the interior of an American home or inn, church or school. We have descriptions of the exterior of taverns and houses, and a few pictures of them, but the inside is left to the imagination. Travellers tell of congregating in the bar-room of the inns or hotels, and of despatching hasty meals in the dining room, without telling us what either of these rooms looked like. The same is true of the bedrooms; all of the attention of the average traveller seems to have been concentrated on the question of the cleanliness and comfort of the bed.

In the descriptions of the American home we miss many small details which would help to make the picture vivid. We get no conception of the furniture, of the pictures on the walls, of the numberless objects of utility important in the life of the household. We are told comparatively little about the clothing which Americans wore; what information we have on the subject is so fragmentary that we can form only a very unsatisfactory mental picture of the actual appearance of a typical American. We are constantly impressed by the lack of discrimination in the choosing of subjects for discussion. It was perhaps natural that each traveller should set down in his note book mention of those objects which at the moment struck his fancy, but it is an inconvenient method for the historian who is attempting to reconstruct the life which the Englishman observed.

On matters outside the home, we are baffled by the same silence in regard to certain points. Many travellers tell us, for instance, of the turnpikes, which were generally regarded as admirable. We are told by what method and under whose supervision they were constructed and how they differed from other American roads, but only one traveller, Abdy, tells us what kind of vehicles were exempt from the payment of tolls, and not one tells us the rate of toll. In regard to statistics too, there are few complete and authentic statements. Assertions which would naturally call for verification seem to have been offered with sublime indifference to authority. Far too frequent for accurate information is the occurrence of the phrases, "I was told by the citizens of the town," and "I have the information from a gentleman of good standing." In most cases the omission of adequate authority leads the seeker after truth a chase in an attempt at verification. Most astonishing stories are told by observers on the slightest basis. Fidler, for instance, tells us that American clergymen are not permitted to sit in Congress. The origin of this prohibition he gives as follows: "One of the members of Congress, a clergyman, was very desirous that some permanent provision should be made for the episcopal church, and was urgent with a friend of his, a member also, to use his endeavors to accomplish it. This friend, probably annoyed by frequent solicitations, and being, as Americans in general are represented, a summer's-day friend, promised his word of honour that he would do something for the church. Accordingly, he mentioned this circumstance in Congress on the first opportunity, and relating his promise, moved that no clergyman should thenceforth sit in that house. The motion was carried by a vast majority, and clergymen, with their golden anticipations, vanished from it forever. This was told me by a divine of prominence."

Considering that a great deal was said by English travellers about the interest of the Americans in politics, we are surprised to find that there was not more discussion in travel literature of the principles of the political system. The space devoted to this by most writers who mentioned the subject is occupied by quotations from the Federal constitution. The Englishman at home must have been rather at a loss if he depended on the travel books for any discussion of American politics and principles. Hamilton, it is true, includes a somewhat lengthy discussion of these subjects rather by way of warning to his own country. The one notable exception, however, is Kendall, whose detailed exposition of the constitution of Connecticut is still regarded as authoritative.

It was the very unusual things that naturally commanded the most attention. Such curiosities as fireflies, rattlesnakes, frogs, and mocking birds are seldom omitted from the accounts. The coloring of the American forests in the autumn and the severity of American thunderstorms were apparently subjects more worthy of comment than some of the greater issues of American life. It would be untrue to say that the average English traveller had no interest in the vital part of the "American scene," but it is quite true that many of these visitors had much the same attitude as most of us have who visit foreign countries today; the things that we recount in our travel tales are the strikingly unusual and interesting circumstances.

One must take into account, too, the particular bias of

certain authors. Many of these travellers were especially interested in one subject, in the light of which they interpreted everything that they saw. This attitude is quite distinct from the interest in trade revealed by Melish and Boardman and other writers who came for commercial reasons, or the botanical predilections of Bradbury. The religious and the philanthropic inclinations seem to have been the most pronounced. A notable case is that of Abdy, whose whole interpretation of American life is colored by his sympathy for the negro. Hardly a chapter of his three volumes is free from some reference to the injustice of the white man to the black. The result is an unusual though not very reliable book.

In the same way, though not to the same degree, Duncan was interested in religious matters, and a strong strain of piety may be perceived throughout his work. He remarks in his preface that very little has been said as to the moral condition of the inhabitants of the United States, or as to their literary and religious characteristics, and he proposes to set right the misapprehension on the subject. Fidler, too, looked at everything from the point of view of the religious conditions of the United States; his account is colored, as well, by his personal disappointment. This last factor plays an important part in travel literature, as we have seen, in the case of such widely different people as Parkinson and Mrs. Trollope.

The question of the relative value of these accounts is a puzzling one. In most cases, it is almost impossible to say which facts were borrowed from other sources and which ones were original. Some books were palpably compilations of other works. In this class is Kingdom's "America and the British Colonies" (1820, 2nd ed.) The author says in his preface that his information has been collected for the guidance of a friend and himself, both of whom at that period entertained some intention of emigrating. In making the book, he has consulted the publications which have met with the greatest share of public approbation. Evidently these are the works of Melish, Bristed, Bradbury, Michaux, Birkbeck, and Fearon. Much of his information is taken from the last-named author, whom he evidently regards as an authority. Another compilation is "A Geographical, Historical, Commercial, and Agricultural View of the United States, Forming a Complete Emigrant's Directory, through Every Part of the Republic, Compiled by Several Gentlemen" (1820). When one looks through the large, closely-printed volume, it is easy to believe the statement that "recourse has been had to every work of reputation on these subjects that has appeared since the year 1788." The compilers do not name the authors to whom they are indebted, but transfer bodily to their pages long quotations apparently given on their own authority.

A rather charming book which is drawn from other than original sources is Priscilla Wakefield's "Excursions in North America." In her preface, the author says that her chief sources have been Jefferson, Weld, Rochefoucault, Bartram, Michaux, Carver, Mackenzie, and Hearn. As has already been noted, this book was compiled primarily for young people, and gives a particularly good account of both Canada and the United States. William Bingley's "Travels in North America, from Modern Writers," has also been cited as having been written for young people. "It has been the design of the author," Bingley says, "by a detail of anecdotes of extraordinary adventures, connected by illustrative remarks and observations, to allure young persons to a study of geography, and to the attainment of a knowledge of the character, habits, customs, and productions of foreign nations." He quotes from Fearon, Weld,

Birkbeck, Francis Hall, Michaux, Bartram, Mackenzie, Pike, and Lewis and Clark.

In regard to the books of travel professedly original, some caution is necessary. The works which are in the form of letters written from America, or journals of the tour, kept more or less regularly and written down on the spot, inspire us with more confidence than do the more unified and much better written discussions. On the whole, it may be said that most of the travellers are rather scrupulous about attributing credit to the authorities from whom they borrow. Englishmen had recourse to many American books; several writers, Bristed, Francis Hall, and Priest, for instance, quote from Jefferson's "Notes on Virginia." Another favorite authority was Jedidiah Morse's "Geography." Many gaps in the accounts of Palmer, Bristed, Francis Hall, and Francis Baily were filled by information from this standard work. Few visitors were as careful borrowers as was Ouseley, whose chief authority was government records; however, Pitkin's "Statistical View of the United States" and Tench Coxe's "View of the United States of America" were consulted with profit. Bristed's book, for instance, is based largely on these two authorities, as well as on Brown's "Western Gazetteer," which other travellers also found helpful. James Stuart and Blane depended on Darby, whose "Louisiana" and "View of the United States" were universally accepted as authoritative. Stuart also used Timothy Flint's "Geography and History of the United States." Another useful American publication was Imlay's "Topographical Description of the Western Territory of North America," which was quoted by Baily; Bristed considered it, however, too flattering an account.

English travellers seem to have depended little on one another. Melish is perhaps the most generally known; his map of the United States was considered very accurate; both Palmer and Blane copy it in their books. But if the average traveller took his information from the fellow-countrymen who preceded him, the fact is not apparent. That he was aware of the work of other observers is evident not only from the mention of English books of travel in the prefaces of the various works, but from the fact that many travellers refute the statements of other writers. This has already been shown to be true in the case of the distorted statements offered by Captain Hall and Mrs. Trollope, and the optimistic accounts of Birkbeck. Other instances occur here and there in this travel literature. Madame D'Arusmont, for example, speaks of Francis Hall's work in terms of commendation, and severely criticises Fearon's book. Bristed makes his opening chapter a discussion of other writers on America, both English and French. He exposes the credulity of Weld and the misrepresentations of Thomas Moore and discusses the authoritativeness of Beaujour, Brissot, Volney, Melish, Bradbury, and Birkbeck. Such mention of other observers bears witness to the fact that English travellers were well known to one another; in regard to actual transmission of statement, however, one cannot be sure. If borrowing was done without giving authority, the evidence of it was rather well-concealed.

A question which occurs to one at the very beginning of the preparation of the material for this book, is — did the English travellers, as a whole, tell the truth about America? By way of answer, one may trace a consistent development in the attitude of these observers. It is noticeable that in the days immediately following the Revolution, the general ideas entertained of the United States were unjust and untrue. Perhaps it was because so little was really known about America that writers like Parkinson, Weld, Janson, and Moore felt at liberty to let their imagination wander where it would. Just after the beginning of the nineteenth century, a change becomes quite apparent to the reader of travel literature. One has an increasing sense of treading upon the firmer ground of fact rather than upon the quagmire of imagination and prejudice. A book like Melish's "Travels," for instance, is a landmark in this evolution of a correct idea of American life. It is true that writers like Fearon, Faux, and Welby come after this time, but we have also, in the second decade of the century, Duncan, Lambert, and Hodgson, all of whom are to be generally trusted. As time went on, the books of travel not only multiplied but became more and more reliable; about 1830, we have a large number of more or less authentic accounts — those of Miss Martineau, Stuart, Coke, Ferrall, Vigne, Murray, and Hamilton, for instance. It is true that this last part of our period witnessed the publication of the works of Basil Hall and Mrs. Trollope, but these are to be regarded not as well-balanced and thoughtful accounts of American life, but rather as the product of two unfortunate dispositions. In regard to most matters, we may say that these later English travellers told the truth; at least they were not palpably delighting in misrepresentation.

The value of this travel literature, though it cannot be definitely estimated, is very real. If, as individuals, we are helped by the criticism of our friends or our enemies, we may expect as a nation to reap the same benefit from the opinions of those who came from other lands. Even the most prejudiced accounts contain some germs of truth. The effect on America of this vast bulk of English travel, and the part it played in the subsequent development of American institutions can, of course, only be guessed at. At any rate, the detailed analysis of English attitude toward the United States in the critical fifty-year period after the founding of the nation, cannot fail to make some contribution to our knowledge of American conditions of the time, and to present in a new and interesting light many of the institutions which we Americans have come to take more or less for granted.

ENGLISH TRAVEL IN AMERICA, 1785-1835

ABDY, EDWARD STRUTT. Journal of a Residence and Tour in the United States of North America from April, 1833, to October, 1834. 3 vols. London, 1835.

ALEXANDER, J. E. Transatlantic Sketches. 2 vols. London, 1833.

ASHE, THOMAS. Travels in America Performed in 1806 for the purpose of exploring the rivers Alleghany, Monongahela, Ohio and Mississippi, and ascertaining the produce and condition of their banks and vicinity. London, 1808.

BAILY, FRANCIS. Journal of a Tour in unsettled parts of North America in 1796-1797. London, 1856.

BERNARD, JOHN. Retrospections of America (1797-1811). Edited from the manuscript by Mrs. Bayle Bernard, with an Introduction, Notes and Index by Laurence Hutton and Brander Matthews. New York, 1887.

BINGLEY, WILLIAM. Travels in North America, from Modern Writers. With Remarks and Observations, Exhibiting a Connected View of the Geography and Present State of that Quarter of the Globe. London, 1821.

BIRKBECK, MORRIS. Notes on a Journey in America from the coast of Virginia to the territory of Illinois. 2nd ed. London, 1818.

———— ————. Letters from Illinois. London, 1818.

BLANE, WILLIAM NEWNHAM. An excursion through the United States and Canada during the years 1822-23. By an English Gentleman. London, 1824.

BOARDMAN, JAMES. America and the Americans, by a Citizen of the World. London, 1833.

BRADBURY, JOHN. Travels in the Interior of America, in the Years 1809, 1810, and 1811. 2nd ed. London, 1819.

BRISTED, JOHN. The Resources of the United States of America; or, A View of the Agricultural, Commercial, Manufacturing, Financial, Political, Literary, Moral, and Religious Capacity and Character of the American People. New York, 1818.

BROTHERS, THOMAS. The United States as They Are: not as they are generally Described, being a cure for radicalism. London, 1840.

BUTLER, FRANCES ANNE. Journal (1832-1833). 2 vols. London, 1835.

CANDLER, ISAAC. A Summary View of America. London, 1824.

COBBETT, WILLIAM. A Year's Residence in the United States of America. 3rd ed. London, 1828.

COKE, E. T. (LIEUT.). A Subaltern's Furlough . . . during the summer and autumn of 1832. 2 vols. New York, 1833.

COKE, THOMAS. A Journal of the Rev. Dr. Coke's Fourth Tour on the Continent of America. London, 1792.

COOPER, THOMAS. Some Information Respecting America. Dublin, 1794.

CUMING, F. Sketches of a Tour to the Western Country through the States of Ohio and Kentucky. Pittsburgh, 1810. (Reprinted in R. G. Thwaites' Early Western Travels, Vol. X.)

DALTON, WILLIAM. Travels in the United States of America and Part of Upper Canada. Appleby, 1821.

D'ARUSMONT, FRANCES WRIGHT. Views of Society and Manners in America: in a series of Letters from that Country to a Friend in England during the years 1818, 1819, and 1820. By an Englishwoman. New York, 1821.

DAVIS, JOHN. Travels of Four Years and a Half in the United States of America During 1798, 1799, 1800, 1801, and 1802. London, 1803.

DAVIS, STEPHEN. Notes of a Tour in America, in 1832 and 1833. Edinburg, 1833.

DeRoos, Frederick Fitzgerald. Personal Narrative of Travels in the United States and Canada in 1826. . . . With Remarks on the Present State of the American Navy. 3rd ed. London, 1827.

Duhring, Henry. Remarks on the United States of America with regard to the actual state of Europe. London, 1833.

Duncan, John M. Travels through Part of the United States and Canada in 1818 and 1819. 2 vols. Glasgow, 1823.

Faux, William. Memorable Days in America, Being a Journal of a Tour of the United States . . . (1818-1820). London, 1823. (Thwaites' Early Western Travels, Vol. XI.)

Fearon, Henry Bradshaw. Sketches of America: a Narrative of a Journey of Five Thousand Miles through the Eastern and Western States of America. London, 1819.

Ferrall, S. A. A Ramble of Six Thousand Miles through the United States of America. London, 1832.

Fidler, Isaac. Observations on Professions, Literature, Manners and Emigration in the United States and Canada, made during a Residence there in 1832. New York, 1833.

Finch, J. Travels in the United States of America and Canada. London, 1833.

Flint, James. Letters from America. Edinburgh, 1822. (Thwaites' Early Western Travels, Vol. IX.)

Flower, Richard. Letters from Lexington and the Illinois. London, 1819. (Thwaites' Early Western Travels, Vol. X.)

Fowler, John. Journal of a Tour in the State of New York in the Year 1830. London, 1831.

Hall, Basil. Travels in North America in the Years 1827 and 1828. 3 vols. 3rd ed. Edinburgh, 1830.

Hall, Francis. Travels in Canada and the United States in 1816 and 1817. Boston, 1818.

Hamilton, Thomas. Men and Manners in America. 2 vols. Edinburgh, 1834.

Harris, William Tell. Remarks Made During a Tour through the United States of America in the Years 1817, 1818, and 1819. In a series of Letters to Friends in England. London, 1821.

HODGSON, ADAM. Letters from North America, Written during a Tour in the United States and Canada. 2 vols. London, 1824.
HOLMES, ISAAC. An Account of the United States of America, Derived from Actual Observation during a Residence of Four Years. London, n. d. (1823).
HOWISON, JOHN. Sketches of Upper Canada. 3rd ed. Edinburgh, 1825.
HULME, THOMAS. A Journal Made during a Tour in the Western Countries of America, September 30, 1818-August 7, 1819. (Reprinted from Cobbett's A Year's Residence in the United States of America. London, 1828. Thwaites' Early Western Travels, Vol. X.)
JANSON, CHARLES WILLIAM. The Stranger in America. London, 1807.
KENDALL, EDWARD AUGUSTUS. Travels through the Northern Parts of the United States in the Years 1807 and 1808. 3 vols. New York, 1809.
KINGDOM, WILLIAM. America and the British Colonies. 2nd ed. London, 1820.
LAMBERT, JOHN. Travels through Canada and the United States of North America in the Years 1806, 1807, and 1808. 2 vols. 3rd ed. London, 1816.
LATROBE, CHARLES JOSEPH. The Rambler in North America (1832-1833). 2 vols. New York, 1835.
MACKENZIE, WILLIAM LYON. Sketches of Canada and the United States. London, 1833.
MARTINEAU, HARRIET. Society in America. 2 vols. New York, 1837.
MATTHEWS, W. Historical Review of North America, . . . by a gentleman immediately returned from a tour of that country. 2 vols. Dublin, 1789.
MAUDE, JOHN. Visit to the Falls of Niagara in 1800. London, 1826.
MELISH, JOHN. Travels in the United States of America in the Years 1806 and 1807 and 1809, 1810 and 1811. 2 vols. Philadelphia, 1812.

MOORE, THOMAS. "Poems Relating to America" in Vol. II, "Poetical Works." Boston, 1856.

MURRAY, CHARLES AUGUSTUS. Travels in North America during the Years 1834, 1835, and 1836. 2 vols. New York, 1839.

NEILSON, PETER. Recollections of a Six Years' Residence in the United States of America. Glasgow, 1830.

OUSELEY, WILLIAM GORE. Remarks on the Statistics and Political Institutions of the United States. London, 1832.

PALMER, JOHN. Journal of Travels in the United States of North America and in Lower Canada. London, 1818.

PARKINSON, RICHARD. A Tour in America in 1798, 1799, and 1800. 2 vols. London, 1805.

PICKERING, JOSEPH. Inquiries of an Emigrant, being the narrative of an English farmer from the year 1824 to 1830. 4th ed. London, 1832.

POWER, TYRONE. Impressions of America during the Years 1833, 1834, and 1835. 2 vols. London, 1836.

PRIEST, WILLIAM. Travels in the United States of America; Commencing in the Year 1793 and Ending in 1797. London, 1802.

RICH, OBADIAH. Bibliotheca Americana Nova. London, 1835. A General View of the United States. 2nd ed. London, 1836.

SHIRREFF, PATRICK. A Tour through North America; together with a Comprehensive View of the Canadas and United States. As Adapted for Agricultural Emigration. By Patrick Shirreff, Farmer. Edinburgh, 1835.

SUTCLIFFE, ROBERT. Travels in Some Parts of North America, 1804, 1805, and 1806. York, 1811.

STUART, JAMES. Three Years in North America. From the second London ed. 2 vols. New York, 1833.

TROLLOPE, FRANCES M. Domestic Manners of the Americans. Ed. by Harry Thurston Peck. 2 vols. in one. New York, 1901.

TUDOR, HENRY. Narrative of a Tour in North America . . . in a series of letters written in the Years 1831-32. 2 vols. London, 1834.

TWINING, THOMAS. Travels in America One Hundred Years Ago. New York, 1894.

VIGNE, GODFREY THOMAS. Six Months in America. 2 vols. London, 1832.

WAKEFIELD, PRISCILLA BELL. Excursions in North America. Described in Letters from a Gentleman and his Young Companion to their Friends in England. London, 1806.

WANSEY, HENRY. An Excursion to the United States of North America in the Summer of 1794. Salisbury, 1798.

WELBY, ADLARD. A Visit to North America and the English Settlements in Illinois, with a Winter Residence at Philadelphia. London, 1821.

WELD, ISAAC. Travels through the States of North America and the Provinces of Upper and Lower Canada during the years 1795, 1796, and 1797. 2nd ed. London, 1799.

WESTON, RICHARD. "A Visit to the United States and Canada in 1833; with a View to Settling in America." Glasgow, 1836.

WILSON, CHARLES HENRY. The Wanderer in America, or Truth at Home. 4th ed. Thirsk, 1823.

WINTERBOTHAM, WILLIAM. An Historical, Geographical, Commercial and Philosophical View of the American United States. 4 vols. London, 1795.

WOODS, JOHN. Two Years' Residence in the Settlement on the English Prairie in the Illinois Country. London, 1822. (Thwaites' Early Western Travels, Vol. X.)

INDEX

Abdy, Edward Strutt, experience in stagecoach, 78; on early marriages, 98; on American family life, 106-107; visits insane asylum, 113; on amalgamation of negro and white races, 124, 125; on education in the United States, 203-204; on Yale College, 214-215; visits Dr. Channing, 260; on Universalists, 262, 305; on American love of money, 310; on American hospitality, 317-318; 338; 340

Academies, 209

African Repository, The, on the negro, 134

Agriculture, Necessity for, 149; interest in, 150

"Airs of Palestine," criticised, 223

Alabama, rich land in, 158

Alexander, J. E., on American society, 97

Allibone, Samuel, on Walsh's "An Appeal from the Judgments of Great Britain," 279

Allston, Washington, 239

Almshouses, 108-109

American Bible Society, The, 251-252

American books of advice to emigrants, 31-32

"American Chesterfield, The," 78

American Annals of Education, The, quoted by Abdy, 203-204

American Monthly Review, The, 226

American Museum, The, tells story of cruelty to slaves, 135

American Philosophical Society, The, discusses cause of poor teeth among Americans, 90; 238

Annapolis, Reason for neglect of, as trading port, 190

Anomaly of slavery in a free country, 122

Apathy in citizenship, 329

Ark, Description of the Ohio River, 36

Army, Expense of the American, 195-196

Arts, American progress in, 238-240

Ashe, Thomas, interested in archaeology, 10; 26; 271; 272

Atheists, Scarcity of, in America, 247-249

Athenaeum, The, at Boston, the finest library in the country, 237

Attachment, Lack of local, 319-320

Attitude, American, toward travellers, 61-63; 316-318

Auburn prison, 117; system of, 118-119; espionage at, 119-120

Awkwardness in social forms, Reasons for, 66-67

"Backwoodsman, The," criticised, 224
Baily, Francis, 9, 16; penetrates wilderness east of the Mississippi River, 22; 337
Baltimore, Prettiest women seen in, 89; as a trading port, 190; "headquarters of Catholicism," 261
Baltimore and Ohio Railroad, The, 24
Banks, Increase in number of, 200-201 (See also United States Bank)
Baptists, 262-263
Barlow, Joel, "The Columbiad," criticised, 223; 225; 274; 278; 282
Beggars, Lack of, 28
Bernard, John, becomes stage manager in America, 8, 16; remarks on condition of American stage, 233-234; 235
Biddle, Richard, "Captain Hall in America," 289
Bingley, William, 16 n., 341
Bird, Robert M., "The Gladiator" acted, 235
Birkbeck, Morris, experiments with Flower in the English Prairie, 5-6, 294-295; on price of crops in the West, 160; opposition to, 295-297; 310; 343
Blackwood's Magazine, on Faux, 15; on Mrs. Trollope, 292
Blair, Hugh, Popularity of, 219
Blane, William N., comments on the English Prairie, 6; sympathetic attitude toward America, 12; 17; 22; uses Cumberland Road, 24; on the negro, 140-141; on paper money, 199; on the Waverley novels, 218-219; 247; on the Jews, 266; 286; on the difference between the North and the South, 300-301; on American lack of gaiety, 319
Boardman, James, 74; on freedmen, 125; on American newspapers, 228-229; on pronunciation, 242; on Unitarians, 259; 340
Books, English, most in demand in the United States, 218-219; reprints of English, 218; poor quality of American, 220-221
Booksellers, Influence of the American, 220
Boone's Trail, 24
Boston, Distinctive character of, 71; women the best educated, 93; as a trading port, 183; schools in, 204-205
Bradbury, John, explores the Missouri, 22; advises emigrants, 34; 38; defends American hospitality, 61; on domestic manufactures in the West, 167; on mining, 176; 337; 340
Braddock's Road, oldest thoroughfare to the West, 23
Bribery in American politics, 325
Bridges, Lack of, 52; poor quality of, 52-53
Bristed, John, "Resources of America," 11; 165; statistics on export trade, 183; on American trade with Great Britain, 185; on the cost of the Revolution,

INDEX 355

197; on American colleges, 211; quotes Buffon's theory, 216; on American literature, 216, 219; on American fiction, 223; on America's progress in arts, 239-240; on atheism, 249; on American national vanity, 304; quotes President Monroe, 306; on lotteries, 313; on lack of local attachment, 319; 330; 343
Brothers, Thomas, an enthusiastic detractor, 15; attacks Philadelphia almshouse, 110
Brown, Charles Brockden, 223
Brown, Samuel R., "The Western Gazetteer," 68; 342
Bryant, William Cullen, 223
Bulwer-Lytton, Popularity of, 219
Burnaby, Andrew, 276
Byron, Lord, Popularity of, 218

Campmeetings, 264-265
Canada, Approximate number of visitors to, 19; buying of, prophesied, 334
Candler, Isaac, "Summary View of America," 12; 16; makes pedestrian journey, 46; 48; 62; on smoking, 72-73; on moral purity of American conversation, 81; on amalgamation of negro and white races, 124; on Irving, 222; on American slang, 241; on American pronunciation, 242; on Catholics, 262; on Jews, 266; on national vanity, 302-303; 315; on American hospitality, 317
Carey and Lea's publishing house, 220
Carlyle, Influence of, 219
Catholics, 261-262

"Chancellor Livington" steamboat, 53
Channing, W. E., 127; as a preacher, 259-260
Character, American, Tradition of uniformity of, 299; diversity of, 299-301
Charleston, Popularity of, 68; orphan asylum in, 110; as a trading port, 190-191; schools in, 207
Chesapeake and Ohio Canal, The, 24
Children, Precocity of American, 83-84; 310
Choice of routes on landing in New York, 18; of routes to the West, 22-24
Christmas Day in America, 85
Church, Possible results of lack of an established, 246; variety of forms of, in America, 255 ff.
Cincinnati, Importance of, as manufacturing city, 175
Circuit Riders, 251-252
Classes of people encouraged to emigrate, 37-39
Classics, Attitude toward, in American colleges, 212
Clay, Henry, on the colonization scheme, 133
Clergy, Usurpation of college chairs by, 211; effect on literature of ignorance of, 217; circumstances surrounding, 252; income of, 252-253; lack of education of, 254; social segregation of, 254-255; influence of, 255; exclusion of, from official positions, 328

INDEX

Climate, Sudden changes of, 31; enervating in South, 39
Coachee, Description of, 48-49
Cobbett, William, on drunkenness, 74; on pauperism, 109; on the American farm laborer, 152; 276; attacks the English Prairie, 295-296; defends American civility, 306-307; 309
Coke, Lieutenant E. T., attends theatre at Philadelphia, 232; 235; on the American language, 240; on income of clergy, 253; on Captain Hall's book, 290; 292; 344
Colden, Cadwallader D., "Life of Fulton," 281
Coleridge, S. T., 219
College, Inferiority of the American, 210-212; curriculum of, 210-212; American attitude toward, 211; William and Mary, 212-213; Harvard, 213-214; Yale, 214-215; other colleges, 215
Colonization Society, 131-134; opposition to, by negroes, 132; by whites, 133-134; real purpose of, 134
Columbia College, Description of, 215
Congregationalists, Nature of worship of, 260; prevalence of, in Boston, 261
Connecticut, Land in, 154; cotton mills in, 169-170; woolen mills in Hartford, 172; education in, 205-206
Conservatism, American, 314-315
Conversation, American, Tone of, 78-80; limitations of, 78-79; pedantry among women, 79; lack of repartee in, 79; native wit in, 79; well-informed quality of, 79; brevity of Western speech, 80; moral purity of, 81; profanity in, 82; inquisitiveness in, 82-83
Cooking, Poor quality of American, 104
Cooper, James Fenimore, Criticism of, 223; 253; 283
Cooper, Thomas, first great American tragedian, 235
Cooper, Thomas, 6; 27; 30; 48; 33; 71; describes typical American farm, 151; on the price of land, 164; on the manufacture of military supplies, 173; on American literature, 216; on American hospitality, 316
Copyright, Complaint concerning, 221
Cost of board in America, 60-61; of passage to America, 34; of travel in America, 35-36; by stagecoach, 48; by steamboat, 53-54
Cotton, Profit in growing, 157; ease of growing, 157-158; manufactories in New England, 169, 171-172; cheapness of, 171-172
Coxe, Tench, "View of the United States of America," 342
Crevecoeur, Hector St. J., 135 n.
Crime, Absence of, in United States, 114-115; 313
Crops, in Pennsylvania, 155-156; in the West, 160
Cumberland Road, The, 24
Currency, System of, 198; necessity for new, 198
"Cut money," 200

INDEX

Dalton, William, quotes Philadelphia police record, 114-115; visits Philadelphia penitentiary, 117; visits Auburn prison, 118; on banks, 201; on increase of Baptists, 262; on American independence, 308
Dancing, American interest in, 95-96
Darby, William, "The Emigrant's Guide," 32; "Louisiana," 32; 342; "View of the United States," 342
D'Arusmont, Frances Wright, 12; 16; praises lot of farmer, 151; organizes "Workies," 179; as promoter of religious infidelity, 248-249; criticised by *The Quarterly Review*, 284; 328; 343
Davis, John, 9; makes pedestrian journey, 46; 281; on American lack of gaiety, 318-319
Debt, National, Reduction of the, 197-198
Delaware, Land in, 156
De Roos, F. Fitzgerald, 7-8; 96; attends Episcopal Church, 256; defends Americans, 286; on pauperism, 328-329
Destiny, Importance of, of United States, 321
Details, Lack of, of American life in travel literature, 337-338
Diderot, 219
Dishonesty, Commercial, of Americans, 311-312
Disparity of interests in different parts of United States, 329-331
Dress, Women's foolish, 91-92; of country girls, 102; of men, 102-103; of both sexes, 102-103

Driver of stagecoach, Description of, 49; importance of, 49; good nature of, 49
Duels, in New Orleans, 69; Timothy Flint on, 70; 314
Duncan, John, on American children, 83; at funeral, 87; on death rate by consumption, 91; on Harvard College, 214, 227; on American use of words, 243; describes American Sunday Schools, 251; on universal suffrage, 326; 340; 344
Dutch Reformed Church, 265
Dwight, Timothy, 153; 225; "Remarks on the Review of Inchiquin the Jesuit's Letters," 277-278

Eastburn's publishing house, 220
Edgeworth, Maria, Popularity of, 218, 219
Edinburgh Review, The, on American literature, 225; 226; discusses Janson, Ashe and Parkinson, 273-274; criticised by T. Dwight, 277; 280; defends itself against Walsh, 282; ridicules Mrs. Trollope, 292
Education (See also Schools), Universality of, in the United States, 203; in New England, 204-205; cheapness of, in Massachusetts, 205; in Connecticut, 205-206; in New York, 206; in Pennsylvania, 206; in the South, 206-207; in the West, 207-208; practical nature of American, 207-208; in the home, 208; Lancastrian system of, 208-209

358 INDEX

Elections, Frequency of, 65-66; defects of, 323-324
Emancipation, Problems of, 145-148; dangers of sudden, 145-146; suggestions for, 146-148
Emigration, Reasons for, 26-29; arguments against, 29-31
English Prairie, The, 5-6; controversy concerning, 294-297
Engraving, Excellence of American, 240
Episcopalians, 256-258
Equality, Spirit of, 64-65; 306-307
Erie Canal, The, 18-19, 24, 39, 53, 154, 303
Espionage in prisons, 119-120
Executives, Attitude toward, 326-327
Export Trade, American, Freedom of, 182; variety of, 182-183; value of, 183-184

Factory girls, in Lowell, 170-171; purity of morals of, 171; in New York State, 174
Family, the typical American, 100-102; good feeling in, 106-107
Farmer, Importance of the, 151-152; general difficulties of the, 152-153; in the West, 160
Farm labor, overstocked in the East, 30-31; 101; excellence of, 152
Faux, William, Criticism of, by *Blackwood's*, 15, 284; 30; on the effects of drinking cold water, 74-75; on Birkbeck's land, 161; on the tariff, 194; praised by *The Quarterly*, 284-285; attacks English Prairie, 296; on American independence, 308-309; on American dishonesty, 312; 344
Fearon, Henry B., 4-5; 17; uses Cumberland Road, 24; 30; 42; on redemptioners, 45; on the steamboat, 53; 61; on American reserve, 65, 80; on the abuse of freedmen, 124-125; on Western emigration, 159; on price of wheat, 160; on price of land, 163; on manufactures in Pittsburgh, 173-174; on trades, 178; on labor discontent, 178; on the tariff, 193; on paper money, 199; 218; on "Salmagundi Papers," 222; on behavior at the theatre, 233; attacked by Walsh, 280; attacks English Prairie, 296-297; 343; 344.
Fences, Varieties of, 161-162
Ferrall, S. A., 14; 54; describes American fences, 162; on agrarian "Workies," 179; on the national debt, 197-198; visits Lancastrian schools, 209; on religious infidelity, 248-249; 344
Fidler, Rev. Isaac, 6; on high price of board, 61; tries to establish school of Eastern languages, 212; tells why American clergymen do not sit in Congress, 338-339; 340
Fifth of July celebration, 85
Financial system, Admiration of, among Englishmen, 195; cheapness of, 195; efficiency of, 196
Finch, J., visits Columbia College, 215
First Day or Sunday School Society, earliest form of American Sunday School, 250

INDEX

Fires, Frequency of, 100
Flatboat, 52
Flint, James, on the backwoods tavern, 60; on American hospitality, 61-62; on manners in the West, 69-70; on American profanity, 82; on men's dress, 102; 152; on mechanics, 177; on price of labor, 178; on paper money, 199; on banks in Kentucky, 200-201; on national vanity, 305; on fondness for titles, 307-308; 309; on disparity of interests, 330-331; prophesies prosperity of the Union, 333-334
Flint, Timothy, on duelling, 70; 342
Flower, George, experiment of the English Prairie, 5, 294-297
Flower, Richard, "Letters from Lexington and the Illinois" criticised by *The Quarterly*, 284; refutes Cobbett, 296
Food (See also Meals), Effect of heavy or animal, 59; abundance of, at inns, 59; effect of too great a variety of, 91; lack of serious interest in, 104; abundance of, in home, 103-104
Forbes' Road, 23
Formal intercourse, 96-97
Forrest, Edwin, "The Roscius of America," 235
Fourth of July celebrations, 84-85
Fowler, John, 74; on New York land, 154; on price of land, 164; on the salt industry in New York, 174-175; on the Society Library, 237; 309-310; 337
Franklin, Benjamin, "Information to Those Who Would Remove to America, 31; 33; 225

Franklin Library, The, 236
"Fredoniad, The," criticised, 224
Free Masons, longest funeral trains, 87
French books read in America, 219-220
Friends (See Quakers)
"Frolics," 104-105
Funerals, American, 87-88

Gaiety, lack of, among Americans, 318-319
Genesee Road, The, 18, 19
"Geographical, Historical, Commercial and Agricultural View of the United States," 341
Georgia, Poor land in, 158; domestic manufacture in, 167; trade of, 190-191; education in, 207
Gold, Discovery of, in the South, 177
Good humor of Americans, 318
"Gouging," practiced in the West, 69-70; 301
Government, Unifying influence of the, 320; defects in the policy of, 323-327; relation of legislative and executive, 326; relation of state and Federal, 327; predicted changes in, 332; ideal quality of, 334-335
Grammar, American carelessness in, 241

Hall, Captain Basil, 11; archtraitor to American hospitality, 12; 52; 61; 68; 76; on social intercourse of men and women, 96-97; 109; on houses of refuge, 111; on cheapness of American prison system, 150; on pardons,

120-121; altercation on American pronunciation, 241-242; on Shakers, 268; "Travels in America," 287-288; criticism of, 288-290; 291; 302; on American hospitality, 316; 326; 343; 344

Hall, Lieutenant Francis, 11-12; on roads, 50; on reserve of American women, 94; praises lot of the farmer, 151; on Irving, 222; 286; 313-314; on American hospitality, 316-317; on American gravity, 318; on influence of government, 320; 343

Hall, Judge James, 25, 222

Hamilton, Captain Thomas, 14; on the American inn, 56-57; on reserve, 65; on Boston women, 93; on houses of refuge, 111; visits insane asylum, 113; on freedmen in the North, 123-124; on necessity for slavery in the South, 126; on University of Pennsylvania, 215; on lack of literary taste, 218; on use of words, 244; attends Episcopal church, 256; on Unitarians, 258; on Methodists, 263-264; on standard of morality, 314; on conservatism, 314-315; on lack of gaiety, 318; on political relations of the United States, 320; on state representation, 324-325; on "Workies," 328; 339; 344

Harmony, Indiana, Rich land in, 161; home of Rapp's community, 269

Harris, William Tell, "Remarks Made During a Tour . . ." criticised, 283-284

Harvard College, 213-214; 227; Unitarianism in, 259

Hemans, Mrs., Popularity of, 219

Hodgson, Adam, 30-31; on drunkenness, 74; on sleighing parties, 86-87; on cruelty to slaves, 135-136; on tobacco-growing in Virginia, 157; on price of crops, 160; on domestic manufacture, 167; on manufacture, 172-173; on "bank mania," 201; on Unitarianism, 259; 286

Holidays, American, 84-86

Holmes, Abiel, "American Annals," criticised, 271

Holmes, Isaac, on American ships, 185; 193; on the financial system, 196; on paper money, 199; on schools, 209; on Samuel Woodworth, 224

Hospitality, American, 316-317

Hospitals, 111-112

Houses of refuge, 111

Howison, John, 77; visits cotton mill at Utica, New York, 174; on behavior of Americans at the theatre, 232-233; on libraries, 237; on Trumbull's paintings, 239; 344

Hulbert, A. B., "Historic Highways," 23

Hulme, Thomas, "Journal" used by Cobbett, 296

Hunt, Gaillard, 113

Hunter, John D., "Captivity among the Indians," criticised, 224

Illinois, Superior advantages of, 42-43; richness of, 161

Imlay, Gilbert, cited as authority, 342

Import trade, American, Statistics of, 183; variety of, 184
Inchbald, Mrs., 231
"Inchiquin the Jesuit's Letters," 274-275; Remarks on, by *The Quarterly*, 275-276; 281
Independence, American, 306-309
Independents (See Congregationalists)
Indians, Early Fear of, as deterrent to emigration, 29; money paid by the government to, 196
Ingersoll, C. Jared, 274
Innkeeper, Indifference of the American, 57; importance of, 59
Inns, American, Inconvenience of, 55-56
Inquisitiveness, American, 82
Insane, Treatment of the, 112-113; asylums for, 113-114
Intemperance, Emigrant advised against, 37; theories of American, 37, 74, 75; frequency of bars, 59; lack of actual drunkenness, 74; widespread prevalence of, 74; ease with which liquor was obtained, 75; conviviality in South, 75-76; cause of increase in pauperism, 109
Interstate slave trade, 137-140
Irish, redemptioners, 44-45; inhabitants of Virginia and Kentucky compared to, 69
Iroquois Trail, The, 18
Irving, Washington, Criticisms of, 221-222; 225; "English Writers on America," 285

Jackson, President, refuses to renew charter of the United States Bank, 201-202

Janson, Charles William, on drunkenness, 74; on American women, 94; on Sunday in the Carolinas, 249; 271-272; 343-344
Jealousy, Sectional, 24, 331
Jefferson, Thomas, quoted on slavery, 141-142; on the dangers of a manufacturing class, 165; Embargo Act, 186; on William and Mary College, 212; considered an authority on literature, 315; 342
Jews in the United States, 255, 266
Johnson, Samuel, 219

Keel boat, The, 53
Kemble, Frances, 16; début in New York, 232
Kendall, Edward Augustus, visits prison in old copper mine, 115; visits Maine, 336; discusses constitution of Connecticut, 339
Kennedy, John P., 222
Kentucky, Insecurity of land titles in, 41; uncivilized character of inhabitants of, 41; prevalence of fever in, 41-42; slavery in, 42; good climate of, 160-161; fine quality of land in, 163; center of hemp industry, 175; other industries in, 175; paper money in, 199; banks in, 200-201
Kindness of Americans to one another, 315-316; to strangers, 313-314, 316-317
Kingdom, William, "America and the British Colonies," 340-341

Lamb, Charles, 219
Lambert, John, on turnpikes, 51-52; 55-56; 60-61; on poor teeth,

90; on orphan asylums, 110; on importation of slaves, 129; cites instance of cruelty to slaves, 135; on hiring out of slaves, 138; on Long Embargo, 186-187; on trade of South Carolina, 190-191; on "Salmagundi Papers," 221-222; on cost of newspapers, 228; on advertisements, 230; on salary of clergymen, 253; on Congregationalists, 261; on Jews, 266

Lancastrian system of public schools, 208-209

Land, Price of government, 26-27; cheapness of, 30; system of public, 150; method of working, 150-151; care of, 153-154; in New England, 154; in New York State, 154-155; in Pennsylvania, 155-156; in Delaware and New Jersey, 156; in the South, 156-157; in the West, 159-161; price of, 162-164

Language, American, Beliefs concerning, 240; uniformity of, 241; carelessness in, 241; changes made in, 241-245

Latrobe, Charles Joseph, 22; on future of mechanic arts, 179-180; on diversity of American character, 300; on national vanity, 305; on importance of the United States, 321

Laws, Difference in state, 331

Lectures, Popularity of, 237-238

Libraries, American, 236-237

Literature, American, English opinion of, 215-218; obstacles to, 216-217; effect of inferior education on, 217-218; scanty evidences of, 221; poor quality of American novels, 222-223

Local histories, Excellence of American, 224-225

Log house, earliest form of American habitation, 100

Long, John, "Expedition to the Rocky Mountains," criticised, 224

Long Embargo, The, 166; effects of, 186-187

Long Island, Prosperity of, 155

Lotteries, Prevalence of, 313

Louisiana, Growing of cotton and sugar in, 158-159

Lounging, American habit of, 77-78

Lowell, the best-known manufacturing city in the United States, 170

Loyalsock Creek, English colony on, 39-40

Lynn, Shoe trade in, 172

Maine, as place of settlement, 39; seldom visited, 336

"Manfred," 218

Manners, Local differences in, 67; in the South, 67-69; in Kentucky and Virginia, 69-70; reason for demoralization of, in the West, 70-71; in cities of the East, 71; among rural classes in the East, 71-72; at table, 78

Manufacture, in early period after the Revolution, 29-30; early attitude toward, 164-166; Jefferson's remarks on, 165; later necessity for, 166; in the home, 166-168; English attitude toward, 168-169; scarcity of, in the South, 175-176; value of, 176

INDEX

Marriage, Early, 97-98; civil nature of, 97; encouragement to, 98
Marshall, John, 224, 225, 274, 282
Martineau, Harriet, 13; 16; explores unsettled region, 21, 22; on roads, 50; 56; on New England manners, 72; on spitting, 73; pleads for more interests for women, 92; 99; on paupers, 109-110; visits Auburn prison, 119-120; 127; 166; visits Lowell, 170; visits factory in Richmond, 176; on trade, 183; on Salem, 187-188; on popularity of English novels, 219; on Irving, 222; on Sunday observance, 250; on American clergy, 253-254; on Presbyterians, 261; on Catholics, 262; 316; on American hospitality, 317; on moral effect of slavery, 322-323; on apathy in citizenship, 329; 344

Maryland, Poor land in, 156; schools in, 206

Massachusetts, Trade in, 187-188 (See also New England)

Matthews, W., "Historical Review of North America . . ." 2

Meals (See also Food), Lack of privacy at, 57-58; description of, 58, 59; as the cause of American diseases, 59; plentiful, at inns, 59; in the home, 103-104

Mechanic, Importance of the, 177-178; wages of, 178; discontent of, 178-179; future of mechanic arts, 179-180

Medicine, Ignorance of, 111

Melish, John, 7; 20; on New England land, 154; on Georgia land, 158; 161; on manufacture in the home, 167-168; on manufacture, 169; on cheapness of cotton, 171-172; on manufactures in Pennsylvania, 173-174; on price of labor, 178; on trade in Massachusetts, 187; on trade in New York City, 189; on Virginia trade, 190; on Maryland trade, 190; on South Carolina trade, 191; on Georgia trade, 191; on education in South, 206-207; on newspapers, 227; on the Franklin Library, 236; 237; 286; on American commercial dishonesty, 312-313; 333; 340; as an authority, 342-343; 344

Methodists, Customs at funerals of, 87; 263-264

Milton, John 219

Mining, Early lack of interest in, 176; unlimited possibilities of, 177

Missouri region, Possibilities of, 42

Money, 37; American love of, 309-313

Moore, Thomas, 218, 276, 343

Morals, Standard of American, 95; 314

Moravians, 266

More, Mrs. Hannah, Popularity of, 219

Morgan, Lady, 218

Mormons, 266-267

Morse, Jedidiah, 342

Motives for coming to America, 3-13

Motives for writing books of travel, 14-17

Murray, Charles Augustus, 13-14; on Charleston, 68; on emancipation of slaves, 148; visits Lowell mills, 170; on American education, 210; on increase of Catholics, 262; on Universalists, 262; on fondness for titles, 307; on American hospitality, 317; 344

Museums, Americans, 236

Napoleonic Wars, Effects of, 3-5

Natural Bridge, Side trips to the, 21

Navy, Cost of, 196

Negro (See also Slavery), Condition of, in North, 123-125; amalgamation of, with white race, 124; fear of, 126-128; legislation against, 127-131; scheme of transporting, 131-134; defense of intellect of, 140-141, 260

Neilson, Peter, on advertisements in newspapers, 230

New England, Land in, 154; furnishes largest proportion of factory girls, 166; particularly adapted to manufacture, 169; cotton mills in, 169-170; other factory industries in, 172-173; education in, 204-205; observance of Sunday in, 249-250; Unitarianism in, 258, 259

New Englanders in the West, 70, 191, 247

New Jersey, as a place of settlement, 39; land in, 156

New Orleans, Unhealthfulness of, 41; fascination of, 41; 68-69; importance of, 192

Newport, Reason for neglect of, as trading port, 183

Newspapers, Interest in, 225, 227; number of, in the United States, 227-228; contents of, 228-229; virulence of, 229; advertisements in, 229-230

New Year's Day, Celebration of, 85-86

New York City, as a trading port, 189

New York State, as place of settlement, 39; abolition of slavery in, 123; one of two leading states, 154; domestic manufacture in, 167; manufactures in, 174-175; education in, 206

Niagara Falls, 19

Niles' Weekly Register, urges scheme for expatriation of female negroes, 147

Norfolk, as a trading port, 189-190

North American Review, The, Criticism of, 226-227; on Janson, 272; defends "Inchiquin's Letters," 276-277; defends Walsh, 282-283; exposes Faux, 285; criticises Captain Hall, 288-289; on Mrs. Trollope, 294

North Carolina, schools in, 207; Sunday observance in, 249

Ohio country, Advantages and drawbacks of the, 40-41

Ohio River, Importance of, 23; bad reputation of settlers along, 301

Opie, Mrs., 218

Organ, in Episcopal churches, 257; largest in Catholic Cathedral in Baltimore, 261

INDEX

Orphan asylums, 110-111
Ouseley, William Gore, on the financial system, 195-196; on salary of clergy, 252-253; on Mrs. Trollope, 293; work based on government records, 342

Palmer, John, 33; 40; on redemptioners, 46; on "Chancellor Livingston," 53; on dress in Philadelphia, 102-103; on social life, 105-106; on price of wheat in Maryland, 160; on Illinois land, 161; on price of farm land, 163
Paper money, Flooding of country with, 198-199; inconvenience of, 199
Parkinson, Richard, on redemptioners, 44; 271; 276; 340; 343
Parsimony, American, 310
Paulding, James K., 224; exposes Janson, 272; 278-279; 283; 285; 290; 299
Paupers, Care of, 108, 109; increase of, 109; few native, 109-110; increase of, feared, 328-329
Peale's Museum, 106, 236
Penitentiary system, Institution of the, 115; failure of early attempts, 116-117; Philadelphia, 117-118; Auburn, 118-119
Pennsylvania, Advantages of, as place of settlement, 39-40; instigator of humane policies, 114; institutes penitentiary system, 115; one of two leading states, 155; land in, 155-156; domestic manufactures in, 167; manufacture of firearms in, 173; flour mills in, 173; education in, 206

Pennsylvania Canal, The, 25
Pennsylvania Railroad, The, 23, 25
Percival, James G., 223-224
Periodicals, Poor quality of, 226; list of, 226
Philadelphia, Distinctive character of, 71; charitable activities of, 110; penitentiary system of, 115-118; as trading port, 188-189
Pickering, Joseph, "Inquiries of an Emigrant . . ." 5; 33
Pitkin, Timothy, "Statistical View of North America," 342
Pittsburg, called "Birmingham," 173; manufactures in, 173-174
"Planters," in the Mississippi River, 54
Poetry, Poor quality of American, 223-224
Political pamphlets, Quality of American, 225-226
Politics, Interest in, 54, 79; lack of discussion of, by English travellers, 339
Porter, Jane, Popularity of, 218
Portfolio, The, 226
Power, Tyrone, 13; 16; 158; plays in New York, 231; 233; on American actresses, 235
Prairie, Theories in regard to the, 161
Presbyterians, 260, 261
Price, of produce, 160; of land, 162-164; of mechanic labor, 178
Priest, William, on redemptioners, 44-45; on sleighing parties, 86; on American manufactures, 168; on trade of Philadelphia, 188-189; on Annapolis as a trading port, 190; on currency system, 198; 276

Primogeniture, Lack of, 65; evils of lack of, 328

Princeton College, not much visited by travellers, 215

Prisons, Condition of early, 115; development of, 115-120; cheapness of system of, 120; frequency of pardons, 120-121; free education in, 120

Provisions for voyage to America, 34-35

Quakers, longest funeral trains, 87; gratify love for beauty, 102; dress of, 102; establish first almshouse, 108; 265-266

Quarterly Review, The, 222; 226; reviews Holmes' "American Annals," 271-273; reviews "Inchiquin's Letters," 275-276; criticised by T. Dwight, 277; ridiculous statements of, 278; 280; 283-284; praises Mrs. Trollope, 292; denounces Birkbeck, 205; 208; on American character, 299

Ramsay, David, "History of the United States," criticised, 224

Rappites, 268-269

Redemptioners, 44-46

Religion, American attitude toward, 246-248; 255-256; scarcity of atheists, 248-249; conservatism in, 269; 314

Representation, Defects of, 324-325

Reserve, of landlord's family, 59, 62, 65-66; of women, 94; probable cause of, 65; 94

Revenue, Sources of, 192, 196; value of, 196; criticism of, 196-197

Reviews, Lack of good, 220

Revivals, 264

Rhode Island, cotton mills in, 169

Rich, Obadiah, on American periodicals, 226; criticises Mrs. Trollope, 290-291

Roads, Poor quality of, 50-51; method of building, 50; corduroy or gridiron, 48, 51; later neglect of, 52

Rousseau, 219

Salem, Commercial importance of, 187-188

"Salmagundi Papers, The," Criticism of, 221-222

Salt, Manufacture of, in New York State, 174-175

Saratoga Springs, a fashionable resort, 19-20

"Sawyers" in the Mississippi River, 54

Schools (See also Education), Lack of punishment in, 84, 209; imitation of Scotch system, 209-210; lack of "fagging" in, 210

Scott, Sir Walter, parts of his poems objectionable to American women, 81; popularity of, 218-219

Seasickness, Advice concerning, 35

Sedgwick, Catherine M., Praise of, 222-223

"Senecan Chief, The," first boat on the Erie Canal, 18

Sensitiveness, American, *The North American Review* on, 294; 301-302

Servants, Unsatisfactory nature of English, in America, 38; indif-

ference of American, 57; professional, 100-101; position in family, 101; lack of, on farms, 152
Shakers, 267-268
Shakespeare, 219, 233
Shamrock Society, "Hints to Emigrants," 32
Ship-building, Advance in, 181
Ships, Advantages of American, 181-182
Shirreff, Patrick, 22; on American children, 84; 153; on hedges, 162; on price of land, 163; on Boston schools, 205, 232; criticises Mrs. Trollope, 292-293
Silliman, Benjamin, "Tour in England," criticised, 224
Sing Sing prison, founded on Auburn model, 119
Slavery (See also Negro), as a drawback to settlement in the South, 39; as encouragement to hospitality, 67; attitude toward, in North, 122; abolition of, in New England, 122-123; in New York, 123; attitude toward, in South, 125-128; necessity for, 126; laws against slave education, 128; laws against cruelty to slaves, 128; rights of slaves, 128, 140; prohibition of importation of, 129-130; personal personal treatment of, 134-136; degraded condition of, 137, 140; interstate slave trade, 137-139, 140; schemes for abolition of, 145-148; effect on whites of, 141-144; effect on economic conditions, 142-143; effect on morale, 143-144; 281-282; as disintegrating influence, 321-323

Sleighing parties, Popularity of, 86-87
Smith, Sydney, 216
Social Life, Uniformity of, in cities, 105-106; character of, 105
Society Library, The, 237
Soil, Differences in, 153; false promise of, 153
Somerville, William C., "Letters from Paris," 224
South Carolina, Trade of, 190-191; schools in, 207; observance of Sunday in, 249
South Carolina Railway, The, 18
Southey, Robert, Review of "Inchiquin's Letters" attributed to, 275-276, 278-179
Speculators, Danger of, 36-37
"Spirit shops," or "grog shops," 76; as cause of pauperism, 109
Spitting, Prevalence of, 72-74
"Squatters," along Western river banks, 42
Stagecoach, Description of typical, 47-48
Stage horses, Fine quality of, 49
Steamboat, The, on Eastern waters, 53-54; universal praise of, 53; rules of conduct on, 53-54; on Western waters, 54; dangers of navigating, 54-55
St. Paul's, New York City, one of the best-known Episcopal churches, 257
Strike, in New York City, 1833, 178-179
Stuart, James, 21; 28; on advantages of Illinois region, 42-43; on roads, 50; on "The Constitution," 54; on drunkenness, 74; on negroes, 131; on colonization,

132-133; on the silk industry, 174; on Boston schools, 204-205; attacks Mrs. Trollope, 293; 344

Styles, Fondness for French, 90

Suffrage, Dangers of universal, 325-326

Sugar, Manufacture of, in Louisiana, 158-159

Sunday, Passing of observance of, 249-250

Sunday Schools, Development of, 250-251; influence of, 251

Sutcliffe, Robert, on redemptioners, 46; on children's smoking, 73; on atheists, 248

Swedish Lutherans, 266

Tariff, an important question, 192; arguments of the English against, 193; struggle for higher, 193-194; English tariff on American goods, 194

Tavern, Description of backwoods, 60

Temperance campaigns, 76; influence of, 77; report of Society, 109

Tennessee, Fine climate of, 160-161

Thanksgiving rarely celebrated, 85

Theatre, Early attitude toward, 230-231; in Boston, 231; many visited by English travellers, 231; American behavior at, 231-233; nature of plays at, 233, 235; condition of, at this time, 233-234

Thwaites, Reuben, G., 297

Time of year, Best, for emigration, 33

"Tipping," Lack of, 57

Titles, American fondness for, 307-308

Tobacco, Use of, 72-73; theories concerning use of, 72-73; cultivation of, in Virginia, 156-157

Tolls, Turnpike, 52, 338

Trade, General discussion of, 181-184; with West Indies and China, 184; with Great Britain, 184-186; cheapness of American carrying, 185; in New England, 187-188; in Middle Atlantic States, 188-189; in the South, 189-191; in the West, 191-192

"Travels of Lewis and Clark," 281, 342

Trinity, New York City, one of the best-known Episcopal churches, 257

Trollope, Anthony, 13, 293

Trollope, Mrs. Frances, her work the best-known of travel books on America, 12-13; 15; 24; 73; 77; visits girls' school, 209; on American fiction, 223; 230; on manners at the theatre, 232; defends Captain Hall, 290; popularity of her book, 290-291; influence of, 292-293; 302; on love of money, 310; on standards of morality, 314; 315; 340; 343; 344

Trumbull, John, American artist, 239

Trumbull, John, "Mac Fingal," 278

Tuckerman, Henry T., on English books of travel, 286-287; 294

Tudor, Henry, 13; struggle with American landlord, 62; visits Philadelphia hospital, 112; visits Auburn prison, 119; on sugar growing, 158-159; on Boston schools, 205; on number of students in New England colleges 210; on Yale, 214; meets atheists, 248; on Mrs. Trollope, 293; on American sensitiveness, 302; on national vanity, 303-304

Turnpikes, 51-52; maintenance of, 195; 338

Union, Necessity for the preservation of the, 332-333

Unitarianism, rival of Episcopacy, 258; divided attitude toward, 258; in New England, 258-259; spread of, 259; 266

United States, The, a unique experiment in statecraft, 1; divided opinion on future of, 2

United States Bank, History of the, 200-202

Universalism, Hostile attitude toward, 262; misunderstanding of, 262; 266

University of Pennsylvania, Curriculum of, 210-211; noted for medical school, 215

Unpopularity of the South as a place of settlement, 39

Value of English travel literature, 344-345

Van Buren, Martin, quoted, 305-306

Vanity, National, 302-306

Vigne, Godfrey, 13; on the stagecoach, 47; visits Philadelphia penitentiary, 117; on the United States Bank, 200; on Harvard College, 214; sees Cooper, the tragedian, 235; on uniformity of language, 241; on American pronunciation, 242-243; on wrong use of words, 243; on Shaker meeting, 268; on fondness for titles, 307; predicts dissolution of the United States, 332; 344

Virginia, Treatment of slaves in, 137; slave trade in, 138-139; worst example of farming economy, 156-157; domestic manufactures in, 167; factory in Richmond, 176; bad reputation in trade with Great Britain, 189-190; trade of, 190; education in, 206-207; observance of Sunday in, 249

Voice, The American, 80-81

Voltaire, 219

Voting, by ballot, Dangers of, 323

Wagon, Description of emigrant's, 36

Wakefield, Priscilla, 16 n, 341

Walsh, Robert, 45, 279-282, 284

Waltzing, Attitude toward, 95

Wansey, Henry, 48; 165; visits a copper mine, 176-177; on Massachusetts trade, 187; on internal revenue, 195; on Yale, 214; 231; 276

Washington's Tomb, 20-21

Wastefulness, American, 311

Waverley Novels, Popularity of the, 218-219

Webster, Noah, 225

Welby, Adlard, 92; on price of farm land, 163; praised by *The Quarterly*, 284; on lack of gaiety, 319; 344

Weld, Isaac, 3-4; 50; visits Philadelphia almshouse, 108; at hospital, 112; visits prison, 115-116; on Pennsylvania mills, 173; on mines, 176; on the Virginia trade, 189-190; describes William and Mary College, 212-213; visits theatre, 231; on Sunday in Virginia, 249; 271; on American incivility, 306; 343

"Western Gazetteer, The," on New Orleans, 68; 342

White Mountains, Visits to the, 20, 336

Whitlocke, Mrs., acts on American stage, 231

William and Mary College, described, 212-213

Wilmington, N. C., as a trading port, 190

Wilson, Alexander, "Ornithology," 224

Wirt, William, defends Virginia, 69; criticism of, 224

"Wistar parties," 238

Women, American, Reserve of, 58-59, 94-95; importance of, in a new country, 88; lack of beauty, 89; early fading of, 89, 90-91; gait of, 89; features and figure of, 89-90; poor teeth, 90; reasons for poor health, 90-91; dress of, 91-92; education of, 92-94; fondness for novels, 93; social manner of, 94-95; modesty of, 95-96; freedom of, 96; high position of, 98-99; lack of unwomanly employment, 99; seldom seen at theatre, 231

Woodworth, Samuel, Criticism of, 224

Wordsworth, 219

"Workies," 179; a menace to the government, 328

Wright, Fanny (See D'Arusmont, Frances Wright)

Yale College, 214-215

Yankee, Character of the, 301, 312-313

Yawning, a trait of American manners, 78

"Year in Europe, A," criticised, 224

Yellow fever, 111